Additional Praise for Phyllis Chesler's *The Death of Feminism*

"Ms. Chesler's book is a welcome critique of the Feminist Left's willful and shameful neglect of their sisters' plight in the Islamic World. Rejecting cultural relativism or political correctness, Ms. Chesler paints a depressing but truthful picture of the world that women under Islam have to live in. One hopes Ms. Chesler's book will bring about not only a change in attitudes but some sort of political and social action on behalf of women suffering because of the totalitarian and misogynistic tenets of Islam."

—Ibn Warraq, author of, most recently,
Leaving Islam: Apostates Speak Out

"With great talent and in a vivid style, Phyllis Chesler observes every aspect of today's American culture, politics, and society through a feminist lens. This enlightening picture unveils the most dramatic domestic and international problems of our times, including that of Islamic gender apartheid, analyzed by a politically incorrect and daring lover of truth."

—Bat Ye'or, author of *Eurabia* and *Islam and Dhimmitude*

"Phyllis Chesler has written a brave and passionate book. Let the hypocrites she denounces on the feminist Left and their politically correct allies quail."

—Hillel Halkin, author of *Letters to an American Jewish Friend,
Across the Sabbath River,* and *A Strange Death*

"Feminism is dead; long live new feminism! This is the message of Phyllis Chesler's fascinating study of Islamic gender apartheid that, transcending the traditional frontiers of Islam, is spreading to the West, including the United States. Anyone interested in understanding Islamism, this latest enemy of open societies, should read this book."

—Amir Taheri, author of *The Cauldron:
The Middle East Behind the Headlines*

The Death of Feminism

What's Next in the Struggle
for Women's Freedom

PHYLLIS CHESLER

palgrave
macmillan

First published 2005 by
PALGRAVE MACMILLAN™
175 Fifth Avenue, New York, N.Y. 10010 and
Houndmills, Basingstoke, Hampshire, England RG21 6XS.
Companies and representatives throughout the world.

PALGRAVE MACMILLAN is the global academic imprint of the Palgrave Macmillan division of St. Martin's Press, LLC and of Palgrave Macmillan Ltd. Macmillan® is a registered trademark in the United States, United Kingdom and other countries. Palgrave is a registered trademark in the European Union and other countries.

ISBN 1–4039–6898–5

Library of Congress Cataloging-in-Publication Data
Chesler, Phyllis.
The death of feminism : what's next in the struggle for women's freedom / Phyllis Chesler.
    p. cm.
  Includes bibliographical references and index.
  ISBN 1–4039–6898–5 (alk. paper)
  1. Feminism.   2. Women's studies.   3. Women—Violence against.   4. Women—Islamic countries.   5. Muslim women.   I. Title.

HQ1155.C44   2005
323.3'4—dc22

2005049890

A catalogue record for this book is available from the British Library.

Design by Letra Libre, Inc.

First edition: November 2005
10 9 8 7 6 5 4 3 2 1

Printed in the United States of America.

Contents

Acknowledgments

I would like to thank all those feminist and human rights activists whose work I have drawn upon and without which my work would have been impossible. The fact that I have reached different conclusions or may be critical of their work in no way detracts from the importance and influence of that work. Thus, I am deeply indebted to the feminist work in the area of Islamic gender apartheid that has been done by Dr. Lila Abu-Lughod, Amnesty International, Equality Now, Eve Ensler, the Feminist Majority, Jan Goodwin, Dr. Donna Hughes (who distributes selected news about sex trafficking on the Dignity list), Dr. Kate Millett, Robin Morgan, Judith A. Montoya (who distributes "It's Happening with Women," a compendium of newsworthy items), *Ms. Magazine,* Human Rights Watch, Dr. Suha Sabbagh, Dr. Bouthaina Shaaban, Dr. Gayatri Chakravorty Spivak, Womens E-News, and Women Living Under Muslim Laws.

I would like to thank all those scholars, conservatives, Christians, Republicans, and libertarians whose work in the area of Islamic jihad, terrorism, Islamic religious apartheid, sex trafficking, and western academic biases has strengthened my own work in these areas.

I am indebted to the work of *Azure* magazine; Dr. Fouad Ajami; Bat Ye'or; Julien Benda; Paul Berman; Dr. Andrew Bostom; David Brooks; Tammy Bruce; Christopher Caldwell; *Commentary* magazine; *Conservative Monitor;* Dr. Rachel Ehrenfeld; Orianna Fallaci; Carol Gould; Joseph Farah (in general and for WorldNetDaily); Jamie Glazov, my ever-cheerful editor at *FrontPage* magazine; Dr. Victor Davis Hanson; David Horowitz, the author and publisher of *FrontPage* magazine; Yossi Klein Halevi; Hillel Halkin; Shirley Hazzard; Chris Hedges; Christopher Hitchens; Dr. Michael Ignatieff; *The Intellectual Conservative;* Dr. Nancy Kobrin; Nicholas D. Kristof; Michelle Malkin; Jason Maoz, my supportive editor at *The Jewish Press;* Dr. Daniel Pipes; the *New York Sun;* Glyn O'Malley; Nidra Poller; Jean Raspail; Lance Morrow; George Orwell; the *National Review;* Dr. Barry Rubin and Judith Colp Rubin; Natan Sharansky and Ron Dermer for their work about democracy and tyranny; Maria Sliwa for her important e-mail news services about the persecution of Christians in the

Islamic world and about the Arab enslavement of Africans; SOS Femmes en de-tresse (SOS Women in Distress); Robert Spencer for his excellent books and for his important website Jihadwatch; Andrew Sullivan; Amir Taheri; Kenneth R. Timmerman; the *Wall Street Journal;* the *Washington Times;* the *Weekly Standard;* The Youth Advocacy Program International; and Dr. Fareed Zakaria.

I would like to acknowledge the important work of the following individuals and groups: Alex Satian's and Andrea Levin's CAMERA (the Committee for Accuracy in Middle East Reporting); DEBKA; Professor Alan Dershowitz; Helen Freedman of Americans for a Safe Israel; Vera Golovensky; HonestReporting.com; Morton Klein and Dror Elner of the Zionist Organization of America; Rabbi Michael Lerner; Stephen Stalinsky, who publishes the Middle East Media Institute (MEMRI) reports; and Rabbi Avi Weiss.

I am a board member of Scholars for Peace in the Middle East. It is a most worthy organization, led by Professors Ed Beck and Judy Jacobson, whose exis-tence and intellectual and moral clarity have made a solitary and dangerous mis-sion less lonely and more effective.

In addition, I am very grateful to my Jewish, Muslim, Christian, Arab, and feminist interviewees, both those whom I can—and cannot—name, and to the published writings of the following people: Ayaan Hirsi Ali; Dr. Mahnaz Afkhami; Drs. Margot Badran and Miriam Cooke; Dr. Lois Beck and Nikkie Keddie; Carmen bin Laden; Banahfsheh Zand-Bonazzi; Elio Bonazzi; Dr. Leila Beckwith; Geraldine Brooks; Dr. Paula Caplan; Nonie Darwish; Dr. Nawal El-Saadawii; Elizabeth Warnock Fernea; Brigitte Gabriel; Roya Hakakian; Ellen Francis Harris; Dr. Donna Hughes; Khaled Husseini; Dr. Barbara Joans; Lee Kaplan; Naomi Katz and Nancy Milton; Drs. Nikkie R. Keddie and Beth Baron; Laura Lederer, Esq.; Dorchen Leitholdt, Esq.; Irshad Manji; Dr. Fatima Mernissi; Merry Merrell; Rabbi Etan Mintz; Dr. Azar Nafisi; Dr. Taslima Nas-rin; Rachel Neuwirth; Dr. Arlene Raven; Alifa Rifaat; Tricia Roth; Roz Roth-stein; Salman Rushdie; Freidoune Sahebjam; Jean Sasson; Asne Seierstad; Ramesh Sepehrrad; Soona Samsami; Souad; Barbara Seaman; Saira Shah; Walid Shoebat; Dr. Norman Simms; and Shekaiba Wakili and Sultana Wakili.

I am especially grateful to my researchers. Alyssa Lappen has been superb, effi-cient, available, and knowledgeable. Christi Foist helped out in a pinch as did Pro-fessor Leanna Keith, and my friends, Sonia Nussenbaum and Michael Skakun.

I want to acknowledge the steady support of my assistant William (Bill) Lange; the superb efficiency of my new assistant Robin Eldridge; my computer "guys," Jeff Levine and Doug Macomber; my website master, John C. Burke; and my most excellent bookkeeper, Zulema N. George.

This book literally would not exist without my editor Airié Stuart's enthusi-asm, vision, and commitment. Melissa Nosal has been an exceptionally friendly and efficient assistant editor. I thank my agent, Joëlle Delbourgo, for having led me to exactly the right editor at the right time. Thanks also to the team at Palgrave Macmillan, including Debra Manette, who has done an excellent job of copyediting the manuscript; Donna Cherry, for going the extra mile in terms of the schedule; Ellis Levine, Esq., for his insightful and delightful counsel; and Paige Casey, my marketing manager, for managing a complex marketing and publicity campaign.

In addition, I want to thank Sanda Balaban; Joan Casamo; Jerome Chanes; Linda Clarke; Anselma Dell'Olio; Nancy Dier; Shirley Erlitz; Guiuliano Ferrara; Eva Fogelman; my longtime Torah study partner; Rivka Haut; William Hoffman; Ruth Jody; Nancy Kobrin; Edith Kurzweil; Sam Merians; Kate Millet; and Rabbi Michal and Chaie Shmidman, the Congregation of Orach Chayim for the many varied ways in which their presence in the universe has enlightened and consoled me.

I am, as ever, very grateful to Helene Kostre, Harvey Rossell, David Zimmerman, Gina Solovianova, and Joanna Wilczynska, all of whom make it possible for me to devote myself entirely to reading, writing, thinking, and lecturing.

I honor my extended Afghan, Turkish, and Muslim family who, for obvious reasons, shall remain nameless. We have remained connected for nearly fifty years, and it is a cherished connection.

Finally, I am deeply indebted to my son, Ariel David Chesler Esq., and to his longtime girlfriend, Shannon Berkowsky, for their family love and support. Finally, I have been truly blessed by my benefactor, first reader, and companion, Susan L. Bender, Esq.

I thank God for seeing me through many difficulties and for allowing me to finish this book.

This work is dedicated to freethinkers, truth-tellers, dissidents, and whistleblowers, and to all those who fight for and risk their lives in the eternal struggle for humanity's dignity and freedom.

The Death of Feminism

Introduction

Is feminism really dead? Well, yes and no.

Doing so gives me no pleasure, but someone must finally tell the truth about how feminists have failed their own ideals and their mandate to think both clearly and morally. Only an insider can really do this, someone who cares deeply about feminist values and goals. I have been on the front lines for nearly forty years, and I feel called upon to explain how many feminists—who should be the first among freedom- and democracy-loving peoples have instead become cowardly herd animals and grim totalitarian thinkers. This must be said, and my goal in saying so is a hopeful one. We live at a time when women can and must make a difference in the world.

From the start, feminism has been unfairly, even viciously, attacked. I do not want to do that without cause here. The truth is, that in less than forty years, a visionary feminism has managed to challenge, if not transform, world consciousness.

For example, you can find feminists on every continent who have mounted brave and determined battles against rape, incest, domestic violence, economic and professional inequality, and local "cultural" practices such as honor killings, dowry burnings, female genital mutilation, and the global trafficking in women and children. I don't want to minimize or simplify what feminism has accomplished.

In some ways, feminism has also been inclusive. Feminists are Republicans and Democrats, right-wing conservatives and left-wing radicals; feminists are both religious and antireligious, anti-abortion and pro-abortion, antipornography and pro-pornography, anti–gay marriage and pro–gay marriage. Feminists come in all ages and colors, belong to every caste, class, and religion, and live everywhere. Many feminists are married, are parents, and care about family values. Some feminists march in demonstrations; other feminists police those marches. Some feminists work in government and serve in the armed forces; other feminists oppose these organizations' every decision and action.

Nevertheless, feminists are often perceived as marginal and irrelevant; and in some important ways the perception is accurate.

Today the cause of justice for women around the world is as urgent as it's ever been. The plight of both women and men in the Islamic world (and increasingly in Europe) requires a sober analysis of reality and a heroic response. World events have made feminism more important, yet, at the same time, feminism has lost much of its power.

To my horror, most western academic and mainstream feminists have not focused on what I call gender apartheid in the Islamic world or on its steady penetration of Europe. Such feminists have also failed to adequately wrestle with the complex realities of freedom, tyranny, patriotism, self-defense, and the concept of a just war.

Islamic terrorists have declared jihad against the "infidel West" and against all those who yearn for freedom. Women in the Islamic world are treated as subhumans. Although some feminists have sounded the alarm about this, a much larger number have remained silent. Why is it that many have misguidedly romanticized Islamikaze terrorists as freedom fighters and condemned both America and Israel as the real terrorists or as the root cause of terrorism? In the name of multicultural correctness (all cultures are equal, but formerly colonized cultures are more equal), the feminist academy and media appear to have all but abandoned vulnerable people: Muslims, as well as Christians, Jews, and Hindus, to the forces of reactionary Islamism.

Because feminist academics and journalists are now so heavily influenced by left ways of thinking, many now believe that speaking out against head scarves, face veils, the chador, arranged and child marriages, polygamy, forced pregnancies, or female genital mutilation is either "imperialist" or "crusade-ist."[1] Postmodernist ways of thinking have also led feminists to believe that confronting narratives on the academic page is as important and world-shattering as confronting jihadists in the flesh and rescuing living beings from captivity.

Jihadists do not think women are human beings. However, as yet there have been no feminist foreign policy initiatives emanating from mainstream feminists and the academy. On the contrary, I believe traditional feminism has supported an isolationist and America-blaming position. A knee-jerk hatred for President Bush has all but blinded many feminists and progressives to the greater danger of terrorism and Saudi-based Wahabi and Algerian-based Salafist Islamism (both are radical fundamentalist ideologies that view other Islamic sects as heretical). While extreme fundamentalism exists in every religion, it also exists among secular western intellectuals.

I am disheartened by what has happened to feminism and by what I see as the new powerlessness of women. I did not foresee the extent to which feminists—who, philosophically, are universalists and therefore interventionists—would, paradoxically, become both multiculturalists and isolationists. Such cultural relativism (in the presumed service of antiracism) is perhaps the greatest failing of the feminist establishment. Despite our opponents' considerable fears that feminism would radicalize the campuses and the world, most feminists refuse to take risky, real-world positions. By choosing that path, they have lost their individualism, radicalism, and, in a sense, some of their own freedom.

I recant none of the visionary ideals of Second Wave feminism. Rather, it is as a feminist—not as an antifeminist—that I have felt the need to write a book to show that something has gone terribly wrong among our thinking classes. The multicultural feminist canon has not led to independent, tolerant, diverse, or objective ways of thinking. On the contrary: It has led to conformity, totalitarian thinking, and political passivity. Although feminists indulge in considerable nostalgia for the activist 1960s and 1970s, in some ways they are no different from the rest of the left-leaning academy, which also suffers from the disease of politically correct passivity.

Nostalgia can blind. Thus, many essentially inactive feminists long for "action," even in jihadic form. That may be why they confuse Islamikaze terrorists and misogynists with freedom fighters. The academy, where ideology is often disassociated from reality and from activism, is where such passivity starts.

Dorchen Leidholdt, director of Legal Services for Battered Women in New York City (Sanctuary for Families), supervises a staff of 20 lawyers plus 300 pro bono lawyers. According to Leidholdt, "Although Women's studies courses originally promoted a feminist understanding of women's experience, most have lost touch with the reality of women's lives and have become part of the problem, not the solution. Women's studies has been infected by postmodernism—which is antithetical to feminism."

Massachusetts psychologist Dr. Paula Caplan, author of *The Myth of Female Masochism* and many other excellent books, agrees. She describes one Ivy League campus this way: "The campus has a women's center. If you're a woman from Southeast Asia who thinks she might be bisexual, there's a group for that. There is nowhere for a woman who is being battered to turn. There are no courses in Violence against Women and no Psychology of Women courses either."

California anthropology professor and author Dr. Barbara Joans no longer calls herself a feminist. She explains: "The word has been so misused. I talk about women's rights, not about feminism. University feminists are so far away from the feminism we all worked for in the late '60s and early '70s. It may share a name but that's all. Academic feminists are profoundly self-righteous and are now all left-wing in orientation. They are unable to consider that any position other than their own exists or has a right to a fair hearing."

According to New York and Maryland–based feminist art historian and critic Dr. Arlene Raven: "Women's studies started out as an activist intervention, a way to transform the academy and it has become the most retrograde of disciplines. Everything is constructed, nothing is real. This way of thinking leads feminist scholars to antifeminist positions. The new regime wants to make absolutely no waves."

Barbara Seaman, with whom I cofounded the National Woman's Health Network in 1974, is the author of many important books, including the influential *The Doctor's Case Against the Pill* and, most recently, *The Greatest Experiment Ever Performed on Women: Exploding the Estrogen Myth*. Seaman says: "There is an almost complete disconnect between the grassroots feminist health movement and the feminist academy. Many will not research or teach our history. They will not publish the truth about our positions and activism. Right now Harvard University Press is about to publish a work, *Hot and Bothered*, by Dr. Judy Houck, which disappears or misunderstands the long history of feminist opposition to hormone replacement therapy. The press wanted a quote from the Health Network's current director, Cynthia A. Pearson. But Cindy replied, 'I'm afraid that I can't.'"

Is women's studies to blame for all this? Well—yes and no. Had the academy been slightly more hospitable to original, radical, and activist feminist energies and had funding been plentiful, there might have been no need to ghettoize the study of gender. But that was not the case. In addition, with some exceptions, the kind of feminist faculty who could survive in academe were, like their male counterparts, far too dutiful.

Today feminists are also seen as marginal because of their obsessive focus on "personal" body rights and sexual issues. This is no crime, but it is simply not good enough. It may shock some to hear me say this, but we have other important things on our agenda.

For example, what began as an absolutely essential conversation about "our bodies ourselves" in the late 1960s continues today. Back then, most young and educated women did not know they had clitorises or how to have orgasms, and they were strangers to their own bodies in terms of menstruation, pregnancy, childbirth, and menopause. However, the concern with women's bodies has increasingly gotten more extreme and more public. I am not only talking about the sexual objectification of women by pornographers and some fashion designers, but also about the feminist-created cult of the vagina, which has become somewhat fetishistic.

Eighteen thousand girls and women screaming out "vagina" in Madison Square Garden does not a revolution make. Removing a woman's chador in Madison Square Garden (which, when last I looked, was not located in Mecca, Kabul, or Tehran) might be dramatically thrilling—but does not a revolution make. I agree: Symbols are important, and such V-day ("Victory," "Vagina,") events are legitimate as theater or propaganda. And yet the branding of feminist ideas and ideals has always struck me as a bit strange and in poor taste. "Vulva" cookies? "Vagina warrior" T-shirts? Such merchandise is not pornographic, but it is adolescent and superficial.

How would V-Day play in the Islamic world? Would the women who put on the play be jailed or merely stoned to death on the spot? Would such theater empower sheeted women to rise, or would it further endanger them? How would *Vagina Monologue* performances help women who are being held captive in brothels?

I do not mean to single V-Day out for scorn. Playwright Eve Ensler and company are persistently and visibly talking about women's issues. They are not attacking feminist ideas or mocking feminist efforts. Further, Ensler donates a great deal of money to end violence against women. Still, if this is the most public face of feminism today, I can understand why serious people are not taking feminism all that seriously.

Every year 15 million children die of hunger; the World Health Organization estimates that one-third of the world is underfed and one-third is starving. American girls and women are obsessed with dieting. In the classroom and in therapy offices, feminists focus on the refusal of girls and women to eat and on eating disorders such as bulimia and anorexia.

In Asia, Africa, and the Middle East, women are being horribly disfigured by acid attacks and by facial and bodily mutilation, including genital mutilation; the American media, influenced by the feminist academy (and the commercial sex industry), focuses on a woman's right to have plastic surgery in order to look ever-youthful and "beautiful."

Around the world, girls and women are being systematically, repeatedly, and publicly gang raped as a weapon of war; girl children are sold by their parents, young women are lured by pimps or kidnapped right off the streets and locked into brothels against their will. Many American feminists focus on a woman's right to heterosexual, bisexual, and lesbian sexual pleasure.

I do not want to denigrate such American feminist concerns. They have their place. But at this moment in history, other pressing concerns are being ignored.

Today the mainstream feminist fight to keep abortion legal has become our era's equivalent of the fight for the vote, which consumed sixty years of our grandmothers' feminist energy. I support a woman's right to choose. However, I do think that other equally urgent feminist issues have fallen by the wayside. For example, over the years, mainstream feminists have sponsored more marches, organizations, research, press conferences, and legislation concerning abortion than they have in any other area, with the possible exception of employment discrimination. Far fewer resources have gone toward improving the working conditions of motherhood and parenting or toward the abolition of female sexual slavery.

And other *feminist* views about the politics and morality (or immorality) of abortion do exist.

Washington D.C.-based lawyer Laura Lederer is a former member of the feminist movement. According to Lederer:

> An epic battle for women's rights and lives was sacrificed by mainstream feminists when they marginalized the commercial sexual exploitation of women, when they stood down in terms of pornography and prostitution and chose to focus only on abortion rights and domestic violence—narrowly defined at that time as spousal abuse. And, in order to fund the battle for abortion, deals were made in the feminist equivalent of the smoky backroom. For example, money was raised in the Playboy mansion for the abortion struggle. I saw a fascinating alliance develop between abortion and sexual liberals and pornographers. We endured a lot of arm-twisting in the women's movement in those days: we were essentially told to "stand down" on the violence, rape, and commercial sexual exploitation of prostitution and pornography while what were deemed "more important" women's issues were moved front and center. In my opinion, the mainstream women's movement has not emerged or "never recovered" from that. They have lost their way. I don't know if we—or they—can get back on path again.

Rhode Island–based women's studies professor Donna Hughes is an expert in trafficking and female sexual slavery. She concurs, saying: "I believe that the decline and narrowing of academic and mainstream feminism is due to certain political choices that were made. The life has drained out of most feminists. This began when feminists made a major compromise in the war on pornography and sided with men, gay groups, and the left. Their support of legalizing prostitution drained more life out of them."

So, what am I saying?

I am saying that women can no longer afford to navel-gaze—not if they want to play vital roles on the world historical stage, not if they want to continue to struggle for women's and humanity's global freedom.

And women in America can no longer allow themselves to be rendered inactive, anti-activist, by outdated left and European views of colonial-era racism that are meant to trump and silence concerns about gender. This was precisely what Columbia University professor Edward Said's book, *Orientalism*, accomplished. Published in 1978, it replaced academic views of woman as worthy victim with that of the brown-skinned Arab man as the worthiest victim of them all. Professor Said stole our feminist thunder when it was at its academic height. Ultimately, even feminists came to believe that the "occupation of Palestine" was far more important than the worldwide occupation of women's bodies.

Educated, feminist Americans may not want to believe that Islamic jihad is here and that the survival of western civilization is at stake. But how can educated feminist Americans not "get" the exceptionally bloody jihad that Islam has long declared against women—not only in Muslim countries but also in Europe and North America? How can feminists remain so morally and intellectually passive?

Of course, not all feminists are passive. Many have been helping the female victims of violence in a hands-on way; this includes helping Muslim women and children who are trying to escape extreme fundamentalist violence. Feminists in every country, including Muslim and Hindu feminists, have written about such cases and have provided shelter and legal representation. They have also fought for political asylum on the women's behalf. Feminists in America have also worked with progressive elements within Christian, Jewish, Muslim, and other immigrant fundamentalist communities to rescue women and children who are being battered, tortured, and threatened with death.

However, this work is not often taught in women's studies programs nor does such hands-on work take place on campus. Many law schools have domestic violence clinics; most graduate liberal arts programs do not. Antifeminist professors in medical and graduate school do not often teach the pioneering work of feminist mental health professionals, such as Dr. Judith Lewis Herman, author of *Trauma and Recovery*, and Dr. Lenore Walker, author of *The Battered Woman*. Over the years, when I have been invited to medical and graduate school campuses to talk about my 1972 book, *Women and Madness*, students attend in large numbers; their professors do not.

Some might say that I am being unnecessarily harsh on women who have, indeed, been sounding the alarm about the global rise in fundamentalist misogyny. Perhaps I am. But I think we can really make a difference. I want more of us to put our shoulder to freedom's wheel.

For example, I know that many feminists enjoyed talking about the plight of Afghan women under the Taliban; and why not? This tragedy proved that Feminism 101 was right all along, that men really did oppress women. But few of the televised feminist talking heads wanted to systematically sponsor Afghan women as immigrants or as political refugees. I know because I suggested, privately, that the anti-Taliban American feminists do so. Needless to say, neither did these feminists want to launch a military invasion of Afghanistan on behalf of women. I know—I raised the idea many times. All I got were pitying looks.

Safely railing against oppressors was one thing; actually going up against them personally, physically, risking anything, was something else. After all, many feminists were pacifists, or they were "ladies." But mainly, an increasing number of feminists were leftists and left-dominated liberals. As such, they would happily and repeatedly talk (and scream) about going up against America as an oppressor, but they would not even whisper words that opposed any (brown-skinned, formerly colonized) Third World Muslim tyrant—not even when he was systematically terrorizing and slaughtering equally brown-skinned and formerly colonized women, children, men—and Muslim feminists, both male and female.

And the moment the United States Army actually invaded Afghanistan, most feminists immediately and loudly condemned the action. Somewhat bitterly, many feminists said, "President Bush is not really doing it for the women."

Some personal disclosures are now in order.

First, I am a feminist *and* an American patriot. Yes, one can be both. I am also an internationalist. There is no contradiction here. Finally, I am a religious Jew and am sympathetic to both religious and secular worldviews. Being religious does not compromise my feminism. On the contrary, it gives me the strength and a necessarily humbled perspective to continue the struggle for justice.

Second, Afghanistan matters to me; it has touched my life. Once, long ago, in 1961, I was held captive there and kept in purdah; some women were exceptionally kind to me. I will never forget them. I write about my Afghan sojourn here at length for the first time in chapter 4 in the hope that it will render the situation of women living under Islamism clearer, more real to academic and mainstream feminists.

I believe that my western feminism was forged in that most beautiful and tragic of countries. And yes, I also understand that America has not yet done all that is necessary to build up the country, that ethnic warlords and drug lords continue to tyrannize civilians, that women are still imprisoned in chadaris (full body sheets) and in brutal arranged marriages with limited access to medical care, education, and employment.

Most academics and activists do not actually *do* anything; they read, they write, they deliver papers. They may not be able to free slaves or prisoners the way an entering army might, but they can think clearly, and in complex and courageous ways, and they can enunciate a vision of freedom and dignity for women and men. It is crucial, even heroic, that they do so. In this regard, let me quote from Natan Sharansky and Ron Dermer's book, *The Case for Democracy: The Power of Freedom to Overcome Tyranny and Terror:*

> I am convinced that all peoples desire to be free. I am convinced that freedom anywhere will make the world safer everywhere. And I am convinced that democratic nations, led by the United States, have a critical role to play in expanding freedom around the globe. By pursuing clear and consistent policies that link its relations with nondemocratic regimes to the degree of freedom enjoyed by the subjects of those regimes, the free world can transform any society on earth, including those that dominate the current landscape in the Middle East. In so doing, tyranny can become like slavery, an evil without a future.

I share Sharansky and Dermer's vision. Both women and religious minorities in non-western and Muslim countries, and in an increasingly Islamized Europe, are endangered as never before. In this book I argue that America must begin to factor both gender and religious apartheid into our evolving foreign policies.

❈ ❈ ❈

In 2004 Dutch filmmaker Theo van Gogh was butchered by a jihadist on the streets of Amsterdam for having made a film, *Submission,* that denounced the abuse of women under Koranic Islam. For a period of time, van Gogh's co-creator, Somali-born feminist and Dutch parliamentarian, Ayaan Hirsi Ali, went into hiding. The multiculturally sensitive Dutch finally began to wrestle with what it might mean to tolerate intolerant Muslim immigrants and quickly passed their version of the American Patriot Act.

However, the eerie silence from both feminists and filmmakers about van Gogh's assassination is deafening and disheartening. The same Hollywood loudmouths so quick to condemn and shame President Bush for having invaded Afghanistan and Iraq have, as of this writing, remained silent about the chilling effect that such an assassination in broad daylight can have on academic and artistic freedom. According to screenwriter and filmmaker Bridget Johnson, "Hollywood has long walked on eggshells regarding the topic of Islamic fundamentalism. The film version of Tom Clancy's *The Sum of All Fears* changed Palestinian terrorists to neo-Nazis out of a desire to avoid offending Arabs or Muslims. The war on terror is a Tinseltown taboo."

In December 2004 my dear friend, Italian film critic and journalist Anselma Dell'Olio attended the European Film Awards in Barcelona. At least 1,500 of Europe's most prominent and powerful directors, producers, and actors were present at Europe's equivalent of the Oscars. According to Dell'Olio, German director Wim Wenders, the president, delivered an opening speech in which he hurriedly, "in embarrassment, and only in passing," mentioned "the passing of Dutch filmmaker Theo van Gogh." The *passing?* Was he wafted away by a gentle breeze, did he die of old age? He did not ask the assembled to bow their heads in silent mourning or to rise in protest. According to Dell'Olio, Wenders did not decry the fact that van Gogh had been brutally assassinated or that van Gogh's film partner, Ayaan Hirsi Ali, has been similarly threatened.

No one publicly discussed the importance of free expression or the allegedly sacred right to make films that "offend" various sensibilities.

This silence and embarrassment are forms of appeasement. I suspect that Wenders and others who behave like him are multiculturally correct liberals who feel that Islamic jihad is either justified or that Islamist barbarism represents a native custom that Europe dare not oppose.

I strongly, urgently, disagree with this.

In January 2005 the International Film Festival in Rotterdam decided *not* to show van Gogh and Ali's film for "security reasons." The film was to have been part of a debate on freedom of speech as well as an homage to van Gogh.

'Tis a season that requires heroes. Luckily, there are many. Dhimmi-status peoples (infidels) have been exposing Islam's long history of religious apartheid. Islam's persecution of non-Muslims and of Muslims who convert to other religions is being documented by, among others, Bat Ye'or, the author of *Eurabia: The Euro-Arab Axis, Land of Dhimmitude,* and *Land of Islam;* Andrew G. Bostom, the editor of *The Legacy of Jihad;* Daniel Pipes, the author of *Miniatures: Views of Islamic and Middle Eastern Politics;* Robert Spencer, the author of *Islam Unveiled: Disturbing Questions about the World's Fastest Growing Faith* and *The Politically Incorrect Guide to Islam and the Crusades;* Joseph Farah, *Taking America Back;* Kenneth R. Timmerman, the author of *Preachers of Hate: Islam and the War on America;* and Ibn Warraq, *Leaving Islam: Apostates Speak Out.*

We also have many feminist heroes. Some are Muslims who have no ambivalence about exposing and opposing gender apartheid and other Islamist atrocities. For example, Bengali physician Taslima Nasrin, the author of *Shame* and sixteen other books, immediately comes to mind—as does Irshad Manji, a Uganda-born Southeast Asian Muslim who grew up in Vancouver, Canada, and who is the author of *The Trouble with Islam: A Wake-Up Call for Honesty and Change.*

Nasrin's many articles criticized Islamic religious practices and customs. Therefore, fundamentalist leaders in Bangladesh put a price on her head. Thousands demonstrated for her arrest and hanging. Nasrin escaped and was granted political asylum in Sweden, where she lives in hiding. Manji has had to lecture with bodyguards. Their clarity and bravery grace my life.

Although Muslim extremists were still threatening to kill Ayaan Hirsi Ali, in late January 2005, after seventy-five days in hiding, she returned to her parliamentary duties in order to spotlight Islamic honor killings in Holland. Although Muslim women constitute only 6 percent of the Dutch population, 60 percent of those in Dutch shelters for battered women are Muslim.

For example, in 2003, one eighteen-year-old Dutch-Turkish student, Zarife, was taken by her father to Ankara, where he shot her to death. Her crime? She had "been seen going out with Dutch girls, and without her scarf." That same year, Nuray's father allegedly shot her while she was sleeping because she had been seeking a divorce. Her uncle and mother watched as she was murdered. Female genital mutilation is also practiced on Muslim women in Holland.

The suicide rate for Muslim women living in Holland is five times higher than that of non-Muslims. Hirsi Ali believes that some of these suicides are really honor killings that have all been kept quiet because the "government believed tolerance required respecting different cultures and traditions." Such tolerance has condemned girls and women—who are Dutch citizens—to torture and death.

So much for the Dutch government. What excuse can feminists give for allowing their politically correct multiculturalism to morally blind them to the clear and present danger of Islamic gender apartheid?

As we shall see, gender apartheid and pernicious Islamism exists in fifty-six non-western countries. Let me note a mere handful of examples.

- In 1997, in Cairo, Egypt, twenty-five-year-old Nora Marzouk Ahmed's honeymoon ended when her father chopped off her head and carried it down the street. "Now," he said, "the family has regained its honor." Nora's crime? She had eloped.
- In 1999, in Amman, Jordan, a brother put four bullets into his sister's head—in their living room—and was proud of it. His sister's rape had "dishonored" the family.
- Also in 1999, in Lahore, Pakistan, Samia Imran was shot dead in her feminist lawyer's office by a man whom her parents had hired to kill her. Her crime? Seeking a divorce.
- In 2001, in Gujar Khan, Pakistan, Zahida Perveen's husband attacked her, gouged out both her eyes, her nose, and her ears. He wrongly suspected her of adultery. He was arrested, but male relatives shook his hand and men decided she "must have deserved it" and that a "husband has to do what a man has to do." (An American doctor has since fitted Zahida with glass eyes and prostheses for her ears and nose.)
- In 2002, in Tehran, an Iranian man cut off his seven-year-old daughter's head after suspecting she had been raped by her uncle. "The motive behind the killing was to defend my honor, fame, and dignity." Some people called for this man's death under Islamic law, but ironically, only the father of the victim has the right to demand the death sentence.
- Also in 2002, a tribal council in the Punjab, in Pakistan, sentenced eighteen-year-old Mukhtaran Bibi to be gang raped as punishment for something her twelve-year-old brother had allegedly done: walking with a girl from a higher-status tribe. (Actually, he had been sexually abused by Mastoi men who sought to cover up their crime in this way.) Members of the wealthy Mastoi tribe and the tribal council had threatened that all the women of the accused boy's family would be abducted and raped if the boy's sister refused to accept her punishment.

  Mukhtaran Bibi's father was forced to witness her gang rape, after which she was driven naked through the streets of her village while hundreds looked on. Amazingly, the rapists were eventually arrested and convicted, and round-the-clock protection was given to Mukhtaran Bibi and her family. However, the rapists' relatives said they are waiting for the police to leave. Then they will slaughter Mukhtaran Bibi and her entire family. According to *The Guardian,* six of the fourteen men were sentenced to death but an appeals court overturned the verdict and freed five of the men. The sixth had his sentence reduced to life in prison.

In 2005, as Mukhtaran Bibi was preparing to visit the United States, the Pakistani government suddenly freed her gang-rapists and detained her, their victim. She was held incommunicado for a period of days. An international outcry led to her release. Within a week, the Pakistani Supreme Court suspended a lower court's acquittal of thirteen men, ordered them re-arrested, and agreed to hear the case.

- In 2004, a sixteen-year-old girl, Atefeh Rajabi, was hanged in a public square in Iran. Her crime? Rajabi was charged with adultery—which probably meant she was raped. Her rapist was not executed. Rajabi told the mullah-judge, Haji Rezaii, that he ought to punish men who rape, not their victims. Haji Rezaii both sentenced and personally hanged Rajabi because, he said, she had a "sharp tongue."

- In 2005, in Gaza, five masked members of Hamas, a Palestinian terrorist group, shot Yusra Azzumi, a twenty-year-old Palestianian woman, to death, brutalized her corpse, and savagely beat both her brother, Rami, and her fiancé, Ziad Zaranda, whom she was to marry within days. This self-appointed Morality Squad wrongly suspected Yusra (herself a Hamas member) of "immoral behavior."

Many immigrants from non-western countries live in Europe. Many continue to practice gender apartheid and commit culturally approved crimes against women in their new countries. (I deal with this at length in chapter 7.)

- In 1998, in the Midlands in England, twenty-two-year-old Pakistani Rukhsana Naz's mother, Shakeela, held her down while her brother strangled her to death. Her crime? She had escaped an arranged marriage and was now seven months pregnant with her boyfriend's child.

- In 2001, Sikh Anita Gindha fled her home in Glasgow, Scotland, to avoid an arranged marriage. She married her non-Sikh boyfriend. In 2003, while she was heavily pregnant with her second child, she was strangled to death in front of her eighteen-month-old son, in what Scotland Yard suspected was an honor killing.

- In 2003, in Holland, a thirty-six-year-old Afghan woman was murdered together with her ten-year-old daughter by her estranged husband. The

Dutch were uncertain as to whether this murderer should be prosecuted under Dutch or under Islamic religious law.

- In 2004, an eighteen-year-old ethnic Turkish girl who lived in Germany and was a German citizen refused to marry a wealthy Pakistani whom her family had chosen for her. Her parents went to her place of employment and threatened to kill her if she did not immediately leave her job and marry. They refused to leave the premises. With the help of a supervisor and friends, "Jasmin" was smuggled out of the building and fled to a shelter in Berlin.
- In 2004, in Holland, thirty-two-year-old Gul's husband shot her for daring to request a divorce. She died at the door of a Dutch women's shelter.

Western feminists cannot turn their backs on the plight of such women. Our vision of freedom for women must become part of American foreign policy. We must work with our government and with our international allies on this, because it is one of the most important feminist priorities of the twenty-first century.

While some western men are also domestically violent, woman-battering is no longer culturally acceptable. Indeed, thanks to Second Wave feminism, it is increasingly prosecuted. Also, western woman-battering does not spring from a *culturally* induced source of shame and honor. Because of this, preventing, tracking, and abolishing woman-battering among Muslims and non-westerners may need to evolve in different ways.

Recently I received a letter from a Syrian American poet named Merry Merrell thanking me for my work. She told me that two years ago, when she lived in London, a young Arab girl had been shot and another beheaded for refusing to wear the burqua. She said: "Upon my return to the United States when telling feminists about this, they preferred to talk about the 'abuse' at Abu Ghraib and the Palestinian problem, which I do not think are minor problems. But, as an old warrior feminist, this ability to worry about trivia while dismissing routine devastating abuse of women has left me speechless."

Dr. Donna Hughes described how excited she was to finally meet with Iranian dissident feminists. They told her that her enthusiasm was unusual for an American feminist, many of whom, they said, seemed to lack "intellectual curiosity and engagement" with the cause of women's freedom in Iran.

According to Hughes, in 1996 Paris-based Iranian feminists invited a group of British feminists (Women Against Fundamentalism) to attend a conference, "Women, Islam, and Fundamentalism." The British group refused to participate because the conference title was "too narrow and did not include critiques against other fundamentalisms such as Hindu, Christian, and Jewish."

Feminists did not start out as isolationists or intolerant conformists. We were not all leftists or anti-activist academics, or so removed from reality. We did not all hate America or Israel with such passion. Most of us did not hate men or children either.

Once we were giants in the earth. Some of us still are. Certainly the first, or suffragist, wave of feminism (1850–1920) was amazing and persistent, in both theory and action. Included in this group were Susan B. Anthony, Elizabeth Cady Stanton, Josephine Butler, Matilda Joslyn Gage, Charlotte Perkins Gilman, and the suffragist-activist Pankhursts in England.

Many early Second Wave feminists such as Sidney Abbott, Bella Abzug, Louise Armstrong, Ti-Grace Atkinson, Ros Baxandall, Rita Mae Brown, Charlotte Bunch, Susan Brownmiller, Z Budapest, Aselma Dell'Olio, Dr. Roxanne Dunbar-Ortiz, Andrea Dworkin, Barbara Ehrenreich, Shulamith Firestone, Ellen Frankfurt, Betty Friedan, Vivian Gornick, Dr. Germaine Greer, Susan Griffin, Dr. Barbara Jones, Flo Kennedy, Audre Lorde, Barbara Love, Dr. Kate Millett, Dr. Eleanor Holmes Norton, Our Bodies Ourselves Collective, Pat Parker, Marge Piercy, Dr. Ruby Rohrlich, Sheila Rowbotham, Dr. Joanna Russ, Dr. Diana Russell, Barbara Seaman, Martha Shelley, Dale Spender, Gloria Steinem, Merlin Stone, Alice Walker, Dr. Lenore Walker, and Monique Wettig were their honorable heirs. We were far more concerned with women's sexual freedom than our grandmothers were but, like our grandmothers, we also knew how to take risks and did not weigh the consequences to our "careers" or even to our lives. We spoke truth clearly, not in postmodern academic voices. We did not follow politically correct lines—they did not yet exist. We were idealists and global activists.

The best of us were anarchic, eccentric, and highly independent nonconformists. We often got into trouble with grassroots feminist nonauthors, also known as the "sisterhood," for being uncontrollable, egotistical "stars."

Feminist thinking was not something that I had learned from someone else. It was, rather, the kind of thinking that many of us were pioneering, independently, at the same moment in history. As a pioneer, I did not consider the possibility that the ideas I had arrived at on my own and in solitude could be turned into propaganda and used to stifle free thinking.

In chapter 1, "The 'Good' Feminist," I discuss the nature of the problem we are facing, one in which the "good" people, including feminists, are increasingly removed from both reality and activism. The academy has been hijacked by a mainly left-wing and left-dominated liberal point of view; academics insist that propaganda must be protected by the First Amendment and by academic freedom; and that truth is so "relative" that it may not even exist.

In chapter 2, "Women and the Crisis of Independent Thinking," I discuss the unique psychological and social problems that independent thinking may pose for women, including feminists. I discuss why feminists have a problem, psychologically, with patriotism and hold double standards about nationalism. Finally, I discuss why it is important to talk to the so-called enemy, or rather to consider civilized discussions with one's opponents as something less than a high crime.

In chapter 3, "The New Intolerance," I discuss how free speech and free thought is stifled on countless feminist listserv groups—and in the name of anti-racism, anti-imperialism, and anti-Americanism. In addition, feminists who oppose pornography and prostitution or who have a kind word to say about America or Israel are often harassed and silenced online; sometimes such feminist dissidents are even purged from the online group.

Chapter 4, "My Afghan Captivity," describes what it was like for me in 1961, as the young bride of a western-educated Afghan, when my American passport was taken away and I was thrown into (fairly posh) purdah in Kabul. The curtailment of my freedom was as awful as it was unexpected; yet it was not as tragic as the lives of most Afghan women whom I also write about in this chapter. I nearly died there, and I write about how I finally escaped. From the moment I returned to America, most progressive westerners did not want to understand what I had to say about my experience. I hope that will now change.

Chapter 5, titled "The One-Sided Feminist Academy," discusses dominant feminist views of terrorism, women, and the Middle East, both pre- and post-9/11.

Chapter 6, "In Their Own Words: Portraits of Arab, Muslim, and Middle Eastern Women," describes daily life as well as the increasing atrocities that afflict so many women in the Islamic world. I also create a cultural and psychoanalytic portrait of Arab and Muslim women today. So many women are quiet heroes, so many are doomed and tragic figures, but many are also active, even ardent collaborators with Islamism against women. Their counterparts exist all over the world. However, Muslim and Arab women are unlikely to oppose tyranny unless they are specially and persistently "deprogrammed" and also militarily and legally protected from domestic terrorism.

Chapter 7 discusses Islamic gender apartheid in Europe and in North America. Honor murders now flourish in the West, as do arranged marriages, polygamy, female genital mutilation, the face veil, and the head scarf. The Canadian province of Ontario has recently passed a law that allows Islamic Shari'a (religious) law to govern Canadian Muslims; Muslim feminists are fighting it. American physicians are dealing with issues related to female genital mutilation practices, and American lawyers are representing Muslim and other non-western immigrant women who are being battered and tortured in culturally approved ways. North American lawyers and governments are also dealing with female and male immigrants from Muslim countries who are seeking political asylum.

Chapter 8, "Toward a New Feminism," discusses the policy implications of Islamic gender apartheid from a psychological point of view; the consequences of Islamic woman-hating and the psychological reasons that western feminists deny this reality; the importance of independent thought and of moral and intellectual clarity; and what a feminist foreign policy might be like.

❋ ❋ ❋

In the last quarter century, some well-entrenched but nevertheless distinguished intellectuals such as Alan Bloom, author of *The Closing of the American Mind,* grumbled, fumed, thundered, and despaired as they defended what has become known as the Dead White Male Canon. They viewed the growing "politically correct" influence on campus with horror and considered it both below standard and civilly dangerous. At the time, I did not read any of their books. I was far too busy dismantling the master's house. I, and a groundswell of other intellectuals and academics, viewed the academy's refusal to teach the work of the most excellent women and minority group members or to employ them as professors as an even more egregious danger. Thus, from the late 1960s on, I pioneered women's studies and psychology courses whose interdisciplinary and multi-cultural points of view have come to prevail on most American and European campuses.

Looking back, I now see that both sides in this debate were right—but also wrong. Indoctrinating students into an ideology is not the same as teaching them how to think. Indoctrination leads to what George Orwell termed "groupthink" and what I call "totalitarian thought." As we shall see, such nonthinking is alive and well, not only in academia, but on the Internet in countless listserv groups. I discuss this in chapter 3.

Those who defended the Dead White Male Canon refused to recognize excellence in women or among racial minorities/majorities. To do so threatened their perches and challenged their prejudices. Those who defended the academic canon against the feminist mob tended to be phobic about feminism and about other liberation movements. The patriarchal professorate did not routinely teach work by women or by feminists.

In the 1950s and 1960s, when I was in college and graduate school, we read work mainly by men. We did not read Mary Wollstonecraft (1792), or Susan B. Anthony and Elizabeth Cady Stanton (1860s–1890s), nor did we read Emma Goldman (1910–1930) or Simone de Beauvoir (1949). Patriarchal professors saw women and feminists as intellectual riffraff, rude pretenders to their ivory, Solomonic thrones.

In those days, I was not looking for any female role models; I did not know that any existed. In graduate school, we read Sigmund Freud, Alfred Adler, and Carl Gustav Jung, but not Karen Horney, Anna Freud, and Melanie Klein.

A curriculum change was definitely in order. This long-overdue change was accomplished by Second Wave feminists over and against enormous resistance. The price we paid for accomplishing our ends was very high. Few of us gained admittance to the groves of academe. (I was among those who did.) Increasingly, over time, women's studies professors stopped teaching our radical and visionary work.

But back to today's classroom for a moment. According to Dr. Paula Caplan, many Ivy League women's studies programs are filled with contempt for radical and original feminist thinkers. They often personalize that contempt. For example, Dr. Caplan describes one such campus, which she does not want to name: "The Chair of the program held Catherine MacKinnon's work aloft and said: 'No one should own this book.' Every faculty member took turns trashing it. When I tried to explain that the Ordinance was not censorship, that it was tort law, no one responded. It's as if I had not spoken. A few weeks later, MacKinnon came up again. 'Did you hear, she's engaged to Jeff Masson? What do they do in bed?' They laughed a lot about that. Someone else said that she didn't want to think about what Andrea Dworkin might do in bed."

This is how adolescent "mean girls" and "queen bees" sound. Such chatter has no place in a feminist venue.

In an age where being entertained is confused with learning how to think, and where books are not necessarily or primarily valued, feminist students and their teachers have increasingly become spectators at theatrical-confessional events such as a campus production of *The Vagina Monologues* or a dramatic reading from the latest *Perils of the Transgendered Warrior*.

I am questioning whether what one learns via public group catharsis is precisely the same as what one learns from reading in solitude, listening to an expert lecture, and then participating in a focused and informed discussion about the material. I question the highly theatrical and emotional nature of how information is being imparted. I view the teaching technique as not only lazy but also as proto-fascist.

How did the feminist academy go wrong? Of course, the academy itself was patriarchal and as such would allow only a handful of feminist academics in— and then only if they were not really radical or activist. The gates opened wide only for those feminists who held certain politically correct positions that their male academic allies and mentors also held.

My cohort of Second Wave thinkers and psychological anarchists were not all scholars, although many were. Few were interested in or capable of taking over institutions; only the socialists, communists, and careerists knew how to do that. And, to our enormous, collective detriment, they proceeded to do so.

Those who get ahead within institutions tend to institute and follow party lines far more seriously than independent thinkers or activists ever do. Academic feminists who received tenure, promotion, and funding tended to be pro-abortion, pro-pornography (anti-censorship), pro-prostitution (pro-sex workers), pro-surrogacy, and anti-colonialist, anti-imperialist, and anti-American. It's as simple as that. Some were proponents of simplistic gender-neutrality: Women and men are exactly the same. Others were essentialists: Men and women are completely different, and women are better.

Also, unsurprisingly, the kind of people who prevail within social and tribal infrastructures tend to be politicians and bureaucrats and not independent thinkers. They are loyal to their careers and to their cliques, not to the truth. This is tragic when the infrastructure is informational-educational, as both the academy and the media are supposed to be.

Today, as our anti-feminist opponents feared, true dissent and diversity are gone. In fact, the only dissenters in sight are, amazingly, libertarian conservatives who have been all but banished from the faculty and the lone radical feminist here or there.

I could never have predicted that feminists would become so dutifully post-modern so quickly, that they would join the ongoing strike against writing clearly. For years now, academics have pretended that brilliance and originality can best be conveyed in a secret, Mandarin language that absolutely no one, including themselves, can possibly understand. In my view, this obfuscation of language has been employed to hide a considerable lack of brilliance and originality and to avoid the consequences of making oneself clear.

When I first started out, I never imagined that feminists would one day become as rigid and intolerant as those whom we had once opposed. I did not foresee that feminists would join the rest of the western academy in embracing an anti-Americanism that is toxic, heartless, mindless, and suicidal. Finally, I did not expect feminists and other academics and activists to betray the truth in favor of "subjective relativism."

I do not think that all truth is subjective or relative. I do think that "the" truth of a matter really does exist, although we may experience, interpret, and act on it differently. The consequences of speaking truth are always very high.

I want intellectuals, including feminists, to tell the truth. I want us to write clearly and passionately. I want us to think independently and morally. I want us to be tolerant, to adopt fewer, perhaps even no, party lines, and to welcome independent and diverse thought in others. What "tolerance" do we demonstrate if we only allow those who agree with us to be heard and scornfully silence those with whom we disagree?

While my publisher views this book as unique, it may also be seen as part of a growing body of ideas, most of which is not particularly feminist, but all of which provides the proper intellectual context for this work.

For example, in 1973, Jean Raspail published an extraordinary and prescient novel, *The Camp of the Saints.* He imagined a flotilla of millions of immigrants traveling from the Ganges to France. An all-powerful, multiculturally correct intelligentsia that has taught Europe that it must atone for its racist, colonial guilt welcomes the invasion. Europe (European culture) is destroyed, both from within and without. The novel is raw, thrilling, overwhelming, ironic, cruel, bitter, and every bit as brilliant as George Orwell's *1984.* At first, Raspail was attacked as a racist. Within a decade, European government leaders were all reading his work. Now what Raspail feared has indeed seemingly come to pass, at least in Europe.

In 2002, Orianna Fallaci, the incomparable Italian journalist, published *The Rage and the Pride.* In it, and in subsequent articles, she has both exposed and railed against the Islamic "invasion" of Europe and the Islamic terrorist threat. She understands that the point of jihad is to subdue and conquer. Despite the high and unpredictable risks of war, she throws her lot in with "Mr. Bush and Mr. Blair." And she defends the Jews and Israel with a morally hot passion.

In 2005, my esteemed colleague Bat Ye'or documented the exact reality that Raspail prophetically fictionalized in her book *Eurabia: The Euro-Arab Axis, Land of Dhimmitude, Land of Islam.* The work is scholarly, scary, daunting, and very carefully, cogently argued. Bat Ye'or focuses mainly on Islam's religious apartheid, not on its gender apartheid. I will begin that conversation here.

In my view, Raspail, Fallaci, and Bat Ye'or are not racists. Islamization of the West involves profound cultural, religious, and class differences. What will happen to a pluralist, democratic, and modern but class-based and historically racist civilization when anti-modern, anti-western, and anti-tolerant class-based and historically racist cultures come to live among them? What will happen when economic discrimination exacerbates non-western and Islamist civilizational "shame"?

Indeed, as I've noted, a number of Christians and Arabs (such as Joseph Farah and Robert Spencer), as well as Muslims have been asking this question too. Thus, this book expands the work begun by the irrepressible and daring Irshad Manji, whose refreshingly candid book *The Trouble with Islam: A Wake-Up Call for Honesty and Change* has inspired a global dialogue with other Muslim dissidents who want Islam to evolve into a more truth-telling and tolerant religion and culture.

This book also relies upon and expands the work of my esteemed colleague, David Horowitz. His lifetime work, but especially his latest book, *Unholy Alliance: Radical Islam and the American Left* (2004), describes a post-9/11 alliance between totalitarian thinkers in the West and the East. Horowitz correctly describes how radical left ideas have invaded mainstream liberal thought in the West and how such thinking, paradoxically, now seeks to destroy freedom and uphold tyranny. This book further expands Horowitz's work and my own over the last two years, in my book *The New Anti-Semitism: The Current Crisis and What We Must Do About It* and in the 35 articles that I've published in Horowitz's influential online magazine, *Frontpage.* Here I expand on the issue of women's global freedom and the role that feminists are (or are not) playing to bring it about.

As I've previously noted, in late 2004 former Israeli minister Natan Sharansky and Ron Dermer published a very important book, *The Case for Democracy.* The work is being taken quite seriously by President Bush and his administration. Sharansky and Dermer do not focus on how crucial the role of women will be in the evolution of freedom and democracy in the Middle East and in Muslim countries. In this book, I begin to do so.

Finally, together with my colleague Dr. Donna Hughes, I co-authored an article in the *Washington Post* in 2004 that was well-received by conservative feminists and damned by some left and liberal feminists. Hughes has begun to spell out what an American feminist foreign policy might be, for example, toward Iran, a country that has been described as a "giant prison for women." Among her many suggestions are: "Place the freedom of women and girls at the top of the agenda for dealing with Iran; voice support for women and their freedom and equality in every policy statement on Iran; fund communication technology broadcasts that focus on women's freedom; hold hearings on Islamic fundamentalism and women in Iran; grant political asylum to women fleeing misogynist tyranny in Iran; encourage allies to adopt the same anti-misogyny policies."

Perhaps some of the very academics and mainstream feminists whom I am criticizing—but also trying to influence—will devalue what I am saying. Perhaps they will say that I am no longer a feminist, that I have betrayed feminism, not they. It will not change the truth of what I'm saying. My hope is that this book will resonate with people of all ages: men and women who are quietly doing feminist work within their professions—and there are many; feminists of faith—and there are also many; both Republicans and Democrats; educators, both here and abroad; and especially with the so-called ordinary people whose lives and freedom are at stake.

One

The "Good" Feminist

In the fall of 2004, I found myself in conversation with a woman who in no way wished to offend or argue with me. Indeed, she assumed we stood on common ground (she is a feminist professor) and thus became increasingly agitated by my silence as she recited the usual litany: President Bush is the terrorist, not bin Laden, the war in Iraq is worse than Vietnam, America's reputation is ruined, we need to work in concert with the United Nations, and so on. I said nothing. Finally she blurted out: "But after what we did in Guatemala and all our other dirty doings in South America, you can't say that we didn't deserve having it thrown back at us on 9/11. You *do* understand that America deserves being hated everywhere. Don't you?"

The reality is, I don't. So I responded: "What justice means to those both living and dead in Guatemala and elsewhere is no doubt a burning issue. But you can't possibly believe that al-Qaeda's terrorism is a form of retributive justice, can you?"

Ah, but she can and does. I tell this story to illustrate a very important point: She is not a bad person, she is being a "good feminist."

And she is not alone. This kind of thinking is the first article of faith among "good" people, not only in Manhattan, where I live, but among their counterparts everywhere else. Decent, educated, progressive people—the kind who donate their still-new clothing to a shelter for battered women, recycle carefully, volunteer in a soup kitchen on holidays, worry about the whales, the seals, the redwood forests, the disappearing infant girls in India, the ravaging injustices of capitalism, and what happened to the American Indians (and I am not being sarcastic about any of these concerns)—are by now so desperate for a solution to such problems, for an end to greed, for "equality now" (formerly known as "revolution now" or "paradise now") that they have lost their ability to think independently about causes and their meaning.

The good people who have in the past condemned American foreign and corporate policies are now ready to die for America's sins; they are quite willing to sacrifice their own way of life, as well as their very lives, for a noble cause: They are ready to surrender to a cleansing, redeeming force—if it will only finally rid the world of its immense suffering. They believe they have caused the world's pain and can therefore cure it. They view themselves as barbarians who have forfeited their right to challenge any other group, culture, religious practice, or idea—no matter how dangerous or inane.[1]

Some of these good people may actually believe that the humbling of America and the destruction of Israel will reduce the suffering of the world's victims. They hope it will also free them from the burden of empire-guilt they so unhappily bear—even if this also means that the whole planet might be bombed back to the seventh century.

My friends, the good people, in some ways view al Qaeda as a force that is trying to level the playing field.

I, on the other hand, think al Qaeda is only an annihilating force that has nothing to do with justice but instead represents a totalitarian war against western ideals such as freedom and democracy; we are in the cross-hairs of the Islamist desire to rule the world. I view Osama bin Laden and the late Yasser Arafat and their minions of mullahs as radically evil, not as noble representatives of their own people—people whom they themselves have tortured, tyrannized, and impoverished. I don't view them as extreme but with good intentions.

Saying things like this, coupled with my spirited defense of Israel, has gotten me into trouble with nearly every politically correct good person I know and has resulted in my being severely ignored or criticized in the liberal, left, secular, and feminist media and led to my being perceived as a right-wing, conservative, reactionary turncoat.

The way I see it: Everything is at stake, it is all up for grabs, this is no time for nihilistic rhetoric or tedious party lines. This is not the time to think in ways calculated to please or to least offend one's peers. My goal is quite the opposite. I do not want to offend my good feminist friends; on the contrary, I would like to bring women and men together—from both the right and the left—in order to make a real difference. This is a time when we, the good people, have to think clearly, creatively, boldly, and morally.

❊ ❊ ❊

Back in the day, I was once considered a good person myself. But I often held the minority position among feminists on most issues and was never a true-blue Marxist-Leninist. My kind did not prevail in the academy or in the media. Today what young people and outsiders may think feminism is really about is not the feminism that many of us once fought for.

In 2002, many feminists congratulated me on my book, *Woman's Inhumanity to Woman,* in which I documented female-female aggression and competition and the ways in which women, like men, have internalized sexist beliefs. Mainstream feminist leaders were far less sanguine about my topic and maintained a grudgingly respectful distance. But I was genuinely surprised by how the air grew still around me when first I began to speak out as an American patriot. Vicious attacks alternated with major silences. My Zionism put me in another category. This time, when feminists called to compliment me on my bravery, they spoke in damnable whispers.

For example, a former president of a state National Organization of Women (NOW) chapter called to say: "Everything you're saying is so true. Jew-hatred and Israel-bashing is at its worst among the feminists we know. Especially if they're Jewish. I've begun losing friends over this issue. I don't want this to happen, nor do my friends, so they've begun to not talk about Israel when I'm around. Truthfully, I don't bring it up myself anymore."

I am not exaggerating; she whispered the entire time we were on the phone.

Another colleague said I was "right on," that "Zionism is the dirtiest word imaginable" among our old crowd of feminists. She privately congratulated me for my clarity and courage but sotto voce. She whispered: "I don't tell anyone what I really think. Why should I? Life is short. Life is sweet. I'm not about to risk all my friendship networks that cushion me from loneliness."

Two dear friends, both longtime feminists, came to offer blessed support. After much conversation, one of them said, almost in wonder, "So, *you* see the Jews as the symbol for western civilization. What happens to them is what will happen to the rest of us if we don't wake up. And *you* see America more as a bright and shining promise to the rest of the world, not as a purveyor of death. What a genuinely radical idea!"

In the last five years, I have observed some fairly strange behavior in public places on the part of the good people. Ordinary civilians better understand that the terrorists mean to kill us and that appeasement is not an option. The good people do not. (Or as Harvard professor and author Michael Ignatieff said, "Both Paul Berman and I share an impatience with liberals who don't yet understand what ruthless enemies we are up against.")

For example, early in 2003, in the midst of a quiet café dinner, a soft-spoken artist friend suddenly began screaming, "I hate President Bush, I hope he dies of cancer." Her face got red, and she screwed up her eyes. I was taken aback. Her rage was extreme and out of context; we had not been discussing politics or al Qaeda's ongoing war against the infidels. How could anyone be so angry or so irrational about a political figure?

I can understand marshaling arguments, point by point, against a particular political policy. I can understand criticizing any public figure as long as it is done in a reasonable, rational way. But in an era of competitive reality shows (one step removed from the Christians versus the lions), tolerant, reasoned discourse has lost its cachet.

In the fall of 2000, two things happened: Arab Muslim jihadists launched their second (or third or fourth) intifada against Israel, and the U.S. Supreme Court declared that George W. Bush had won the presidential election. Immediately thereafter, a "coarse partisanship" (the phrase is Mark Helprin's in the *Wall Street Journal*) permeated nearly every interaction in America, reduced what should have been thoughtful and civilized conversation into vulgar, gladiatorial combat. The enlightened good people—the artists, academics, journalists, scholars, and activists—saw conspiracies everywhere and threatened to depart these shores for those of Europe if the Republicans won the presidency in 2004. Good feminist people insisted that Europe was more receptive to the practice of feminism, now aka anti-Americanism.

For example, one American feminist professor proudly admitted to me that she could no longer "bear" to listen to the American media, that NPR and WBAI could no longer be "trusted," and that to maintain the best "critiques of America," one had to listen to the British and French media. She told all her students to do likewise. She begged me to do so too.

A retired American feminist professor and activist said she was going to move to Italy because she could already hear the sounds of "concentration camp construction" in her San Francisco neighborhood. In my view, this woman lacked moral gravity and all common sense—for which, of course, she was duly lionized by her friends who described her as prescient, prophetic, a force for good in the universe.

I once thought that liberals, progressives, Democrats, leftists, peace activists, academics, feminists, and gay liberationists not only tolerated diversity but verily embraced the concept with passion and principle. Either I was wrong or lately such good people have changed radically. Thus, it is no longer possible to have a civil conversation in America or in Europe, at least not among the good people and not if you don't toe the party line.

I may be overstating this, but it seems that many of the 49 percenters—those who voted for John Kerry—refuse to engage in conversation with anyone who does not agree with them totally and about everything. Thus, one cannot be pro-choice and anti–gay marriage, nor can one oppose both rape and affirmative action. One has to sign on to the entire politically correct agenda or risk being attacked and ostracized.

Many progressives have so circled their wagons that even if you come in peace and are known to agree with much of their agenda, they will still regard you as a traitor if you are not sufficiently anti-American or do not strongly support the Palestinian cause. God forbid if you say that a religion (other than Judaism) is not purely peaceful, or that a culture (other than America's) may be dreadfully misguided. If you say this, the good people will instantly conclude that you are a racist.

The good people are not afraid to speak their truths; indeed, they are shouting them from the world's rooftops. Those who disagree with them, even in minor ways, have grown quieter and perhaps more determined to oppose them. Americans on both sides of this great divide are increasingly reluctant to say what they really think unless they are safely among co-true believers. No one wants to risk the inevitable screaming match or ruptured relationship.

This is a dangerous moment in our history.

For example, a lifelong Democrat and pioneering feminist physician tells me that her grown grandchildren won't talk to her because she voted for President Bush. "My family is deeply divided over this." A judge begs me to advise him. The problem? His thirty-year-old son has become "corrupted by identity politics" and insists on wearing a pro-PLO T-shirt and an Arab kaffiyeh when he comes home for Jewish holidays. "When my wife asked him to come but please, without the political fashion statement, he hung up on her. Now, he won't take our calls."

A Republican politician from the Midwest tells me that he can no longer discuss politics at his family table because his brother views his party as "Satanic." "Out of respect for my mother, I keep quiet. Otherwise we'd come to blows." A West Coast gay playwright tells me that he dares not reveal that he is a patriotic American and that he is anti-jihad. "They'd cut me off at the knees. It's hanging time on the left, and I want to live." A lifelong feminist Democrat in New York tells me that she will no longer talk politics with anyone who did not vote against Bush. "I don't know what world they live in, but it's not mine."

Does she believe that engaging in dialogue with the designated "enemy" somehow constitutes traitorous behavior? If so, and I suspect this is the case, I must ask: Is she only afraid of the Republicans—who have not abolished her First Amendment right to speak out as a feminist and who have not rescinded the Fourth Amendment against improper search and seizure—or is she afraid of the media and academic elite who view civil conversation with anyone who opposes them as a high crime?

It is crucial to note that our government has not criminalized free speech nor have dissidents been jailed for saying whatever they please. In my opinion, the chilling of free speech has been unilaterally imposed by those who claim to act on its behalf.

What sort of group or person refuses to recognize the existence of and refuses even to talk to, no less hire, someone with whom they disagree? What sort of group or person persistently slanders and demonizes those with whom they happen to disagree on key political issues? What sort of group or person demands uniform party-line thinking—and is powerful enough to coerce people into "hiding" their potentially dissident views, sometimes even from themselves?

Surely I must be talking about the power of the former Soviet state or Nazi Germany, Maoist China, or any one of the many Islamic dictatorships; or I must be describing Republican and conservative thinking. Alas, I am not.

Today totalitarian thinking is *also* flourishing among media and academic elites. Oddly enough, such totalitarian thinking and its consequent thought control are flying high under the banners of "free speech" and "political correctness." Dare to question these elites' right to silence or shame those who are trying to expose or challenge them, and you'll quickly be attacked as representing a new and more dreadful form of "McCarthyism" and "witch-hunting."

For example, on March 6, 2005, the Columbia University chapter of Scholars for Peace in the Middle East, and the David Project co-sponsored a daylong academic conference at Columbia to challenge the Palestinianization of the Middle East Asian Language and Culture Department and the professorial intimidation of pro-Israel students. I spoke at this conference and can assure you that the other speakers were dignified, serious, and knowledgeable. Nevertheless, on April 4, under the umbrella of "Stop McCarthyism at Columbia," many speakers condemned the Jewish students' efforts to foster free discovery and eliminate intimidation from the classroom; one called their campaign a "right-wing onslaught" led by "a small number of Zionist students."[2] Dr. Charles Jacobs, the director of the David Project, explains the situation in this way:

> The modern university is severely challenged by radical relativism. Can anyone distinguish between propaganda, lies, and teaching? . . . How then would a university president stop a professor from teaching lies and hate? The conventional theory, expressed by the New York ACLU [American Civil Liberties Union] in this debate, is that universities are inherently protected . . . because they are "open marketplaces of ideas" in which truth will out. But everyone knows that Middle East studies departments are more like captured regions in a war of ideas, which have become fortresses of entrenched power, almost entirely closed off to scholars who do not subscribe to the Palestinianist viewpoint. . . . It is easier to avoid these tough issues and instead throw stones at those who wish to safeguard some standard of truth and decency of discourse. The newest stone thrown at us, ironically by those who wish to silence our opinions, is "McCarthyism!" Yet we have never said anyone should be fired or prevented from getting a job in Middle East studies because of his or her views— or silenced so that his or her words could not be spoken in Columbia's halls. It is they who have done this.

Professor Norman Simms, who has endured similar accusations from college administrators and colleagues, explains what the slurs "McCarthyite" and "witchhunter" are meant to do and why these epithets hurt. Simms is an expatriate

American who left America during the Vietnam War first for Canada and then relocated to New Zealand—a country in which there are no more than 6,000 Jews, many of whom are Holocaust survivors. Simms and other Jewish academics at the University of Waikato have always kept a low and secular profile.

According to Simms, that changed when Hans Joachim Kupka, a high official in the Neo-Nazi Bavarian Republikan Partei, who maintains an anti-Jewish and Holocaust denial website, came to do his master's thesis on 'The Use of German in New Zealand.'" When Simms advised Kupka that most German-speaking Jews would not consent to be interviewed by a Nazi, all hell broke loose at the university. Bryan Gould, the vice chancellor, branded the Jewish academics, led by Simms, as "witch-hunters." Other administrators referred to the Jewish academics as "subterranean people" and as "uninvited outsiders." Simms writes:

> The parents, grandparents, or other relations, and friends of many of the Jews who were calling attention to Kupka's hate mail on the internet had already lived through those persecutions by the witch-hunter supreme, Joe McCarthy. To call these (expatriate) academics who have devoted their lives to liberal causes and to the exposure of McCarthyite tactics, "witch-hunters" was a hurtful, spiteful, and ugly thing [to do]. Second, to bring up the concept of witches in relation to Jews is to evoke archaic hatreds—the slurs that Jews are witches and magicians, worshippers of the Devil, who poison wells.

In my opinion, American campuses have indeed bred a new and diabolical McCarthyism. Academics now presume that they have the right to teach brazen lies and engage in hate speech, which they expect to be protected in the name of "free speech" or academic freedom. Worse, when academics try to teach a non– or anti–left wing view of any subject, they will be accused (by the new McCarthyites) of leading a McCarthyite witch-hunt against the left wing totalitarian suppression of free speech.

As I continually intone: Orwell himself would weep at such extreme linguistic distortions of the truth.

Free speech and academic freedom are very important. However, professors are also supposed to teach the difference between the truth and a lie. The earth is round, not flat; Darwin was right about evolution; communism failed; women are oppressed, and men are too. Many professors have abdicated this responsibility. Professors must be allowed to hold their own political or intellectual point of view; however, they should also teach students that more than one point of view exists. Professors should also allow students to make up their own minds without being publicly shamed or academically punished.

David Horowitz, author, publisher of *FrontPage* magazine, and president of the Center for the Study of Popular Culture (CSPC), has long insisted that college and graduate students are being "indoctrinated or otherwise assaulted by political propagandists." Horowitz has campaigned for an Academic Bill of Rights in which no professor can be "hired or fired or denied promotion or tenure on the basis of his or her political or religious beliefs" and for a campus "environment conducive to the civil exchange of [diverse] ideas." Horowitz wants to "remove partisan politics from the classroom." He writes:

> It is not an education when a mid-term examination contains a required essay on the topic, "Explain Why President Bush Is A War Criminal," as did a criminology exam at the University of Northern Colorado in 2003. . . . At Foothills College in California, a pro-life professor compared women who have abortions to the deranged mother Andrea Yates who drowned her six children. The professor then gave D's and F's to students who expressed opinions in favor of abortion. . . . It is the task of professors—whether they are left or politically conservative—to teach students *how* to think and not *what* to think about matters that are controversial.

This makes sense and seems fair, but Horowitz has been demonized as a right-wing McCarthyite embarked on an anti-left witch-hunt. For example, weblogger Kurt Nimmo, writing in *Counterpunch,* describes Horowitz as occupying a world in which "all of the clocks were lurched backward to a more paranoid and suspicious time, let us say somewhere mid-stride of the McCarthy inquisition." Nimmo further characterizes Horowitz as "cynical," "paranoid," and "misanthropic" and, of course, as a "neo-conservative." Alexander Cockburn, of *The Nation* and *Counterpunch,* characterizes Horowitz as a "whiner," a "howler," and a liar. Dutch mathematician, economist, and pro-Palestinian activist Paul de Roooij also demeans Horowitz for "smearing" leftists, "whitewashing" America and Israel, and for publishing writers, such as the eminent Daniel Pipes, who "froth" and engage in "deranged diatribes." De Rooij declares:

> And who does Horowitz think he is to have the stature to call for an "academic bill of rights"? Perhaps this intellectual and moral pipsqueak should first crawl out of the sewer before pontificating about this topic. Horowitz's dubious projects, his shady past, and his far-right-wing connections suggest that what he is proposing is a frontal assault on academic freedom. His call for this bill is a bit like a pyromaniac urging safe usage of fireworks.

Recently Horowitz has been heckled, harangued, and physically assaulted by leftists at his college lectures.[3] He may indeed be anti-left, but that is no crime. (My saying so amounts to heresy on campus.) Horowitz may indeed be arguing for freedom of expression and intellectual diversity in order to empower conservative professors, but his principles would redress an imbalance and apply to all.

A number of recent surveys and studies have confirmed Horowitz's charges. For example, in 1995, *The American Enterprise* (*TAE*) surveyed professors' voting registration records at Cornell and Stanford. According to editor Karl Zinsmeister, professors at both campuses had overwhelmingly registered to vote as

Democrats.[4] However, these findings were discounted by critics because the survey had looked at only "two campuses" and "considered [only] nine academic departments."

Therefore, in 2002, Horowitz's CSPC and TAE jointly published a yearlong study of nineteen leading colleges and universities, including Brown, Syracuse, and the universities of Maryland and Colorado. They found that professors had registered to vote 10 to 1 for Democrats.[5]

However, both CSPC and TAE are conservative organizations. In addition, their data collection process had not been separately and independently controlled and certified. This does not mean they did anything unethical or that their findings weren't "true." It simply means that a more refined study was required.

Interestingly, also in 2002, a separate study conducted by the Higher Education Research Institute at the University of California at Los Angeles (UCLA), confirmed that Horowitz and Zinsmeister were definitely onto something. The institute published a survey of 55,521 professors at 416 colleges and universities nationwide. They found that 48 percent of college and university professors identified themselves as "liberal" or "far left"; 34 percent identified themselves as "middle of the road."

In 2004, economics professor Daniel B. Klein and Andrew Western published a far more extensive and methodologically rigorous survey of voter registration and the professoriate at the University of California at Berkeley and at Stanford University. Klein and Western studied the voting registration records of 1,005 professors from twenty-three academic departments at both universities. They conclude: "The findings support the [CSPC and TAE] 'one-party campus' conjecture. For UC-Berkeley, we found an overall Democrat to Republican ratio of 9.9:1. For Stanford, we found an overall Democrat to Republican ratio of 7.6:1. Moreover, the breakdown by faculty rank shows that Republicans are an 'endangered species,' (in terms of age and retirement), on the two campuses."[6]

Thus, Klein and Western also found a faculty D:R ratio that ranged between 8 to 1 to 10 to 1. In addition, at both UC-Berkeley and Stanford, the female professors had an overall D:R ratio of *25:1.* Klein and Western do not discuss this rather astounding finding, which may or may not be Berkeley-specific. Might this mean that female faculty are academically acceptable only if they are uniformly and extremely liberal, progressive, and left? Are both female and male faculty hiring female faculty along these lines? Or does this mean that faculty tend to associate only with those with whom they agree ideologically and do not know (or want to know) those who are ideologically or philosophically different? Or is it possible that male faculty is able to tolerate "difference" a bit better than female faculty—at least at Berkeley?

In 2005, Daniel B. Klein and Swedish sociologist Charlotta Stern again confirmed Horowitz and Zinsmeister's point, namely, that intellectual and ideological diversity does not exist on most American campuses. Klein and Stern surveyed 1,678 professors from all over the country who had responded to a questionnaire. They conclude: "The results show that the faculty is heavily skewed towards voting Democratic. The most lopsided fields surveyed are Anthropology with a D to R ratio of 30.2 to 1, and Sociology with 28.0 to 1. The average ratios are about 15 to 1. Thus, the social sciences and the humanities (Anthropology, Economics, English, History, Political Science, and Sociology) are dominated by Democrats. There is little ideological diversity."[7]

In March 2005, Professors Stanley Rothman, S. Robert Lichter, and Neil Nevitte published a study based on a survey of 1,643 full-time faculty at 183 four-year schools. The researchers relied on the latest (1999) data from the North American Academic Study Survey. The co-authors found a "leftward shift on campus over the past two decades." According to the co-authors, in 1984, a similar survey done by the Carnegie Foundation for the Advancement of Teaching found that only 39 percent identified themselves as "liberal." In the current study, 72 percent of those teaching at American universities and colleges described themselves as "liberal" and 15 percent are "conservative." In addition, 87 percent of the faculty at the most elite schools described themselves as "liberal."[8] The study also found that "women and practicing Christians teach at lower quality schools than their professional accomplishments would predict."

Interestingly, in June 2005, the American Council on Education (ACE) and twenty-two other higher education organizations released a statement that called for "intellectual pluralism and the free exchange of ideas" on college campuses in an "environment characterized by openness, tolerance, and civility." They also stated that neither students nor faculty should be "disadvantaged or evaluated on the basis of their political opinions."

David Horowitz hailed this as a major victory in the battle for academic freedom and "an important first step in recognizing that serious problems of political exclusion and political harassment exist on our college campuses."

It is no crime to be a liberal or to register to vote as a Democrat. Until this last election, I did so all my life. However, to be a Democrat today means that one is a liberal, and liberals are no longer what they once were or who they should be. Today liberals are more left than ever before. Many engage in totalitarian groupthink. In some ways, many left-dominated liberals are also utopian and nihilistic. They conform to party lines as a way of obtaining and preserving their academic positions, identities, and funding—and as a way of socializing, fitting in. The fact that so many professors are left-dominated liberal Democrats is therefore worrisome. Although Democrats, liberals, and leftists can be extraordinary teachers, the campus homogeneity is counterproductive. Emory University professor of English Mark Bauerlein concurs: "Academics need to recognize that a one-party campus is bad for the intellectual health of everyone. Groupthink is an anti-intellectual condition, ironically seductive in that the more one feels at ease with compatriots, the more one's mind narrows."

High school teachers or college professors are supposed to teach certain things so that by the time students graduate from college, they know these subjects. Increasingly, this is not the case. For example, in 1990 the National Endowment for the Humanities found that "42% of 700 college seniors could not place the Civil War in the correct half-century, and 31% thought Reconstruction came after World War II."

In 2000 the American Council of Trustees and Alumni (ACT) published a survey of 556 seniors at the "nation's top 55 liberal arts colleges and universities." They found that the "seniors flunked." "They could not identify Valley Forge or even the basic principles of the U.S. Constitution; . . . [only] 22% were able to identify 'Government of the people, by the people, for the people' as a line from the Gettysburg Address. Little more than half (52%) knew that George Washington's Farewell Address warned against permanent alliances with foreign governments. [However], 99% knew who the cartoon characters Beavis and Butthead were and 98% could identify the rap singer Snoop Doggy Dogg."[9]

If high schools insist on graduating students who lack certain basic knowledge, colleges should—but do not—provide the necessary remedial work. In 2002, the National Association of Scholars (NAS) found that in terms of "general knowledge," contemporary college seniors scored on average no higher than the high school graduates of a half-century ago and far below 1955 college graduates. Seventy-three percent of the 1955 college graduates had correct responses as compared to 54 percent of today's college seniors. The authors conclude: "Perhaps the most discouraging finding of our study is that the high-cultural aspirations of contemporary college seniors, as measured by their avowed tastes in reading, and avowed interest in classical music, are not impressively distinct from those of broad samples of the American population at mid-century, only a fraction of which had completed college. [Though] given the recent emphasis our colleges and universities have been putting on the teaching and study of *popular culture,* this may not be that surprising."[10]

I must note that *none* of the thirty-four history questions asked by the American Council of Trustees and Alumni (ACT) concerned the history of American women. (It's not only students who have failed to do their homework.) Similarly, the NAS study asked specific questions about Charles Lindbergh and Albert Einstein, but not about Amelia Earhart or Nobel prize-winners Marie

Curie or Rosalyn S. Yalow. The *only* woman the NAS study specifically referred to was Florence Nightingale.

But the NAS authors fail to discuss one of their most interesting findings. Twenty-four percent of the 2002 sample compared to 17 percent of the 1946 sample volunteered more "high-brow" or "canonical" favorite authors. Overwhelming majorities in both samples either had no favorite author or mentioned only a popular or "lowbrow" author.

However, the 2002 sample volunteered more "highbrow" *women* authors. Only two people in the 1946 sample claimed a favorite woman author: Pearl S. Buck. The 2002 sample claimed eight women favorite authors: Five mentioned Toni Morrison, and five others mentioned Jane Austen; four mentioned Maya Angelou; two mentioned Charlotte Brontë. The following authors were listed, one per student, respectively: Isabelle Allende, Emily Dickinson, Ayn Rand, and Jane Smiley. Two students in the 2002 sample also mentioned W. E. B. Dubois and one mentioned Cornel West. Not a single African American author had been cited in 1946.[11] Perhaps the "politically correct" academy is also doing something right. But not everything.

For example, many professors obsessively believe that Europe is culturally more sophisticated and mature than America. I don't know about you, but for me, Europe lost a great deal of its shining aura during the Holocaust when the non-Nazis allowed the Nazis to murder six million European Jewish civilians and millions of other non-combatants, such as gypsies, homosexuals, anarchists, Catholic priests and nuns, and the mentally retarded and disabled. History shows us that evil people perpetrate genocide, but also that most good people do nothing to stop them, at least not for a long while. (The American government, American Jewish communities, and the Arab League also played ignoble roles in the Holocaust.)

Thus, much as I, too, had once longed to live in Europe (many American intellectuals and artists do), my ardor was always tempered by an awareness that Europe was a more dangerous than utopian reality. Still, my acquired taste for Europe and for its culture did not evaporate. Like all formerly colonized peoples, Americans feel intellectually connected to European languages, literature, painting, music, history, politics, and philosophy.

My first visit to Europe took place in 1961, and I've been back many times since then. Sometime in the 1970s, I began to note the colorful presence of Arab, Indian, and Caribbean peoples on the streets of London and of North Africans on the streets of Paris. Oh, I thought, the colonies have come home to roost. I admit it, I was enjoying a small anti-colonial revenge fantasy, but in truth I also thought that the formerly colonized brought some undeniable color and charm to the cold climates of northern Europe.

This reverie ended once women started appearing veiled, like ghosts, on the streets of Europe. I recognized these shapes from my time in Kabul, Afghanistan. Once it became clear that full-body shrouds, head scarves, and face veils were not disappearing but were instead multiplying; once it became clear that many (not all) Muslim immigrants to Europe had no intention of integrating into a modern, democratic, infidel Europe, I saw the dreadful handwriting on history's wall.

My feminist colleagues and other good people did not—and still do not—see it this way.

I do not understand this because the information is now in, it's not hidden. For example, some American expatriate colleagues of mine who live in London, Paris, and Rome have agreed with the great scholar Bat Ye'or's description of Europe as "Eurabia," and with journalist Orianna Fallaci's rage against the Islamization of Europe, particularly Italy.

My expatriate friends are heartsick, outraged, by how jihadic Islamism—aided and abetted by left-wing intellectualism—has increasingly taken over their countries. Playwright and writer Carol Gould, who lives in London; novelist and translator Nidra Poller, who lives in Paris; and filmmaker and journalist Anselma Dell'Olio, who lives in Rome, have each described a toxic level of anti-Americanism and Jew- and Israel-hatred in their cities.

Their stories are alarming, almost unbelievable, and include unprovoked verbal and physical street assaults against those who are perceived to be Americans or Jews; unprovoked anti-American and anti-Zionist harangues by people whom they have known for a long time (their drycleaner, photo developer, neighbor, office mate, etc.); grotesque, daily anti-Semitic cartoons and graffiti in their most beloved newspapers; huge and angry demonstrations in which American flags are burned and at which "Death to the Jews" and "Death to America" is routinely chanted. Even Britain's Prince Harry wore a Nazi uniform to a costume party. Nazism and its reincarnation is no joke, and Harry's father "sentenced" him to privately visit Auschwitz and to learn about the horror of the Holocaust.

All three expatriates have lost friends and colleagues over the question of Palestine and America, two words that operate as code words, prearranged signals that, when uttered, allow the vast indoctrinated armies of the night to salivate in solidarity with the noblest of all oppressees: the Palestinians. "Palestine" is quintessential shorthand for whether one holds politically correct views on America (as evil), democracy (as only a word debased by America), freedom (not as important as justice or retribution), terrorism (as justified revolution), the Jews (as always to blame), and Israel (as the most Nazi of apartheid states).

The author Paul Berman, in his wonderful book *Terror and Liberalism,* also notes a growing problem with Europe. He writes: "In Europe, and not just there, a new kind of politics did seem to be stirring, which sometimes called itself left-wing and sometimes right-wing—a demagogic politics, irrational, authoritarian, and insanely murderous, a politics of mass mobilization for unachievable ends. . . . Among the many commentators from half a century ago, the philosopher from Algeria [Camus] was the single one who intuitively recognized a crucial reality. He recognized that, at a deep level, totalitarianism and terrorism are one and the same."

I do not understand why American intellectuals need to hate America. Barry and Judith Colp Rubin enlighten us on this subject in their excellent book *Hating America: A History.* European intellectuals have indulged in this affectation for a long time. The Rubins suggest that what bothered Europeans about Americans was their refusal to defer to a refined upper class and to recognize their own inferiority. What's worse, Europeans saw America as a place in which women talked too much and did not know their place. In a recent interview in *Frontpage* magazine, the Rubins make a clear distinction between criticism of America and anti-Americanism. They conclude: "The main carriers of anti-Americanism are intellectuals for whom the American type of society is repugnant both in itself, as a challenge to their own existing society, and a new world in which they will be of little importance. And since these people have such influence in the realm of ideas–books, media, universities–they are successful in spreading their concept. It is also a substitute ideology for a radical left, and sometimes a radical right, that can no longer pose a positive vision of the society they would build. Instead, there is a call for a united front against America."

I am frightened that the American thinking classes today feel it necessary to ape such ideas. It is not unpatriotic to criticize America; there are many things to criticize. However, the thinking classes exercise a double standard. They demonize America and Israel, but fail to hold Third World tyrants and torturers to the same standards.

I hold right-wing conservatives to this same standard. I do not respect the demonization of feminism or of other progressive ideals. But I am closer to and feel more responsible for fundamentalist intolerance among those who have argued most passionately *for* diversity.

Here's one of many dilemmas that I now face: My expatriate friends and I seem to inhabit one universe; the good people live in another universe entirely. When an independent thinker suggests that there is more than one ideological reality and one point of view, she or he is quickly accused of having gone over to the "dark" side and is then "disappeared." What can we do to change this?

As a psychologist, I must ask: Have the good people all been brainwashed? If so, how might they be deprogrammed? How can we each deprogram ourselves so that we know we are thinking independently and not as is expected of us by our significant others?

Professor Michael Ignatieff, author of *The Lesser Evil: Political Ethics in the Age of Terror,* notes that successful societies are "apt to feel guilty about their success." He suggests that we resist this inclination. He writes:

> It is an illusion, dear to liberal democrats everywhere, especially Americans, to believe that we are responsible for all the evils of the world and that we are in a position to cure them, if only we possessed the will to do so. Certainly we have a responsibility to work toward relieving the global burden of injustice. But we should be clear that we are doing so for reasons of justice, not in the delusive hope of greater security. Having responded to injustice with justice, we have no right to expect peace and good feeling in return. This is to misunderstand evil, to forget terrorism's essential connection to nihilism, its indifference to the suffering it purports to represent, its contempt for our gestures of reparation.

I especially want women and intellectuals, both feminist and non-feminist, to acknowledge that Islamic terrorism is evil and has no justification. I would like us to support Muslim and Arab dissidents in their fight against Islamic gender and religious apartheid and despotism. To fail this opportunity betrays all that we believe in, both as good and as a relatively free people.

※ ※ ※

On February 22, 2004, Donna Hughes and I published a piece in the *Washington Post* titled "Feminism in the 21st Century." It caused a stir on both sides of the aisle. We wrote, in part:

> Forty years ago, American women launched a liberation movement for freedom and equality. They achieved a revolution in the Western world and created a vision for women and girls everywhere. Today, women's economic and social participation is considered a standard requirement for a nation's healthy democratic development. But there is a need now, in the opening years of the 21st century, to rethink feminism. Many feminists are out of touch with the realities of the war that has been declared against the secular, Judeo-Christian, modern West. Many feminists continue to condemn the United States, a country in which for the most part, their ideas have triumphed. Human rights work is not the province of any one ideology. Saving lives and defending freedom are more important than loyalty to an outdated and too-limited feminist sisterhood. . . . Twenty-first-century feminists need to reassess the global threats to women and men, rethink their vision, rekindle their passion and work in solidarity with pro-democracy forces around the world to liberate humanity from all forms of tyranny and slavery.

Some might say that the good feminists have indeed been terrified out of their wits because they can no longer distinguish that which is dangerous from that which is harmless. They scapegoat and blame America and Israel for the crimes of Islamic terrorists. They minimize Muslim terrorism or accuse the victims not only of "provoking" the violence but of actually committing it.

My dear colleague, former Israeli minister Natan Sharansky, has it right. In his and Ron Dermer's book, *The Case for Democracy,* Sharansky writes about the "failure of people who live in free societies to distinguish between religious fundamentalists in democratic states and religious terrorists in fundamentalist states." Such a failure endangers us all.

Islamic terrorism is threatening to destroy what feminists and other forces for democracy have accomplished thus far. But even as western feminists decry sexist oppression everywhere (and they do, they do), their own doctrine of multicultural relativism allows them to have one standard for western women and another, much lower, standard for women who live under Islam. In my view, such multicultural relativism is an ingeniously disguised form of racism and sexism. The presumed compassion involved in viewing the veil as a free choice or polygamy as a colorful cultural custom is, I believe, tragically misguided and a betrayal of feminist principles.

I have therefore been wrestling with a series of dilemmas.

For example: Where do I belong now that the good feminists and other progressives are, in my view, no longer as tolerant or as peace-loving as I once thought they were?

My universe of good people is no longer able to tolerate the slightest difference. We need to begin to notice when people are mainly raging. I have seen and heard so-called peace activists scream "fascist," "war criminal," "traitor," and "die" at people holding American or Israeli flags. The peaceniks do not say "Come, let us reason together."

In 1927, the French writer Julien Benda published *La trahison des clercs* (The treason of the intellectuals). In it he analyzes the "pacifism" of intellectuals. He describes "vulgar pacifism" as that which "does nothing but denounce the man who kills, and sneer(s) at the prejudices of patriotism." Benda does not agree that "highway robbers" and "leaders of armies" are the same. He describes a "mystic pacifism" too: One that is "solely animated by a blind hatred of war and refuses to inquire whether a war is just or not, whether those fighting are the attackers or the defenders. . . . It is impossible to exaggerate the consequences of this behavior. . . . Just like mystic militarism, [mystic pacifism] may entirely obliterate the feeling of justice in those who are smitten with it."

Benda's concerns are mine today. They are also the concerns of Iranian journalist Amir Taheri, who has recently described how European "anti-war" activists were planning to demonstrate against the liberation of Iraq. When he asked the organizers in London and Paris whether they would "include any expressions of support for the democracy movements in Arab and other Muslim countries, notably Iraq, Lebanon, and Syria," they told him no. Taheri writes:

"Why are so many Westerners, living in mature democracies, ready to march against the toppling of a despot in Iraq but unwilling to take to the streets in support of the democratic movement in the Middle East? Is it because many of those who will be marching in support of Saddam Hussein this month are the remnants of totalitarian groups in the West plus a variety of misinformed idealists and others blinded by anti-Americanism?"

❋ ❋ ❋

The 1960s is a decade in which I and so many others became of age politically: in the civil rights, anti–Vietnam War, hippie, and feminist movements. The decade's spirit and values as well as nostalgia for one's youth have found a continuing home on the western campus and in the media. Its long-term influence is both positive and pernicious.

My 1960s cohort of academics and activists refuse to wrestle with the fact that sometimes there just is no one to blame: no all-purpose colonial victimizer and no specific social program that can rid the world of evil or that can "cure" individuals who engage in evil behavior.

Those of us who cut our teeth on social protest movements and who came to earn our living teaching and writing automatically thought that all broken things can and must be fixed; that rage, indifference, cruelty, murder can all be understood by examining their social roots and, of course, by changing society. To us (me, too), every killer was Richarrd Wright's Bigger Thomas, and his murderous act could only be understood by coming to grips with the larger murderousness of racism, sexism, and capitalism.

True—but also not true.

Apart from the specific dilemma of the battered woman and of other victims of chronic sexual and family violence, I do not believe that being "victimized" entitles victims (of verbal slights, economic discrimination, or sexual harassment) to kill their personal or collective victimizers.[12] Indeed, not all poor and oppressed people commit murder; being oppressed does not justify killing someone else.

But my 1960s generation believed and still believes that immoral and criminal behavior must be understood in context and then "cured" by a more revolutionary and humane system of economics, education, justice, therapy, and social bonding.

I once believed this, too, but I don't anymore—at least not exactly.

Does that mean that I am no longer a feminist, that I've deserted the cause of social progress and am now in favor of hourly televised public executions, mullah-style?

It does not.

So where is "home" for an independent thinker?

Perhaps the human yearning for "home" is antithetical to independent thinking. Most people are willing to sacrifice what makes them "different" in order to belong, to be liked—and to avoid getting physically, economically, or socially killed. People either keep their "different" views to themselves or slowly, subtly begin to doubt or modify such views. The tension between our need to belong and our need to think independently can be unbearable.

Perhaps only someone who is utterly confident about her own point of view can actually tolerate other viewpoints. But, paradoxically, most strong-minded people tend to congregate mainly with like-minded others. Why would anyone subject themselves to the tension that "difference" seems to breed? Why sacrifice the stability of intimacy that "sameness" seems to confer?

Thus, anyone who is "too" different, even in small ways, is often seen as risky in friendship, business, and politics. More important, anyone whose primary allegiance is to truth-telling rather than to a particular group; anyone who dares depart from an approved party line—especially if that line has failed its own most cherished principles—anyone who is actually ready to wash this dirty, dirty laundry in public is usually seen as disloyal, a "spoiler."

Democracy absolutely cannot flourish without a critical mass of just such "spoilers" and whistle-blowers. Great ideas cannot flourish without them either.

I have always expected good people to be smart, fair, tolerant, even-tempered, and socially civil. I still believe they can be.[13]

In 2002, the Higher Education Research Institute at UCLA (mentioned above) noted that "the movement toward 'liberal' or 'far left' political identification over the last 12 years has been especially strong among women faculty: from 45 percent to 54 percent." This may indeed be "attributable to their dissatisfaction with the Republican Party's current position on issues . . . such as abortion, welfare, and equal rights."

Ordinarily, pro-feminist views among female faculty would please me very much. In this instance, however, based on everything I have written in this chapter, I must question whether these "liberal" views have been arrived at independently or whether they reflect a culture of conformity and uniformity among feminist academics. From a psychological point of view, this difference is crucial. If one's views are only part of "herd" behavior, then one may not remain loyal to them when and if the herd changes direction.

How do intellectuals and academics resist party lines? How do some people manage to retain an independent point of view? In my opinion, women are both uniquely equipped and uniquely disadvantaged to become whistle-blowers. The next chapter considers the difficulties women face as they attempt to resist party lines and adopt unpopular or dissident positions.

Two

Women and the Crisis
of Independent Thinking

Women especially value dyadic bonding with other women. In my research and in my practice as a therapist, I have found that women crave emotional intimacy from other women in ways that most men do not crave from either women or men. Women need ongoing sympathy and understanding from their female intimates. Thus, women are far more sensitive than men (they have to be) about pleasing and not offending each other. Of course, women can also envy, mistrust, dislike, and sabotage each other, too, but they usually do this "nicely" or "indirectly," through gossip, slander, and shunning.

Women also know how to compete with other women directly. They might steal their best friend's spouse, job, or social position within a clique without shame or regret. Or they might do it and regret it later. Unsurprisingly, women are as close to the apes as to the angels—just like men.

How do these facts apply to the ideas in this chapter? At the risk of mortally offending the political correctniks, research does suggest that while women are not all alike (nor are men) women as a group, compared to men as a group, tend to communicate and think differently. Neither men nor women are "smarter" than each other, but they do seem to have different cognitive skills and different social-affiliative needs. (I discuss much of this research in previous books, especially in *About Men, Mothers on Trial: The Battle for Children and Custody,* and *Woman's Inhumanity to Woman.*)

For example, studies confirm that girls develop social intelligence sooner and are thus both more interpersonally sensitive and more interpersonally demanding than boys are; girls also excel in coding and decoding nonverbal, interpersonal, and social signals. Boys want to belong to the all-boys' gang or club and are willing to accept a leader and sublieutenants without feeling diminished or personally disliked if they are in neither category. Girls feel more comfortable among equals, shoulder to shoulder.

While men kill openly and directly and know how to enforce party lines, they also know how to give other men (but not necessarily women) some serious personal and ideological breathing room. Men do not take their differences *personally;* women usually do. For the most part, women, more than men, fear that the smallest difference in perceived social status or opinion among female friends or within an all-female circle may lead to conflict and disconnection. It often does. Thus, women usually tend to trust (or feel less threatened by) other women who most resemble themselves in terms of clothing, education, marital status, religion, and ideas. Perhaps unconsciously women hope that such "sameness" or uniformity will assure stable, continuous, and non-envious relationships.

I am not only talking about white middle-class women but about women of all races and classes: secretaries and physicians, homemakers and judges, traditional grandmothers and heads of corporations. Such behavior is also true of women in the non-western world. Of course, there are always exceptions: Some women prefer men as friends; some women never, ever listen to, repeat, or initiate gossip; some women mistrust or despise other women so much that they have no women friends.

If we want to encourage women to think independently, we must first understand the female-female affiliative patterns that might discourage independent thinking lest it hurt someone's feelings or end a friendship.

Most women are so fearful of being disliked or shunned by other women that they tend to self-censor as a way of belonging. They identify who the leaders of an all-female clique are and then try to please them by agreeing with them on all things and by acting as their enforcers within the group. Women need to share the details of their lives, but they must do so very carefully lest what they reveal drives an intimate—or an entire social circle—away.

Thus, unconsciously and automatically, women perpetually juggle their need to speak in their own "voice," to reveal all (as only women can, down to the last detail), against their overwhelming desire for interpersonal stability. Women need each other—but the price for remaining connected seems to include perpetual self-monitoring.

Needing to bond—and knowing precisely how to do so—can be an admirable survival skill as well as a moral virtue. However, the willingness to bond at any price is often less admirable. In fact, we may even argue that women's overwhelming need for intimacy also leads to passivity, conservatism, and a refusal to take responsibility for injustice.

But, like it or not, just like men, women are also herd animals, which means that humanity tends to collaborate with and enforce the patriarchal status quo. Hitler and Stalin also had their ardent female followers. To paraphrase Edmund Burke: Evil flourishes when enough good *wo*men do nothing to stop it.

Dr. Carol Gilligan published her influential book, *In a Different Voice,* in 1982—fifteen years after the Second Wave of feminism began. The work has influenced generations of scholars on every continent; it has also been challenged. Gilligan has gone on to write many more books. Unlike many academics, she writes in a way that can be understood. In the beginning, I felt her work was important. I usually defended it when people attacked it. But over time I came to understand that her work, while very useful, was also flawed.

Gilligan taught us that girls begin to "lose voice" when they are only seven years old. A girl must be "nice" in order to have friends. By the time she is eight years old, a girl is already afraid of being whispered about, slandered, or shunned. Thus, in order to create and maintain dyadic bonds and group membership, girls "lose voice" and become "inauthentic." But girls and, later, women lose voice not because boys or men force them into silence and inauthenticity but mainly because other girls and women do so. Gilligan gives countless examples of this in her work.

For example, Gilligan and her co-authors describe the "tyranny of niceness." Gilligan and Lyn Mikel Brown write that girls quickly "retract . . . strong feelings rather than face the painful consequences (of being ostracized). Girls learn that "authentic encounters" *with other girls* are "dangerous." Expressing a "different" view is "risky." And, therefore, girls learn how to express themselves carefully, minimally, falsely, passively, cleverly, and indirectly as the best way to stay alive both psychologically and socially. They also learn that it is suicidal to come to the aid of the slandered and shunned girl; if they do, they will suffer the same fate.

Gilligan did not notice or focus on what has recently been termed the "mean girl" phenomenon. Perhaps she was so invested in presenting girls and women— who have been unfairly criticized—as morally "different" and superior to men that she failed to note what her own research had so clearly documented.

By the ealy 1990s, researchers had documented that girls can be bullies, too, and that verbal abuse, coupled with social ostracism, can damage girls in a lasting way. Girls also learn (from other girls and from women) that they must look away, refuse to "take sides" when a girl tries to be herself, "authentic"—and is then cruelly targeted by other girls as unacceptably "different." Girls are not necessarily taught how to stand up to bullies or how to protect other girls who are being bullied because they are "different."

Original thinkers are by definition "different"; at least their ideas are. In addition, until quite recently, women were not supposed to be public thinkers at all. Those who were did not always lead safe and happy lives. Imagine the bravery it might take for girls and women trained in false niceness to embrace—or become—original and independent thinkers whom others might publicly oppose and condemn.

Thus, by the time most girls become women, they are well trained in how to censor unpopular or original thinking within themselves and to dissemble. They know how to conform on the outside, while screaming on the inside, without breaking a sweat.

A whistle-blower is an insider who risks everything in order to expose an injustice that, but for her, would remain covered up and would also continue. Whistle-blowers cry incest, rape, racism, embezzlement, police cover-up, economic discrimination, sexual harassment, torture, genocide, and so on.

Democracy and ideas cannot flourish without whistle-blowers.

Given the above niceness training women undergo, we might predict that women would be less likely than men to think independently; less likely to rebel openly against tyranny; less likely to report injustice. To the extent to which feminism has taught women to be bolder, braver, more assertive, more "maternal" to the entire human race, not just to their own personal brood, we must honor this kind of feminism and teach it to our children and grandchildren.

Many women have been whistle-blowers. They have exposed drug companies, product liability, environmental hazards, nuclear danger, and employment discrimination. Rachel Carson, Karen Silkwood, Helen Caldicott, Norma Rae (Crystal Lee Sutton), Barbara Seaman, Enron's Sherron Watkins, and World-Com's Cynthia Cooper all immediately come to mind.

Feminists have historically been the whistle-blowers of patriarchy. At our best and in our time, this is precisely what we did. We exposed the hatred and slow but steady subjugation of women within the family and on the job, within our churches and synagogues, and within universities, courtrooms, doctors' offices, hospitals, brothels. We "spoke out" against domestic violence and against every other gender-based injustice.

Between 1966 and 1975, pioneer Second Wave feminist leaders did think boldly and independently, and were also activists. Sadly enough, very few ever landed tenured or long-term university positions or had their important work continually taught and embraced by the feminist academy. With exceptions, those who did receive tenure led fairly embattled academic lives. Few received funding. Most important, while our books *were* taught in universities in the 1970s, and while we ourselves were much in demand as one-night-stand campus lecturers, by the mid-1980s, this had all changed.

I was among the handful who had a tenured academic appointment. Some of us did not have the proper credentials or did not want full-time jobs. Those of us who were fully credentialed and who also had or wanted academic positions had to fight very hard to both get and keep them.

Those who get ahead within institutions tend to institute and follow party lines far more seriously than independent thinkers or activists, including feminists, ever do.

Most of the early Second Wave feminist pioneers were no worse—but no better—than any other group of human beings, both male and female. Thus, both visionary and party line feminists did not consciously and carefully forbid gossip, slander, shunning, and clique or cult formation, nor did they necessarily place great faith in the importance of the individual thinker.

As feminist professors, we tended to "indoctrinate" students as much as we taught them. I did this, too. However, at the time, the feminist critique of the academy and of patriarchy was intellectually very exciting. We made a most compelling argument for curriculum expansion. I still think we were right.

I sometimes loved to use films to illustrate points in my classes. Their use had its place, as did the critical analysis of popular culture, which became more and more accepted. However, the academy eventually went overboard in these two areas. Perhaps some thought this was a way of bringing otherwise disinterested and passive students to life, namely, by catering to their short attention spans and need for dramatic, visual overstimulation. Fair enough. Gradually, over time, in order to compete with television, movies, video games, and the Internet, pedagogic approaches relied more and more heavily on entertainment and visual presentations and less on book learning. The kind of solitude and privacy that independent and critical thinking requires became secondary. This non- or anti-classical education exerted a profound and unfortunate effect on both feminist students and activists. Let me give you two examples.

First, in the year 2001, I attended a Madre benefit in New York City for the women of Afghanistan. For more than twenty years, I have supported and admired Madre's left-wing work on behalf of women in South America, mainly Nicaragua, and elsewhere around the world. Madre essentially opposes American foreign policy and views it as highly detrimental to Third World women.

This Madre event was staged, not spontaneous or participatory, and it was oddly disappointing, almost embarrassing. I had invited a young Afghan friend to accompany me, and we both found the evening curiously naive. Hollywood and Broadway celebrities, including Susan Sarandon, Danny Glover, and Tony Kushner, were reading and the event was being videotaped. Self-important but very professional technicians with walkie-talkies ordered the crowd around. Most of those who came were in their twenties and thirties and had probably never before demonstrated "in the flesh." They were very obedient to these technicians, awed by the stars. They displayed no humorous rowdiness, did not express themselves at all. They behaved as if they were in "church," so to speak, and their religion was Hollywood and Broadway Entertainment.

To them, attending a theatrical event with a left-feminist political message seemed fully the equivalent of taking political, even revolutionary action. In my hopelessly old-fashioned view, it is not. But these audience members have been empowered to believe that it is by their professors and by the media (who, perhaps, have studied with such professors). The benefit *was* entertaining, and it did raise some money, which the executive director of Madre, Vivian Stromberg, rather sincerely said she'd "personally deliver to the refugee camps in Pakistan."

My point: I doubt that this event empowered such a self-selected audience to throw off their shackles of passivity and become activists, or even entertainers. Nor do I think the event was truly educational. Many poems and speeches were read aloud dramatically. However, no one read a single poem by an Afghan or Muslim poet, nor did any of the readings focus on the plight of women (or intellectuals) in the Islamic world, especially those who had been tortured and executed for their ideas. There were no stirring speeches by Muslim dissidents who were calling for "regime change" anywhere in the Islamic world. Incredibly, the readings consisted of European and American left and pacifist diatribes against various wars, including World War II and the Vietnam war. Post–9/11, this crowd opposed the invasion of Afghanistan and roared its approval when Congresswoman Barbara Lee was recognized in the audience and asked to stand. (Lee had voted against the American invasion of Afghanistan.)

My second example is from the mid-1990s, when I was consulted by a group of lesbian feminist activists (all college and graduate school educated) about the Aileen Wuornos case and about women on death row. Wuornos, the subject of the film *Monster,* was the hitchhiking prostitute who was executed in Florida as the so-called first female serial killer. I had gathered together a "dream" team for her defense and wrote a number of law review articles about the issues her case raised.

I suggested that the activists write to Wuornos or to other women on death row or, if they opposed the death penalty, that they consider volunteering for the many overworked public defenders around the country who need backup researchers for their capital cases. I failed to persuade a single one to do anything that would take too much time or that would not lead to an almost instant photo opportunity. What these "activists" all seemed to want to do was march with "Free Aileen Wuornos" banners in political parades and to climb over the "fence" (I did not know what fence they were talking about) and try to break *into* death row as the best way to get "great" press coverage. They seemed to believe that making the evening news was tantamount to political and legal action.

Ideas take time to develop; activism on behalf of great ideas requires even more time and might involve grave personal sacrifices. Such realities were foreign to both these groups—the Madre audience members and the Wuornos fence-climbing activists. This kind of thinking (or non-thinking) still exists today.

By the mid-1980s, only by being willing to engage in debate could an American intellectual appear on many popular television and radio programs. This had not always been the case and was never the case in Canada and Europe (and in certain American radio venues), where authors and intellectuals were listened to at great length and treated respectfully, not as gladiatorial entertainers.

I can be as quick with a quip as the next intellectual performer, but I do not delight in clever debates. For example, on college campuses, when I'd deftly deal with a hostile, anti-feminist comment, the feminist audience would applaud me wildly and boo my opponent. I used to say: "Please don't applaud. This is not a football game. We are exchanging ideas and trying to arrive at the truth of the matter or at least to understand what we truly disagree about and why. Please try and show some respect for the importance, even sacredness, of this undertaking."

My earnest sobriety rarely worked. Students increasingly seemed "hardwired" for fighting—but from an essentially passive, spectator's point of view. Many—of course, not all—students did not seem to have the patience or ability to accept the kind of doubts and contradictions that thinking and sustained activism require.

Many people seem to need interaction, immediate feedback, stimulation, approval. However, learning how to think, how to draw conclusions, how to communicate, defend, or even change one's mind also requires uninterrupted time, solitude, silence, and self-esteem. Among women, learning how to think requires something further, namely the ability to withstand any and all pressure to conform and the psychological strength to go it alone, no matter the cost, to absorb scorn or slander for the sake of one's truth.

Also, in my opinion, people cannot think or communicate properly if they must scream in order to be heard. Real thinking is not the same as a savage and witty sound bite. Debating an adversary is only one way to explore a topic. In my view, debating may be "entertaining," but it's not always educational nor does it often lead to a meeting of minds. Snappy one-liners and instant conclusions do not necessarily represent the mind at its best.

By the mid-1980s in America, many television producers routinely demanded that I and other intellectual performers provide our own ideal debating opponent! They would also want us to provide what I came to refer to as "fresh kill," namely a weeping victim to illustrate or "dramatize" our expert remarks. Perhaps they really understood their audiences. One had to have a definite point of view and a specific plan of action—even if it was a pose.

Indeed, some media was quickly overrun by non-intellectuals who were really ideologues but who loved to perform, and by non-revolutionaries who loved to pretend that they were or had been revolutionaries and who also loved to perform. No one knew who anyone really was, but what did it matter? The media had room for all of us. Good-looking fast talkers "spun" the news. In addition to talking fast, people also came to believe that if you had two people from opposite sides of a continuum, or from two opposing political parties, presenting both extremes amounted to telling the truth or constituted a fair and "balanced" view of things.

I used to say: "This is like saying you can't interview an Auschwitz survivor without also talking to Adolf Hitler because you need to hear both sides before you can make up your mind." About what—about whether racism and genocide are alright?

Somewhere along the way, both the truth and moral gravity were lost.

Academics, the public, and the media all continued to confuse debates-as-entertainment with education, expertise, and wisdom. Over the decades, one had to speak louder and more simplistically in order to be heard. If you weren't "over the top," or if circumstances demanded some "different" thoughts, you might not be listened to. Feminist health activist and author Barbara Seaman told me the following story.

"I was talking to a group of feminists who seemed to be focused only on abortion and on a narrow definition of civil rights. Then 9/11 happened. For me, things changed. I became very aware that my children and grandchildren could be killed. I wanted to do whatever I could to protect them as best I could. I was in favor of Wesley Clark for the presidency for this reason. I wanted to be sure that our commander in chief had military experience. When I said this, at first no one 'heard' me. Then, when I persisted, they disparaged what I was saying and tried to shame me for having security concerns. Eventually I stopped trying to make my point. But it hurt, not being listened to by my own people."

I have had similar experiences among feminists. But lectures of mine have also been invaded by Fathers' rights groups. I have been harassed by anti-abortion ideologues who did not seek an exchange of ideas but who only wanted to silence me through intimidation and to shame me and my point of view before an audience. In this they are very similar to politically correct left-wingers who do the same thing. However, the anti-abortion fanatics do not present themselves as the advocates of free speech and tolerance; the left-wingers and liberals do.

Let me be clear: I oppose this tactic on both the right and the left. It is one that only fascist goon squads employ. It should have no place in civilized, tolerant conversations and therefore no place in the academic world.

These days, disagreement seems to preclude the possibility of dialogue. People are not willing to listen to you if you're "off point" on any subject about which they've already made up their minds. Thus, you can talk about abortion with feminists, but only if you're *strongly* pro-abortion and avidly anti-Republican. Among Republicans and conservatives, you can easily talk about the importance of democracy and about defending Israel and America from Islamic terrorism but probably not about gay marriage and abortion. Nevertheless, let me share a personal story.

In 2003, after I published *The New Anti-Semitism*, the Reverend Pat Robertson interviewed me on the *700 Club*. We discussed Israel, anti-Semitism, the importance of democracy, and the danger of Islamo-fascist terrorism. We agreed that appeasement is not an option and that western intellectuals have lost all common sense. I could probably have also talked with him about trafficking in women and pornography, but these subjects were not what I'd come to talk about. He was very respectful, and I did not say anything I did not mean.

Then the Reverend Robertson sent a crew to my home for a second interview. At a certain point, the cameraman could not contain himself and asked: "How does it feel talking to the Christian right?" I quipped, "Well, how does it feel to be in bed, intellectually, with a radical feminist?" We all laughed. The moment was wonderful because we'd asserted our common humanity over and against what we'd feared might have been unbridgeable ideological differences. It was a taboo-breaking moment.

But word that I'd done the program got out. A number of feminist liberals and leftists denounced me both behind my back and to my face. The fact that I had not recanted a single feminist principle did not matter. In fact, I'd never spoken a word about "women's issues" per se. The fact that a feminist leader was actually engaged in dialogue with the so-called enemy was not viewed as a good thing but as a betrayal. In my view, loyalty to feminism does not consist of talking only to those with whom you are already in total agreement; it also consists of expanding the conversation to include those with whom you may agree on some but not on all issues.

Was my truly unpardonable sin that of finally venturing beyond the 1960s and '70s? It would seem so.

For example, when it became clear that the now-defunct left feminist *Women's Review of Books* would not be reviewing my book about anti-Semitism I called the editor and thanked her for *not* reviewing it. Since in my view the publication was run by staunch anti-imperialists, anticolonialists, and therefore anti-Zionists, I knew my book would probably not be fairly reviewed. "But," I said, "you've reviewed nearly every book I've published since you've been in existence. Perhaps your readers might want to hear directly from me about what I'm saying and why I think it's important. Why not interview me?"

She gave no reason and simply declined to do so. I concluded that my long and honorable feminist track record did not stand me in good stead once my views were no longer politically correct.

The conservative media did not hold the fact that I'm a feminist leader against me when it came to that book. Of course, I was saying something compatible with conservative views. But I still concluded that, among the right, there was more willingness to listen to the Other. For example, W. J. Rayment, the editor of the *Conservative Monitor,* wrote: "Now I find myself championing a book written by a feminist. This is a strange turn indeed . . . there is no clearer or more vibrant account of events leading to the current war on terror than the one Ms. Chesler has compiled . . . there is no clearer picture of the danger. . . . If I have to fight in the trenches, I will be happy to have . . . even a feminist [with me] if it comes to that."

The message is clear: You might think differently than I do in some ways, but we can still work together at this moment in history.

Rayment writes that he has a "firm belief that women deserve equal rights with men." Some conservatives are pro-woman and pro-equality. It's a fact that liberals and leftists still fail to note and should acknowledge, especially now.

Another very telling review appeared in *The Weekly Standard,* a conservative magazine, and was written by Werner J. Dannhauser. He concludes: "This book is bound to impress impartial readers by its author's courage. True courage does not so much consist in taking a stand against the majority as in taking a stand against one's peers; it is a willingness to forsake the cozy warmth of one's intimate group when integrity demands it. This proud radical feminist has done just that. It behooves those of us who are neither feminists nor radicals to welcome her to the good fight."

My point: Some conservatives are ready to work with those with whom they disagree on major issues as long as they agree on other major issues. This is admirable. I think that feminists on the liberal left would become stronger by embracing the other in some ways as well.

Some conservatives may embrace my feminist analysis of the plight of women under Islam only because such an analysis may ennoble or justify an American foreign policy that has been undertaken without women in mind. Similarly, I can share feminist views on certain topics with left and liberal feminists—as long as I don't mention God, Israel, pornography, or Islamic terrorism.

How many people, both men and women, in our country feel that they can express only half of what they want to say? How many people feel intellectually "closeted" today? Where do any of us belong in these times?

It is not easy to be an intellectual without an intellectual home. There are people with whom I have shared transcendent and soul-shaking ideas. This is what brought us together in the first place. To purposely *not* share ideas with them seems another kind of betrayal. Thus, I repeat: Women, including feminists, need to encourage others to think independently, no matter what their viewpoint might be.

Over the years, I have often debated those on the "other" side. For example, in January 1977, I flew into Cincinnati in the midst of a blizzard to debate the late, great anthropologist Margaret Mead, whose task it was to oppose feminism. To the chagrin of the thousands of feminists who had gathered to enjoy a matricidal boxing match, we instead engaged and bonded. I presented first. After about ten minutes, Mead got up, leaned on her walking stick, slowly and loudly clumped her way to the microphone, nudged me aside, and interrupted me. "You, young woman, are obviously brilliant. But how many more are there like you in that movement of yours?"

It was a no-win moment. While I was pleased, even thrilled, that I'd impressed her, I was also embarrassed, outraged, that she'd just publicly demeaned and challenged the movement I represented. I told her: "Dr. Mead, no matter what I say I'm in trouble. If I'm not part of a worthy movement because, in your view, one doesn't exist, then I'm not that smart after all, am I?"

We both laughed and I continued. Soon enough, we ran into some profound differences. She said that women deserved to be raped, that it never happened unless they'd violated a taboo. Oh, how we disagreed—but soberly and respectfully. She would not budge. Afterward, the assembled feminists had planned a reception to honor us both. Given what Mead had said about rape, the sisters refused to allow her to join us. I had no choice; I stayed with Mead. It was an important moment, one that inspires me as I write this book. I know it is possible for thoughtful women to respect and support each other even when they profoundly disagree.

Afterward, Mead and I became friendly colleagues. She wanted to blurb my book *About Men,* but only if I took out two pages that dealt with rape. I would have loved her endorsement but told her: "You know I can't do that. I will have to live without it. But thanks for reading the book."

Later that year, when I was seven months' pregnant, Mead insisted on coming to see me. "Being pregnant is more fragile a state than being old." I did not know that she had cancer at the time. Her first question was "What are you doing about your nipples?" My own mother never asked me this question. "Rub them with a rough washcloth, pinch them, toughen them up," she told me. She was blunt, forceful, and unbelievably kind to come.

"How do I keep breast-feeding when I also have to teach and lecture?"

"Take a nursemaid and the baby with you wherever you go. That's what I did when Catherine was born. And don't listen to anyone—I don't care if he's a doctor or your best friend—who discourages breast-feeding."

We talked at length about the many problems that will arise when an ambitious professional woman decides to become a mother. We may not have agreed about rape, but how blessed I was that such a visible grandmother of our American tribe personally came to initiate me into the rites of motherhood.

And it all began because, as serious thinkers, we knew that we did not have to agree with each other; and we did not have to break with each other because we had serious intellectual or political disagreements.

Earlier, in 1973, I had engaged in a public dialogue with the late, great psychiatrist R. D. Laing in the Algonquin Hotel. Newspaper reporters and a videographer treated our meeting as a theatrical "event," which made it impossible for us to talk privately. (Nevertheless, we found a way to do so.) Later, some feminists criticized me because I had talked to a "sexist man." Quite aside from the importance of Laing's pioneering work, I found this comment outrageous. But, because I cared about what feminists thought, I sought to justify myself. Said I: "He was the one who sought me out. It's a measure of feminist power that he did so. What can we gain by only talking to ourselves? I think he really wanted to engage, intellectually, with a feminist."

It amazes me how relevant these experiences are today. Here again, as with Mead, a non-feminist wanted to dialogue with one of us. I thought it was an honorable request. Yet some saw my doing so as treasonous. At that time, my feminist friends were all women. Is it possible that they were afraid they might lose me to "larger" male ideas or to male power? Were they jealous that Laing had asked to talk to me and not to all of us?

My feminist critics were probably right about Laing's sexism—but so what? I would never have had the opportunity to share my feminist views about mental health and illness with an influential, albeit quite bohemian, psychiatrist had I refused to talk to him at all.

※ ※ ※

Please understand: In the early to mid-1970s, the academy had not yet been hijacked by politically correct feminists and leftists. Therefore, those who controlled the campuses opposed feminist intellectuals. I took considerable heat for championing what was seen as a new and dangerous ideology.

Right from the start, and forever after, I bugged the hell out of the anti-feminist high command in academia. First, I was a whistle-blower, involved in the class action lawsuit on behalf of women at my university, the City University of New York. That won me no friends in administrative high places. Also, in my case, it was a case of "Publish *and* Perish." Perhaps I had written too many books and articles, founded too many national organizations, new courses, and university student clubs. Maybe I loved my students too much and they loved learning with me—whatever my offense, it took me twenty-two years to achieve a full professorship. This is not at all unusual for women.

The faculty made decisions about promotion and tenure. Upon reading my quite lengthy curriculum vitae, the tenured physical education professor on the committee stood up and exclaimed: "I don't care how many articles and books she's published! All she researches is women. That doesn't count." Whereupon another leading local light (with absolutely no publications to her credit) observed: "What she writes doesn't count because she's a feminist, which proves that she's biased and isn't a true social scientist."

This anti-feminist academy had to be confronted and transformed. However, from the beginning, contrary to the view of a monolithic feminism (and as I've previously noted), feminists never all agreed with each other. Only outsiders seemed to think so. But we at least were able to understand each other's writings. Over time, feminist writing became fashionably postmodern and entirely incomprehensible. In my view, many feminists dutifully followed the rest of the academy and became bad writers; others became totalitarian thinkers.

Now the times have changed. Today conservatives, including libertarian conservatives and radical feminist activists, are the new politically incorrect minorities on-campus. What I once knew as women's studies has been taken over by totalitarian thinkers who are far more leftist than feminist and whose anti-Americanism and anti-Zionism have become obsessions. Such thinkers (or non-thinkers) are not committed to a democratic or tolerant exchange of ideas but mainly to a "politically correct" party line.

❊ ❊ ❊

I did not set out to write a "tell-all" book about my controversial interactions with some other feminists. However, the feminist reaction to my views is typical and emblematic of how feminist thinkers silence and punish each other for daring to hold independent or "different" points of view. Our disappointments in each other, our partings, and our silences cannot have been easy for any of us. I share these stories with you in the hope that they will illuminate the kind of thinking that has become pro forma among so many feminists today. This conformity must change in order for feminism to regain its vitality.

I was grappling with the dilemma—really the horror—of how independent thinkers had become ideologues when something rather unexpected happened. On October 9, 2004, out of the blue, I received a letter from Muriel Fox, co-founder of NOW, a former president of the Women's Forum, and the current chair of the Board of Veteran Feminists of America. I have been associated with all these groups from the beginning, and still am.

Muriel and I have never been close, but we have always been delighted to see each other and have certainly never crossed swords. She must now be in her seventies.

Her e-mailed letter assured me that the word was "out" that I would be voting for President Bush and that if I did not change this perception and this reality, I would "make enemies." She said that she had been about to buy my book, *The New Anti-Semitism,* but did not do so for this reason. She was not about to read a book written by anyone who might support a Bush presidency. She said she was telling me all this "for my own good." Perhaps she meant well, perhaps she only meant to open a dialogue, but her letter did not do that. Instead, Fox clearly warned me that how I voted could change people's views of me "from here to eternity" and that she worried that my "unique wisdom and creativity" and "credibility" will be "discounted forevermore" as a function of this single vote. She ended by sending me "a big hug and longtime love," which she hoped would not be a "Goodbye Hug to my old feminist heroine friend."

I immediately reached for the phone and called her. I learned that things were worse than I had understood. I was as "good as dead among feminists" if I did not cease, desist, and publicly recant. Muriel kept repeating: "They are going to destroy you." She said that what I ought to do is "pay for an ad in the *New York Times* announcing that I was *not* voting for Bush." Otherwise, she said, "feminists would never forgive" me and would "no longer admire or trust" me. She was not at all interested in hearing what I had to say about why I might be voting for Bush.

Susan B. Anthony and countless others spent sixty years fighting for female suffrage. It would dishonor them if I voted only out of fear or sold my vote to please others. Clearly, Muriel did not view voting as a matter of one's own conscience but as a resource that belongs to one's "team" or party.

When did the feminist movement become a wholly owned subsidiary of the Democratic Party?

Reader: You must understand three things: First, I take Muriel's service to feminism quite seriously and therefore do not dismiss her letter as that of a retired person who is merely expressing her own private opinion. I do not see her as "retired" but as representing the voice of the (mainly Democratic) mainstream feminist movement in America. I respect her enough to take her seriously.

Second, Muriel did not write to me as a friend, since we are not friends. Her letter was from one political person to another about a political matter.

Third, please note the clever carrot-and-stick mother-daughter approach she adopted, one in which she will remain filled with love and admiration for me if I see things her way, but not otherwise.

Muriel then sent me a final email. She insisted that she was "not threatening me" but said, again, that I would not be "forgiven" if I voted for President Bush. She reminded me that "women feel strongly about this election, as if the fate of the world depends on it."

And thus, in many ways, feminist leaders are no different from other kinds of leaders. Fox was not allowing me any political or ideological room to differ or to make an independent choice. She was not content merely to make her case and then, no matter whom I voted for, remain connected to me as a colleague. The "love," approval, and connectivity was tied to whether I conformed to the party line.

The feminist rejection of women who are "different," who do not conform in word and deed to the accepted orthodoxy, has got to stop. First, it is not worthy of us. Second, it is particularly dangerous for women to tie (maternal or sisterly) approval to ideological conformity. Doing so will only reinforce—not exorcise— the conditioning into conformity that most girls have already experienced. Finally, such rigid intolerance of difference has driven too many women away from identifying as feminists: women who choose motherhood over high-powered careers; women who are American patriots; conservative women; many religious women; women who do not identify themselves primarily in terms of sexual preference; and women who oppose abortion, pornography, and prostitution.

Three

The New Intolerance

The two aims of the Party are to conquer the whole surface of the earth and to extinguish once and for all the possibility of independent thought. . . . When people "disappear" no one is allowed to mention it, no one is mourned, no *one* person is important, only the Party and Big Brother are important.

In Oceania there is no law. Thoughts and actions which, when detected, mean certain death are not formally forbidden, and the endless purges, arrests, tortures, imprisonments, and vaporizations are not inflicted as punishment for crimes which have actually been committed but are merely the wiping-out of persons who might perhaps commit a crime at some time in the future.

—George Orwell, *1984*

Communication in cyberspace has, almost overnight, become as important to certain people as having a cell phone. At home, at work, in transit—even on vacation, such people are almost constantly talking on their cell phones or communicating with others on their computers. Often, or so it seems to me, such cell phone and cyberspace communications seem more real than talking to a family member or to a living human being in the same room. Flesh-and-blood appearances do not seem to have the same compelling "reality" (or fantasy appeal) as do cyberspace appearances.

Thus, what happens on a private listserv group may matter very much to each member.

Although one does not usually see or hear someone else in cyberspace, the feeling of intimacy is often quite profound. One "talks" to others at home, or in one's bedclothing. Sometimes one "talks" in the middle of the night or while at work. Membership in a listserv group may make people feel less alone, more important, safer; they "belong" to a family-like group, a clan, a gang, a professional or social alliance that they imagine will fulfill many different needs.

Let me suggest that people may develop some kind of psychoanalytic transference to their listserv groups. In a way, the connection is an umbilical one. One is never alone, one is always connected to another. Many people may become dependent upon, even addicted to the communication. People may feel "witnessed" and supported by their daily cyberspace communications.

But there is another, darker side to cyberspace communications. Sometimes a small group of people may attack the same person over and over again, day after day, for months, even for years. Meanwhile, hundreds of onlookers remain silent. No one stops the attacks or calls for a more civilized fight.

It is also a good example of how mobs work.

Unlike in-person mobs, in the online world, one person attacks and instantly disappears. Often people attack one by one, one after the other. No individual in cyberspace sees herself as part of a lynch mob or as contributing to an atmosphere in which people are systematically demoralized or ultimately silenced. Yet these listserv exchanges can have serious consequences for people's livelihood and reputations. They've provided me with a glimpse of how academic and mainstream communities of students and faculty silence and exclude different or offending points of view. These small communities may serve as examples of how larger communities function.

By now, many people have had some experience with listserv groups being shut down due to an ugly battle run amuck. When this phenomena was first called to my attention and I reviewed some of the e-mail exchanges, I decided that such "flamers" must be sociopaths or mentally ill. I have now changed my mind. While some cyberspace attackers may indeed be interpersonally tone-deaf or even sociopaths, they are also empowered politically and ideologically to intimidate any perceived disbeliever into silence. Thus, the angry, often theatrically staged "yelling" matches on television that I've written about in chapter two may have their counterparts on the Internet.

Some cyberspace attackers do not hesitate to strike hard, even viciously, when their opponent is not physically present. They would probably not physically or verbally attack anyone in person. Another way of saying this is that the Internet is tailor-made for physical and moral cowards who like to attack without having to make eye contact and with no risk of physical retaliation.

Certain cyberspace attackers remind me of the brainwashed, sexually repressed, and super-aggressive mobs in George Orwell's novel *1984*. Big Brother's captive population is literally monitored around the clock through "telescreens" that can view every room, each person. The telescreens broadcast Big Brother's orders and conduct daily "hate" sessions. (Orwell's depiction of how indoctrination through false propaganda turns into group hatred is chilling and masterful.) In addition, concealed microphones are everywhere. People are always anxious and paranoid; everyone has permanent enemies.

This involuntary round-the-clock lack of privacy somewhat resembles our voluntary but highly addictive relationship to the Internet.

Today, Orwell's Thought Police are, rather ominously, everywhere: certainly in the Arab and Islamic world—just as if they've slipped off his pages and into living action like Hollywood computer-generated characters. Orwell's Thought Police sound a lot like the Afghan Taliban or like Iran's or Saudi Arabia's Virtue-and-Vice squads, who arrest men and women for the smallest sign of "individuality" or difference, and who harass and arrest women for showing a single strand of hair, or cheek, or even a glimpse of ankle. Their grim vigilance suggests the enormous sexual repression and consequent sexual violence that is true both in Orwell's *1984* and in the Islamic world today.

Many recent memoirs and novels set in Iran and Afghanistan, such as Azar Nafisi's best-selling *Reading Lolita in Tehran,* Roya Hakakian's *Journey from the Land of No,* and Khaled Hosseini's best-selling *The Kite Runner,* all describe the savage curtailment of private life and thought—and of life itself—by radical Islamists.

According to Nafisi, Khomeini's mullahs and their goon squads closed newspapers and universities and arrested, tortured, and executed beloved teachers, prominent artists, intellectuals, and activists, including feminists, and thousands of other innocent and productive *Muslims.* (The persecution of dhimmi-status [infidel] peoples such as Jews and Ba'hai by Khomeini's minions requires a separate book.) Their actions frightened everyone into silence. The mullah squads constantly harassed women on the street and at work. If a woman failed the dress-code standards even slightly, or by accident, she risked being arrested, probably raped, possibly executed.

Hakakian dedicates her book to the memory of the "unknown number of Iranian women political prisoners who were raped on the eve of their executions by guards who alleged that killing a virgin was a sin in Islam." Of course, others say that they rape the unmarried virgins so that they will be barred from heaven. Nafisi notes that when Iraq bombed Iran during the war, Hashemi Rafsanjani, the speaker of the Iranian parliament, recommended that women dress properly when sleeping, so that if their houses were hit "they would not be indecently exposed to strangers' eyes."

The university where Nafisi taught became highly politicized. Free or prowestern thought was deemed a thought crime. Nafisi's classes were monitored and policed both by Islamist students and government overseers. Western novels were condemned as "sinister assaults" on (Islamic) culture, as "a rape of our culture." Under Khomeini, "there were only two forces in the world, the Army of God and that of Satan. Thus, every event, every social gesture, also embodied a symbolic allegiance." Both Iran and Afghanistan also specialized in publicly stoning women to death. Eventually Nafisi fled Iran.

Let me quote from Khaled Hosseini's fictional description of life in Afghanistan under both the Russians and the pre-Taliban mullahs. In *The Kite Runner,* he writes:

> You couldn't trust anyone in Kabul anymore—for a fee or under threat, people told on each other, neighbor on neighbor, child on parent, brother on brother, servant on master, friend on friend. . . . The rafiqs, the [Afghan] comrades, were everywhere and they'd split Kabul into two groups: those who eavesdropped and those who didn't. . . . A casual remark to the tailor while getting fitted for a suit might land you in the dungeons of Poleh-charkhi. . . . Even at the dinner table, in the privacy of their own home, people had to speak in a calculated manner—the rafiqs were in the classrooms too; they'd taught children to spy on their parents, what to listen for, whom to tell.

Here is his depiction of the Taliban era:

> In Kabul, fear is everywhere, in the streets, in the stadiums, in the markets, it is a part of our lives here. . . . The savages who rule our *watan* [country] don't care about human decency. The other day, I accompanied Farzana jan to the bazaar to buy some potatoes and *naan.* She asked the vendor how much the potatoes cost, but he did not hear her, I think he had a deaf ear. So she asked louder and suddenly a young Talib ran over and hit her on the thighs with his wooden stick. He struck her so hard she fell down. He was screaming at her and cursing and saying the Ministry of Vice and Virtue does not allow women to speak loudly. She had a large purple bruise on her leg for days but what could I do except stand and watch my wife get beaten? If I fought, that dog would have surely put a bullet in me, and gladly!

Hosseini's descriptions are right out of *1984.*

In a way, so are the thousands of stories about Muslim women—some men, too—who, in the last twenty-five years, have been kidnapped, raped, jailed, flogged, and savagely stoned to death by joyful-vengeful mullah-led Muslim mobs for the alleged crimes of prostitution or adultery or free thought. Such mobs do not seem to be composed of individuals with minds of their own. As in *1984,* they are a brainwashed, fanatical, and dangerous collectivity.

In 1990 Iranian journalist Freidoune Sahebjam published a haunting and carefully rendered account of how, on August 15, 1986, a thirty-five-year-old woman was stoned to death in Kupayeh, Iran. It is titled *The Stoning of Soraya M.* This book bears witness and also took great courage to write since Sahebjam himself had been arrested and tortured by Khomeini's ("common law criminal") mullahs in Paris. Soraya (peace be upon her) was lynched by the villagers with whom she had lived all her life. Her own father, her two sons, and her lying, greedy, heartless, petty criminal of a husband, Ghorban-Ali, all threw the first stones.

How did this happen? When Soraya was only thirteen, an arranged marriage with the twenty-year-old Ghorban-Ali took place. Soraya was docile, obedient, and fertile. She did everything uncomplainingly. Her husband routinely insulted, beat, and then abandoned her and their children; he also consorted with prostitutes and brought them into the marital bed. Soraya dared not say a word. A "complaining" wife is easy to divorce.

Ghorban-Ali had begun to work with a group of extortionist mullahs in some distant towns and had been well rewarded. He "did not want to live any longer" with Soraya, who had become a "silent, resigned woman who was old before her time and, what was worse, completely above reproach." Ghorban-Ali had a new wife picked out, and, although he could now afford many houses, he wanted his old mud house back. For him to get it, Soraya had to die.

He therefore falsely accused Soraya of adultery. Soraya's aunt, Zahra, a village elder (and the author's main informant), loved Soraya and knew she was innocent. But she was powerless and could not save her. Ghorban-Ali tricked Soraya's own father into condemning her. He also had the support of one of the many fake, pederast, thieving mullahs who, under Khomeini, enriched themselves personally by jailing and extorting money from their prisoners and by then executing them and confiscating all their wealth—a process very similar to the European Inquisition in which the church amassed great wealth in precisely this way.

After Ghorban-Ali denounced Soraya, she was sentenced to die later that same day. Ghorban-Ali was "radiant, jovial. Men slapped him affectionately and heartily . . . others hugged him." The crowd of villagers began to chant: "The whore has to die. Death to the woman." The villagers—who had known Soraya since her birth—cursed her, spit on her, hit her, and whipped her as she walked to her stoning. A "shudder of pleasure and joy ran through the crowd" as their stones drew blood. According to Sahebjam's account, Soraya died a slow and agonizing death.

When Soraya's aunt Zahra went to retrieve her body for burial, she was greeted by a "hallucinatory spectacle. On the exact same spot where Soraya had been stoned to death, a joyful fire was now burning, and around its flames the villagers were dancing. The strolling performers had started their show. The village women had donned their finest multicolored dresses and were turning in circles."

Afterward, the fake mullah declared that the sinful Soraya could not be buried in a Muslim cemetery. He ordered some women to carry her broken body away. They half-buried her near a stream that Soraya happened to love. But when Zahra returned the next morning, she found that dogs had devoured most of her niece. She sat and wept, collected Soraya's bones, and buried them.

What is the point of this heartrending story? Namely, that as Muslim women are being tortured and stoned to death, many multiculturally correct American and European feminists are deconstructing and justifying the face veil and the head scarf—and strongly opposing American intervention in the Muslim world. Such feminists are also silencing and demonizing all other views on intervention in academic journals, in the media, and on feminist listserv groups.

Sahebjam writes that "being born female is both a capital crime and a death sentence." I must emphasize that this ghastly, local stoning cannot be blamed on the crimes of the American or Israeli empire.

In my opinion, Orwell's novel predicts and describes both Islamic totalitarianism and its western counterpart: politically correct left-dominated liberalism and postcolonial, anti-imperialist feminism—a feminism that has denounced America's vision of freedom and democracy for Muslim countries far more visibly and effusively than it has denounced Islamist horrors.

Thankfully, western governments do not execute people for their ideas or police their dress codes—but Orwellian-style Thought Police tactics are fully in use, among many western academics. A grim policing of ideas and their free expression takes place among academics and intellectuals, especially on Internet listserv groups.

In chapters one and two, I described the ways in which certain feminists and other progressives seem to have stopped talking to anyone who does not agree with them totally. Let me again ask: What sort of person refuses to talk to someone with whom they disagree? What sort of group or person persistently slanders and demonizes someone with whom they happen to disagree on key political issues? What sort of group or person demands uniform party line thinking—and is actually powerful enough to coerce people into "disappearing" their dissident views, sometimes even from themselves?

Religious fundamentalists and totalitarian and tyrannical regimes all do this. But as I've shown, totalitarian thinking is also flourishing in America today among our media and academic elites. Oddly enough, such totalitarian thinking and its consequent thought control are flying high under the banner of "free speech" and "political correctness." Dare to question this elite's right to silence or shame those who are trying to expose or challenge what they are doing, and, as I've noted, you'll be attacked as representing a new and more dreadful form of McCarthyism.

The intolerant progressives also insist on viewing themselves as abused victims. In an inspired article titled "Anti-Semitism: A Psychopathological Disease," Professor Norman Simms discusses the ways in which anti-Semites seek to destroy their prey by *becoming* über-Jews, by "identifying with their Jewish victims so as to encompass, devour, possess and protect [their] own [non-Jewish or Jewish] victim [child] selves." Thus, a Holocaust denier may view himself as the "real" (Jewish-like) victim or as the victim of Jews; similarly, Palestinian terrorists may view themselves as being persecuted by Israeli "Nazis," and so on.

So, too, multiculturally correct leftists and left feminists often view themselves as being persecuted by "fascists," "fundamentalists," "Republicans," "conservatives," and others. They may well be but they do not ever note how they themselves also silence dissenters or demonize their opponents. As I have shown in chapter one, left-dominated liberals control the academy. They also influence the airwaves.

Harvard Law School graduate and journalist Andrew Peyton Thomas describes classrooms and Internet student chatrooms in this way:

> Students who are right of center who dare to speak up in class are routinely hissed at. This is a form of intellectual intimidation that the left practices with impunity, as professors never discourage it. Students who dissent from the far-left orthodoxy of Harvard are harassed in Harvard Law chat rooms that continue classroom discussions; they see their posters or notes advertising upcoming meetings of their student organizations destroyed or effaced by vandals; and hear student opinion leaders dismiss their concerns about this mistreatment as groundless. In March 2003, the student newspaper, the *Harvard Law Record,* encapsulated nicely this groupthink when it devoted an editorial to disparaging these concerns. The title of the editorial captured its thesis—and the sentiment predominant in the student body: "Conservatives Should Shut Up about Silencing." Needless to say, right-leaning students at Harvard Law are in for a tough and often lonely walk.

For years, announcements for marches, demonstrations, and petitions routinely flooded the non-moderated academic listserv groups that I was on; however, they did not usually overpower the ongoing dialogue. This changed in the fall of 2000. After that, an academic conversation might be under way about a research study, a professorial opening, an upcoming convention, a request for a therapist or for a graduate-level bibliography—when suddenly someone would start raging against the "stolen" election or, more often, would dump unasked-for pro-Palestinian, anti-Zionist, and anti-American propaganda into the online discussion. No one would stop these people. And it was assumed that "everyone" felt exactly the same way.

Various Internet listserv groups quickly became as rigidly polarized and politicized as most North American campuses already were. For example, when the late Yasser Arafat unleashed his last intifada against Israel, some members of one academic group began issuing propaganda reports against the "Zionist occupation" and against America's support for it. This had absolutely nothing to do with what we usually talked about online. When I tried to get the conversation back on (a feminist and professional) track, my politics on the Middle East were immediately challenged and scorned. The ensuing attacks became very sharp indeed. This happened to me on two different listserv groups.

Like Islamists, academic left-dominated liberals are comfortable only when they dominate; they also project their own hostile intentions onto their opponents, claim "persecution," then preemptively strike the first blow in "self-defense." Today such intellectuals, including feminists and gay liberationists, patrol Internet listserv groups and punish both thought crimes and future thought crimes. They do so not only through intense, repetitive, simultaneous attack "rants," but also through a system of selective rewards and punishments.

When an academic's or intellectual's worthy successes are ignored by his or her colleagues on a regular basis on a listserv group, that person is meant to become demoralized, to leave the group, or to change (or hide) the offending point of view. This is true especially if the group routinely praises other members' (lesser or equivalent) achievements. Self-appointed members of the thought police repeatedly and obsessively attack one colleague's work only—even as they praise, ever so vaguely and good-naturedly, everyone else's work. Cyberspace attackers are filled with great rage and usually employ sarcasm, contempt, and shaming tactics in their attacks.

Donna Hughes holds the Carlson Endowed Chair in Women's Studies at the University of Rhode Island (URI). She also maintains an important listserv group on trafficking and female sexual slavery. She has worked on legislation in this area and has traveled frequently and widely on behalf of women's freedom. Her work has, in part, led to a far-reaching and new human rights policy aimed at the abolition of sexual violence and exploitation and that advances the freedom and dignity of women and girls around the world.

Hughes belongs to a faculty listserv group at URI. Whatever is written can be read by approximately 375 faculty members. I cannot exaggerate the listserv's influence on each member's career and reputation. Most faculty members are silent. Perhaps they are simply too busy (or too wise) to chime in; perhaps they do not wish to run afoul of the bullies who rule the list and lead the attacks. Whatever the reason, with only a few, recent exceptions, other academics, including feminists on the listserv group, have not supported Hughes's right to hold her views without being viciously and repeatedly attacked.

It is important to understand that the victims of physical, verbal, and psychological violence are always more haunted by the silence of the "good" people than they are by the evil actions of the "bad" people. Therefore, when a member is being unfairly or unprofessionally attacked, listserv silence is a form of collaboration or appeasement. One cannot remain "neutral." Refusing to stop the bullying in progress amounts to siding with the bullies.

The URI women's studies faculty has largely been silent when Hughes has come under attack. Perhaps the feminists disagreed with her politics or envied her visibility. Whatever the reason, their behavior did not rise to the level of professional or sisterly civility. If one can't civilly tolerate a different point of view in the academy, where might one do so? (Please understand: Such uncivil and intolerant behavior is hardly unique to URI or to academic feminists.) Hughes told me: "Two guys [on the listserv group] have declared war on me. They hate that I am publishing feminist work in places like *FrontPage* magazine and the *National Review.* They say that I'm only publishing there because my scholarship is so bad that I can't get published elsewhere or in academic journals. They allege that I support torture. They engage in character assassination and guilt-by-association tactics and absolutely no one stops them."

I reviewed her listserv material; it bears out her every word. Hughes's "crimes" include holding abolitionist views about pornography, prostitution, trafficking, and sexual slavery; viewing freedom as a universal value; and publishing in the "wrong" (conservative) places.

The kind of professors who claim to stand for diversity and tolerance are totally intolerant of "difference," as exemplified by Hughes's work. One of her constant detractors is quite proud of his acquisition for the university library of a collection of pornography films and postmodern feminist books about pornography. He describes their content at length online. He is not inclined to "tolerate" Hughes's analysis of pornography and prostitution; instead, he mocks it at every turn. Interestingly, but not surprisingly, this professor's language is often pornographically sadistic-seductive. For example, when one person finally criticized him for being cruel to Hughes, he asked: "Will you beat me Daddy if I don't stop it?"

Although the few professors who continually attack Hughes seem incapable of civilly tolerating her views, they simultaneously continue to find new ways to "tolerate" the most "intolerant" of Islamic fundamentalist forces and regimes. Such professors seem to think that allowing Sha'ria law to rule Muslims in Europe and North America proves that they are being true to their own liberal values. Or perhaps they recognize a kindred closed-mindedness in the Islamists.

When Hughes shared a *cri de coeur* written by an Iraqi architectural engineer, Sarmad Zangna, about his passionate and courageous desire to defeat the Islamist terrorists in Iraq, one faculty member, committed to baiting and shaming Hughes about pornography, disingenuously claimed that he was not at all clear whether Zangna was referring to the *American* terrorists or to some other group. (Martians, perhaps?)

I spoke with Italian former communist, computer designer, and journalist Elio Bonazzi, who said: "Trying to talk reason to the left is like bouncing off a rubber wall. The left is so well defended against reality that when reality itself opposes their theory, they come up with another theory to rationalize reality. Stalin may have killed millions—but the capitalist nations made him do it. They are cognitively disconnected from reality in the same way that cult members are. Once there was a cult that preached the End of Days. When that last day came and the world continued on, the cult rationalized it by saying that the cult's goodness and faith had clearly persuaded God to spare the world."

Bonazzi told me a poignant story about a prominent anti-fascist in Italy named Norberto Bobbio. Bobbio stood up to Mussolini and joined the resistance. Years later, when Bobbio took a stand against the communist movement in Italy, communist students at his own university booed and jeered him as a "fascist."

But back to Donna Hughes. Not only was she maligned on her faculty listserv group for her anti-trafficking and pro-freedom for Iraq point of view (otherwise known as her pro-war view), she was also baited for her abolitionist views on pornography and prostitution. This is not a politically correct position among many academic feminists; it often offends gays and feminists who fear that it may threaten their sexual privacy and access.

When Hughes posted an article she had published in *FrontPage* magazine about an Iranian woman political prisoner, her pro-pornography nemesis informed her that *FrontPage* is an extreme right-wing rag run by David Horowitz allegedly to fight for academic diversity on college campuses, but what Horowitz is really after is getting rid of anyone who doesn't agree with the extreme right.

FrontPage is an online Internet magazine that began publishing in 2000. In the last year (June 2004–June 2005), *FrontPage* has received nearly one billion "hits." More important, *FrontPage* has interviewed leading intellectuals, politicians, and human rights activists such as Bat Ye'or, Vladimir Bukovsky, Christopher Hitchens, Khaleel Mohammed, Daniel Pipes, Natan Sharansky, and Andrew Sullivan. *FrontPage* has also sought to represent opposing political points of view in symposia and thus has had both left and liberal (Stanley Aronowitz, Susan Estrich, Michael Lerner) and right-wing voices (Tammy Bruce, Ann Coulter, and James Woolsey) at their roundtables. I have been an interviewee and a participant in a number of symposia; I have also written regularly for *FrontPage*. I consider myself in excellent company.

In 2002 Hughes posted an article on her website about a man who was suspected of the illegal trafficking of Eastern European prostitutes' babies for the sake of adoption. He denied the charges and was never convicted. The article remained up during 2003. In October 2003, the man who was the subject of the article threatened to sue Hughes for defamation. The university then removed the article in order to look at it. URI did not repost it nor, according to Hughes, did they return her many phone calls about doing so.

Hughes threatened to repost the article on her own. "That got their attention," she told me. Then, in March 2004, the American Civil Liberties Union (ACLU) came down on Hughes's side; the American Association of University Professors (AAUP) "were also great on this." A number of the URI women's studies faculty were members of AAUP. According to Hughes, they were "cool" to her; they supported her "on principle but did not like the politics. They gave [her] no personal support."

Once Hughes won the battle to have her article reposted, several faculty members quietly congratulated her. URI professor, administrator, and feminist Kat Quina, sent news of the Hughes victory to another listserv group. According to Hughes, "Kat was the only women's studies person who gave me some personal support." Indeed, Quina understood that the issues of trafficking and sex workers are controversial, but that Hughes's work has nevertheless influenced the American State Department in enunciating a new human rights policy.

Luckily, Hughes knows no fear. Thus, she informed the listserv group that syndicated columnist Michelle Malkin had received hate mail that was both racist and sexist. She wrote: "Michelle Malkin is a Filipina-American conservative opinion journalist. I've heard that she takes a lot of abuse from liberals because women of color aren't supposed to be conservative. . . . I have been shocked at the viciousness of liberals lately. Racism, sexism, sexual exploitation have become acceptable. One thing is clear to me, liberals can no longer claim to hold the moral high ground on respect for other people, diversity, multiculturalism, or any kind of anti-oppression politics." Hughes provided the URL for anyone interested in reading the hate mail that Malkin had received and posted (http://michellemalkin.com/archives/001212.htm). Some examples include:

> Hi. Self-hating flat nosed Filipino Bitch! As we used to refer to your kind—little brown Fucking Machines. Looks like this little LBFM learned to whore in a different way to make some pesos.
> Did some minor Republican operative purchase a mail-order bride and train her to do this?
> You're just a Manila whore shaking your ass waiting for the Republican fleet to come in, aren't you?
> Proverbs 69:69 counsels: "Like a whore who infects those she lies with, so doth the ultra-republican faux columnist infect her readers with lies." While you are looking in the mirror, cursing the Left because you weren't born blond, think about the above. Amen.

The sexualized political hate, the brutal misogyny and racism, takes one's breath away. Nevertheless, Hughes's opponents did not even pause to say "Malkin's hate mail is awful. There can be no excuse for it." On the contrary. One professor proceeded to do a postmodern textual analysis of Malkin's e-mail in order to prove that the letter-writers were not necessarily left-dominated liberals and that therefore, as he'd always known, right-wing conservatives are still more racist and sexist than left-wingers could ever be.

Although this professor presumably holds a PhD and teaches at a university, he could not focus on the issue at hand. He was interested only in defending "the left." This is the behavior of a true believer, not that of an independent thinker.

Hughes's second academic opponent, let's call him Professor X, actually suggested that Hughes needs to join a multicultural group that will teach her what "real" racism and sexism are about. He went further. He said that it's the right, not the left, in this country that is morally bankrupt. He provided the usual laundry list, which included, among other things, forcing people into gender roles that do not fit; obstructing the use of alternative sources of energy; increasing the fear of immigrants and aliens; denying adequate health care coverage to the elderly; and continuing to promote a military policy that denies equal rights for sexual minorities.

There is nothing wrong with this professor raising any one of these points. But many of these problems also existed under Democratic president Bill Clinton, who, it must be remembered, supported and signed both the Defense of Marriage Act and the "Don't Ask, Don't Tell" policy regarding gays in the military. However, none of this has anything to do with whether Malkin has received racist and sexist hate mail.

This long and self-righteous list is typical in that Professor X is using it to overwhelm and exhaust his perceived opponent. His list is meant to silence, not to communicate. It is the kind of list that the Thought Police would keep handy.

Hughes is not the only one who has been attacked on a listserv group. Like Hughes, I have also been persistently attacked and studiously ignored on one particular listserv group. I have, in effect, been "purged" by the left-feminist listserv group known as the History in Action group (HIA), for my past and possible future views.

In the novel *1984,* someone named "Goldstein" is the permanent traitor whom Big Brother denounces at regular intervals around the clock. It is no accident that the eternal Traitor has a Jewish name. In his choice of name, Orwell acknowledges the presence of virulent Jew-hatred among Nazi-era fascists and communists. "Goldstein's" alleged, monstrous crimes, coupled with surreal televised news of permanent war, brainwashes everyone into extraordinary group hatred against him. When a nine-year-old boy physically attacks Orwell's protagonist, Winston Smith, the boy calls him "Goldstein."

Among leftists and left-dominated liberals, Israel and the Jews—but sometimes America as well—are the current "Goldsteins." Perhaps I was "Goldstein" on this particular listserv group. Of course, I was also a feminist leader—always an endangered position among other feminists.

For years this group was led primarily by top "Mean Girl," *Nation* columnist Katha Pollitt, whom I have never met. She and her small band of leftist fundamentalists consistently either attacked or ignored my work. Pollitt treated at least two other older Second Wave feminist listserv members similarly. Pollitt had her listserv favorites from whom she loved to solicit ideas and quotes for her column. I never saw anyone on the listserv group object to this use of listserv material. On the contrary, they loved it.

Please understand: Disagreeing with someone is alright. Doing so directly and respectfully is alright. Attacking someone nonstop because she does not agree with you, berating her, trying to shame her for holding a different point of view, is not alright. This is what cults do and what wartime brainwashing is about. This is not how civilized people should exchange ideas and information. This is about coercing conformity and obedience, not about a free and tolerant exchange of ideas.

The reaction and non-reaction of western academics and intellectuals to the 2000 Intifada against Israel—and to 9/11—finally persuaded me that this group had become suicidally intolerant. Thus the issues of terrorism, anti-American-ism, Israel-bashing, and anti-Semitism opened my eyes—but so did the feminist reception to my tenth book, *Woman's Inhumanity to Woman*. The reaction—or non-reaction—to the ideas in this book is one of many examples of feminist closed-mindedness.

Some feminists say that *the* issue of Second Wave feminism was women's un-acknowledged envy, competition, and sexism, which was also known as trash-ing. Although the book focuses on all women, everywhere in the world, and not particularly on feminist women, most party line feminists were defensive, ner-vous, and strangely silent about this book. For example, although I had sent the manuscript to a number of major feminist leaders—who had in the past rou-tinely endorsed my work—they never once said a word about this book. It is lit-erally the only work of mine they have not endorsed. I would have welcomed a private dialogue. Utter silence communicated nothing intellectually useful.

However, many feminist leaders loved the book. For example, when Shulie Firestone, the author of the 1970 classic, *The Dialectic of Sex,* read it, she ex-claimed: "Oh, Phyllis, if only you had published this early in the 1970s, it might have saved our movement." High praise indeed—but I do not agree with it; nothing could have saved us from our own Chinese Cultural Revolution in fem-inist America. Kate Millett, the author of the groundbreaking *Sexual Politics,* read it, laughed, and said: "Oh look what you've gone and done, told all of the truth again." And she gave me a glorious blurb for the book. Many feminists agreed with her and did likewise, including Vivian Gornick, Roxanne Dunbar-Ortiz, and Susan Griffin. Deborah Tannen wrote a front-page *Washington Post* review praising the book.

However, Pollitt and Sonia Robbins Jaffee, who often reviews books for *Pub-lisher's Weekly,* kept challenging and badgering me on this listserv group about this particular work and couldn't seem to let it go. I was quite taken aback by the sustained and simultaneous nature of their attacks because Nation Books was the publisher, and, as I've said, Pollitt is a *Nation* magazine columnist.

Perhaps it was not about the book at all. Perhaps I had disappointed them in some important way. Once I had been the kind of feminist who braved the might of the state on behalf of custodially embattled mothers, especially those whose children had been raped by their fathers. *Nation* magazine had published my letter about my 1986 FBI grand jury experience. Perhaps my pro-religion views and religious activism threatened the reflexive left contempt for religion. And now I had dared suggest that women had flaws.

If a book or a body of work is important and at least partly true, there is a generous versus an envious way of challenging it. Envious criticism tends to be ugly and "mean-girl" personal. It seeks to destroy the work itself by demeaning its creator, often by referring to her appearance or reputation; in short, by focusing outside the work itself.

Pollitt did so in a breathtakingly nasty obituary of feminist writer and activist Andrea Dworkin. Even after she was dead, Pollitt could find nothing kind or measured to say about Dworkin's work, which, in my opinion and that of a great many others, was visionary, both in literary and intellectual terms. While I did not agree with Dworkin about many things, our differences would never, ever lead me to devalue the body of her work or her enormous talent. In her column in *The Nation* Pollitt writes: "Andrea Dworkin died on April 9 [2005] at 58— she of the denim overalls and the wild hair and wilder pronouncements. . . . Dworkin was an oversimplifier and a demagogue. . . . Andrea Dworkin was a living visual stereotype—the feminist as fat, hairy, makeup-scorning, unkempt lesbian. Perhaps that was one reason she was such a media icon—she 'proved' that feminism was for women who couldn't get a man."

Only at the end does Pollitt pull herself back and write: "I never thought I would miss unfair, infuriating, over-the-top Andrea Dworkin. But I do. And even more I miss the movement that had room for her."

Pollitt was kinder to me. She did not write about my weight, hair, clothing, or sexual preferences. Instead, she focused on the presumably questionable methodology I had used in *Woman's Inhumanity to Woman*—but mainly as a way of not dealing with the ideas, the substance of the book. This kind of criticism, this tone, will never lead us to a movement that would have room for Dworkin, for Pollitt, and for me.

According to Pollitt and Robbins Jaffee, the fact that I had not "named names" in the book invalidated what I was saying. But my female interviewees had revealed painful and private facts about their relationships to their mothers, daughters, and best friends. And my interviewees were not necessarily public figures, feminist leaders, or published authors. When they were, or if they asked me to quote them by name, I gladly did so.

Neither Pollitt nor Robbins Jaffee contacted me offline or by phone. (I did not contact them either.) And as they launched and relaunched this critique, everyone else remained silent. I felt isolated, but I also thought that an online exchange still might be fruitful. However, nothing we said ever led any of us to change our minds.

Except now I have changed my mind about the importance of naming names, especially when those names belong to public figures and published authors.

The level of verbal hostility was very high. Perhaps only teenage girls who deal with female bullies might recognize the kind of nonstop hostility unleashed. But this conversation was presumably taking place among like-minded adult thinkers and activists, not among female teenagers.[1]

In my opinion, Pollitt and others, especially Roxanne Dunbar-Ortiz, Sonia Robbins Jaffee, and Judith Ezekiel (who was very good on the issue of anti-Semitism in France, where she lives and works), could not abide my pro-Israel and pro-America point of view. In fact, *Nation* magazine ran a cover story that resembled the jacket art of my book *The New Anti-Semitism*. The review attacked the book (and several others). The *Nation* cover was titled: "The *Myth* of the New Anti-Semitism." The exchanges on the HIA listserv group about Jew-hatred, Islamism in Europe, the danger of jihad, the slaughter of innocent Israeli civilians, and other topics were "hardball" exchanges. I never got the slightest support for my views; everyone supported hard left views. Or they remained silent.

Again: We are each entitled to our opinion. And it is crucial for thinking people to continue talking even when they disagree with each other. This is one reason I chose to remain on the HIA listserv. But I felt increasingly uncomfortable and under siege in a group where I'd hoped for a friendly, respectful, and, perhaps supportive intellectual exchange.

Pollitt and others could not bear that I had begun to publish articles in *FrontPage* magazine and in the *National Review* online. (Hughes was attacked for doing so as well.) I did not hide my new bylines from them. In fact, I was rather proud of the *feminist* and pro-woman pieces I had begun to publish mainly in *FrontPage*.

My first piece was about the trafficking of women and about censorship. A Swedish left-wing filmmaker, Lukas Moodysson, had refused to allow his brilliant anti-trafficking film *Lilya 4-ever* to be shown at a feminist conference in Israel. The Israeli feminists who were sponsoring the anti-trafficking conference turned to me for help. I wrote a piece in which I challenged Moodysson's decision to show his film in every other country on earth where brothels, pimps, and trafficking also flourish but not in Israel. After the piece had been rejected by the major liberal media on both coasts, I offered it to *FrontPage,* which took it and ran it the next day. Within forty-eight hours Moodysson had changed his mind and decided to allow the Israeli feminists to show his film.

I considered this a success story. I sent it to the HIA listserv group and asked for their feedback; really, I wanted their respect. No one would comment on the substance of the matter. The only thing that mattered was *where* I had published the article. This was shocking. I was accused of being a right-wing, neoconservative, a Bush supporter, an enemy. This attitude did not change when, in the context of the genocide in Darfur, Sudan, I published a piece in *FrontPage* about the "gender cleansing" of the Sudanese women. (This is how I viewed the ethnic Arab Muslim practice of publicly and repeatedly gang-raping Sudanese African women, including children.)

I was proud of what I'd written. I wanted feminist support for my anti-trafficking and Sudan-related pieces. I'd also sent this listserv group a piece or two about Jew hatred and Israel-bashing on the left. I was eager for some rational and civilized exchanges. None was forthcoming. In fact, the listserv group refused to discuss my pieces at all because I'd published them in a "right-wing rag."

Where I'd published, not what I'd said, was everything to them.

In a sense, this was part of a familiar pattern. When ideologues disagree with someone's ideas, they often refuse to engage with them substantively; instead, they create a diversion by referring to the author's appearance (as Pollitt did in Andrea Dworkin's case) or to some methodologically irrelevant issue (as Pollitt and Robbins Jaffee did vis-à-vis *Woman's Inhumanity to Woman*). Ideologues also create other kinds of diversions, such as refusing to read or comment on work that has been published in a politically incorrect place, as was done in both Donna Hughes's case and in my own.

I fear that the publication of the book that you are holding will be met with great resistance from just such feminists, although I hope otherwise.

On June 25, 2004, when the publisher announced that it had acquired *Women, War and Allegiance* (its working title), the HIA listserv members made naught but nasty, "catty," comments. Pollitt started it off by sending around the *Publishers Lunch* notice of the book with her own "No comment." My former colleague, Professor Roxanne Dunbar-Ortiz, quickly wrote that I was doing this book for money, because attacking the left and feminism is so "lucrative." Carol Hanish agreed but stressed that it's not just the book contract but the lectures and speaking fees that also had to be taken into account. Pollitt thought that I was writing this book selling out the feminist left in order to have fifteen minutes of fame on the "right-wing gravy train." (Were they already counting the Orwellian "Goldstein's" money?)

Pollitt imagined that she and others would be making appearances in this book as anti-Zionist villains and not as the intolerant leftists some of them truly are. At the time, I had no intention of writing about this listserv group at all. This remained true even though I was horrified by how HIA members had greeted the announcement of my new book, and even though I was disheartened by the listserv's continued hostile and chilly tone toward my ideas.

However, as I began interviewing Donna Hughes about her listserv experience, I recognized similar listserv patterns of disdain, hostility, and intolerance. What was happening was not personal—it was political. Events began to intensify online, and reached a crescendo in November 2004. At that point, I concluded that I was obligated to reveal what had happened to me. Doing so was very painful. Living through a traumatic experience is bad enough; choosing to relive it (many times in order to write about it) is the price that I have chosen to pay for the right to speak my mind.

Third Wave feminist author and activist Jen Baumgardner informed everyone that, actually, I was still on the listserv. (By now, I'd been so discouraged that I rarely "spoke.") Suddenly Pollitt wanted Baumgardner to contact me to make sure that I would abide by a newly suggested "privacy policy." Clearly, one had not been in effect before. Pollitt was concerned that she not end up being quoted in an anti-feminist book—especially if her comments were "scribbled off the top of [her] head."

Professor Ros Baxandall opined that so many women go without attention—and *they* don't become "right-wing turncoats." Baxandall agreed that she was uncomfortable being on a listserv with me since I'd come out for Bush. However, she did not want to afford me a "lucrative" career by "banning me." Then, she said, I'd become just like David Horowitz, the former leftist and publisher of *FrontPage.*

Why didn't I leave? Did I still consider myself "one of them"? (Poor fool, I probably did.) Was I denying to myself that I'd changed, and that the change mattered? (Perhaps I was.) Was I also hedging my ideological bets, unwilling to choose one "side" over another? (Indeed, I did not want to do so.) Did I really want to force them to throw me off the listserv so that I could write about it? No, I did not. I have far too many other things to write about, and being attacked and ultimately "purged" on the listserv was painful.

Perhaps I had truly underestimated how threatening a symbol I had become. I was not appropriately pro-PLO, I was inappropriately pro-Israel and pro-America. But mainly I was threatening because I was "like" them, but no longer *exactly* like them; "like" them, but also *very different* in some important ways.

In retrospect, I think that the nature of the Internet made it easy for us to impart greater power to each other than we actually may have had. It also allowed us to speak "loudly" without being able to soften the blow of our words. In November 2004, the listserv group got very intense. Perhaps if John Kerry had won the election, I might not have posed such a threat. Kerry lost. Bush won. A friend of mine who moves in left feminist circles told me that she'd heard from someone on the listserv that I was already on the Bush payroll. I toughed it out, replying that "if the check was in the mail I would certainly cash it."

Pollitt and company could not get at the president, but they could sure vote against him over and over again by hectoring and bullying me and by driving me away. In mid-November, I committed the greatest sin possible: I joined author and publisher David Horowitz and others, including former Israeli minister Natan Sharansky, Daniel Pipes, Steve Emerson, Bill Kristol, Bernard Goldberg, John Fund, Victor David Hansen, and a number of military officers, and Republican senators and congressmen, at a conference in Florida. It was certainly not my usual crowd—although I had worked with Sharansky before.

I recanted no feminist principle and mainly spoke about jihad, terrorism, Israel, and the plight of women in the Islamic world. I also spoke about the "Palestinianization" of the western academy and how dangerous this was for western values such as women's rights, truth, and democracy. So, I had actually dined with the enemy; I had been in the same room with some of the men who had brought John Kerry down.

The very day the first article about the conference was published (in *Front-Page* magazine), Pollitt singled me out and demanded that I agree never to reveal what she or anyone else had said on the listserv. Had the group been friendly, or even slightly respectful, and had the request been made to everyone, it might have been a fair enough request. But in this instance, coming when it did, why it did, and how it did, and so long after the listserv atmosphere had already become so charged, hostile, and paranoid, I doubted that agreeing would have led to civility or tolerance for my views. Nothing I could do would ever have ensured my "rehabilitation" on this listserv group.

Some members now said that they would not speak if I remained on the listserv. Others said that these were dangerously repressive times and that they would be endangering themselves if they spoke when I was "listening." Many members were talking about how "unsafe" and "anxious" they felt with me on the list. Some members stopped speaking. One whom I do not know threatened me. She said that she knew sixty lawyers whom she'd unleash against me if I hurt anyone in the group. As each member weighed in with pointed questions and demands, I became giddily nervous. What exactly had I done wrong? I kept asking if they were convicting me of a future thought crime. Did they honestly believe that I was spying on them or that their views constituted secret information that I would one day turn over to the government?

In a sense, I was once, unwittingly, a member of a cult—that of left feminism. I never took a loyalty oath as such, but for years the unspoken rules included sharing cherished beliefs about capitalism, colonialism, imperialism, sexism, homophobia, fundamentalism, and feminism. I had come to these beliefs on my own, not as the result of any pressure to conform. Intellectually, and independently, I "fell out of love" with simplistic views of capitalism, colonialism, imperialism, etc. Things had become more complicated for me, not only on the left but among feminists, too. Men were no longer always the "enemy," women were no longer always "pure victims," honorable feminists could honorably disagree with one another. Thus, over time, I came to understand that it is not honorable to remain silent about intolerance and bias wherever one may find it, including in one's own movements. Fundamentalist intolerance exists on both the right and the left and I will not be party to it.

Perhaps I should have confronted the hostility long ago and left. Perhaps some others on the listserv who have since contacted me privately should have called for a friendlier, more respectful, less paranoid tone. I became paranoid, too—I assumed that everyone, even the silent lurkers, were in agreement with Pollitt, when this might not have been the case.

Pollitt consulted lawyers and editors and quit the list. So did Jen Baumgardner.

And then so did I. Technically, I cried "uncle" and finally asked to be removed from the list; in reality, I was "purged." Since we live in America and not in Soviet Russia and since Pollitt and company are not running the American government, I am speaking only metaphorically and psychologically.

It is important to understand that, with the exception of Pollitt, at least sixteen active members on this listserv group are women whom I know personally, some very well, who have waged feminist battles by my side for more than thirty-five years and who know the value of my work. Their silence and, eventually, the jackal chorus calling for me to leave the list, was up close and personal.[2]

Since I left, one listserv member called to say that the list has lost its "pizzazz" and that what had been done to me was wrong. She said: "Every listserv group acts out at least once. Either it finishes them off or it bonds them." Barbara Seaman regularly tells me that the list is mainly quiet.

Right, left, right, wrong—we all had our marching orders, and we marched away from each other. We have now all lost the opportunity to talk to the other and to the almost other. I no longer read *The Nation* magazine. I doubt that anyone on this listserv reads *FrontPage*, the *Wall Street Journal*, the *New York Sun*, or the *Weekly Standard*—all of which I read regularly, as well as the *New York Times*, the *New York Post*, and the Jewish, Palestinian, Arab, and Israeli media. The dialogue is broken, the potential gone.

This is all very similar to the great divide in our country between left and right. Daily, the divide is becoming ever more extreme. The thinking classes, including the feminists, are part of the polarized divide.

What happened to me, to Donna Hughes, and no doubt to many others on left-dominated academic listserv groups might be painful and might even have far-reaching repercussions; however, it still remains a small and private matter. No one forces us to remain on unfriendly listserv groups. More important, the professors and other listserv members do not run the government, they have no state police powers, they are not members of paramilitary organizations. But, given their level of intolerance and paranoia, if they ran the state, they might soon be conducting show trials, demanding public recantations, and exiling dissidents to concentration camps, torture cells, and gulags. It's certainly happened before.

In 399 B.C., the democratic, pagan Athenian state arrested and tried the great philosopher Socrates. He was condemned to death for "corrupting" the youth by teaching them to question everything, especially authority.[3]

Nearly two millennia later, in 1600, the Catholic Church and Inquisition jailed, tortured, and burned Giordano Bruno alive for his "heretical" ideas.[4]

In 1633, the Church arrested, jailed, and convicted Galileo Galilei for "heresy." His crime? He claimed the Earth revolves around the sun. The Church forced both Bruno and Galileo to publicly recant their views.[5]

Nearly four hundred years later the secular, anti-religious, totalitarian Soviet regime murdered at least thirty to forty million people. Let me name just five among the thousands of intellectuals and artists whose truth- and freedom-loving ideas, which included exposing the hypocrisy and crimes of the politically correct ruling classes, led to the banning of their works and to their persecution, torture, imprisonment, and external or internal exile in the Siberian gulag.

In 1921, in order to silence and punish Anna Akhmatova, one of Russia's most beloved poets, the Soviet regime executed her first husband, the poet and theorist Nikolai Gumilyev, for "betraying the revolution." In 1938, the regime imprisoned their son, Lev Gumilyev, for twenty years. In 1949, Stalin also imprisoned Akhmatova's third husband, who died in a Soviet prison camp in 1953. Akhmatova was condemned as both a "bourgeois" and an "aristocrat" and was described as a "harlot nun." She was expelled from the Union of Soviet Writers but was never imprisoned. Like Bruno and Galileo, she also once "recanted"; she wrote a poem praising Stalin in the hope that it might win her son's freedom. Akhmatova's greatest poem, "Requiem," described the suffering of the Russian people under Stalin. It was not published in Russia until 1987—twenty-one years after her death.

In 1963, the Soviets convicted the Russian writer Vladimir Bukovsky for organizing poetry meetings in Moscow and imprisoned him for eight months. When he was released, he led demonstrations to free other Soviet dissidents. For this Bukovsky was sentenced to five years of hard time in a psychiatric-political rehabilitation facility. He documented the abuse of psychiatric institutions for political reasons and smuggled his account out to the West. This led to his third arrest in 1972 and to a sentence of twelve years. In 1976, he was exchanged for former Chilean communist leader Luis Corvalan and moved to England.

In 1978, the Soviets falsely accused and convicted Natan Sharansky, a mathematician, translator, human rights activist, and Jewish refusenik, of treason and of spying for the United States. The state sentenced him to thirteen years in prison, where he spent long periods in solitary confinement and undergoing other tortures. He was also sent into "internal" exile in the gulag. He was freed in 1986 as part of an American-Soviet prisoner exchange. Sharansky moved to Israel, where he was the minister for Jerusalem and diaspora affairs.

In 1980, the Soviets arrested Sharansky's mentor, André Sakharov, a nuclear physicist and human rights activist, sent him into "internal" exile in Gorki, and allowed him no contact with foreigners. Sakharov had played a major role in Soviet Russia's development of the hydrogen bomb. In the 1960s, Sakharov became active against nuclear proliferation. He was banned from all military-related research. In 1970 Sakharov founded the Moscow Human Rights Committee and, in 1975, won the Nobel Peace Prize. His protests against the Soviet invasion of Afghanistan was the "final straw" that led to his arrest. In 1986, Sakharov returned to Moscow and co-led the democratic opposition to Soviet rule.

This pattern of terror was repeated in Hitler's Nazi Germany, Mao's communist China, Castro's communist Cuba, and in many, if not most, Islamic regimes throughout the twentieth and into the twenty-first centuries. A separate chapter—actually many books—would be required to name the names of the heroic dissidents.

The pattern is clear: Dissent is intolerable. The Soviet state did not tolerate it. It murdered its perceived enemies and employed a vast system of torture, prison, and internal exile to subdue its entire population. This totalitarian policy neither wavered nor changed over seventy years. And this regime was romanticized and essentially "whitewashed" by most leftists and by many left-dominated liberal academics whose heirs now run the European and North American academies and are active on listserv groups.

Many leftists and left-dominated liberals have written about their trips to Cuba in the 1950s, 1960s, and 1970s. Few denounced Cuba for its human rights atrocities. Castro's Cuba was not the people's paradise that so many American leftists, myself included, once imagined it was. Free speech was savagely curtailed, and many intellectuals and writers were imprisoned, tortured, and murdered for their anti- or non-communist beliefs or for their exposure of wrongdoing by the politically correct regime. The Cuban regime has zero tolerance for dissent. Please allow me to focus on three Cuban prisoners of conscience.

In 1960, the poet Armando Valladares, who fought against Batista, was condemned to twenty-two years of brutal torture and confinement. Valladares managed to write about prison conditions while he was imprisoned and to smuggle his work out. For this he was denied food, medical attention, and visitors. In 1982, Valladares finally won his freedom due to an international campaign on his behalf.

In 1968, another Cuban poet, Herberto Padilla, published an anti-Castro collection of poems that won Cuba's highest literary prize. The state-sponsored Union of Cuban Writers and Artists was forced to issue a statement that criticized its own publication as a "counterrevolutionary work." Like his many predecessors, Padilla was forced to publicly recant his own work against "the revolution." Padilla endured years of persecution and prison under Castro until Senator Ted Kennedy campaigned and won his freedom and exile to America.

In 1973, Castro imprisoned the poet, novelist, and playwright Reinaldo Arenas, who had fought at Castro's side against Batista. Castro tortured Arenas, not only for his "ideological deviance," but for his homosexuality. The Castro regime banned his work and forced Arenas to publicly "renounce" it. In 1980, he was allowed to leave the country in a mass exodus of "undesirable" homosexuals. In 1987, Arenas was diagnosed with AIDS; he committed suicide in New York City in 1990. Many know about him from his internationally acclaimed memoir, *Before Night Falls,* which the painter Julian Schnabel made into a beautiful, haunting movie.

These four Soviet and three Cuban dissidents ran afoul of the ruling classes. Their principled stand for human rights and for the life of the mind threatened fundamentalist orthodoxies and was punished as "heresy."

Why this rather long digression? What do these dissidents and their fates have to do with feminist listserv fascism or totalitarianism on academic listserv groups?

Left-dominated liberals and conservatives of all stripes would probably condemn the persecution of Socrates, Bruno, and Galileo. But then they'd part company. Many notable leftists have failed to condemn Soviet, Maoist, and Cuban human rights violations, including the persecution of independent thinkers and whistle-blowers; conservatives have not hesitated to do so. Instead, leftists have focused on the oppression of women, poor people, and racial minorities by capitalist nation-states and by religious institutions.

Although exceptions do exist, right-wing fundamentalists are intolerant about abortion and gay rights. Right-wing hard-heartedness has led to a long-term campaign to judicially, legislatively, and politically defeat the civil rights of women in general (there is still no equal rights amendment in the constitution) and women's rights in reproductive matters in particular. Such right-wing intolerance has also led to the refusal to allow gays to be out in the military or to marry or enter into civil unions. The name-calling and outright hatred of feminists as "baby killers" and the bombing of clinics have been far from "Christian" and constitute terrorism.

Extremists on the left and right do not tend to "clean house," that is, they do not expose the crimes committed by one of their own. For example, private industries, such as drug companies, do not usually police themselves. Their goal is profit, not truth-telling or teaching. The Catholic Church did not expose or punish priestly homosexual pederasty; left to their own devices, the leaders covered it up. However, the Church does not view itself as necessarily progressive or objective.

Only the thinking classes view themselves in that way. The fact that most leftists and left-dominated liberals still hesitate to acknowledge that enormous crimes against humanity were committed by communist states in the name of revolution is very troubling, as is their allegiance to rigid party lines and intolerance toward those who challenge or simply fail to espouse them. The fact that such thinkers are running our universities is very worrisome.

I fear for us in North America and in Europe, both bastions of democracy, when the good people, especially our professional thinkers, are so afraid of diversity, "difference," and independent and heretical thinking. If we do not start teaching women and men how to think and how to tolerate different thoughts, we will soon find ourselves living in a new totalitarian world, one forged by Islamist fundamentalists and left-wing ideologues. Neither group can bear opposition. True thinkers, including old-fashioned liberals, can.

Once I nearly lost my life to such closed-minded fundamentalism. It was long ago, in Afghanistan. I believe that what I learned there has not only forged the kind of feminist I am, but may explain why I can't sign on to any party line.

My experience has led me to believe that what's next in the struggle for women's freedom involves taking a strong stand against the Islamic mistreatment of women and intellectuals. Perhaps if feminists can acknowledge the absence of civility and tolerance in our dialogue with each other and with the "other," we may also be able to acknowledge that our multicultural correctness has endangered all those held hostage by jihadic, totalitarian Islam—including ourselves.

Let me share with you my current understanding of what my captivity in Afghanistan was like and what it means for us today.

Four

My Afghan Captivity

If a woman shows her face to a Moslem, he breaks out into violent abuse because the act is intended to let him know that he is looked upon as a small boy, or a eunuch or a Christian in fact not a man.

—Captain Sir Richard F. Burton

On December 21, 1961, when I returned from my captivity in Afghanistan, I literally kissed the ground at Idlewild Airport. (That's what Kennedy Airport used to be called.) I weighed ninety pounds and was infected with hepatitis. Although I would soon become active in the American civil rights, anti–Vietnam war, and feminist movements, what I had learned in Kabul rendered me immune to the various romanticizations of Third World countries that infected so many American radicals back in the day.

I had seen just how badly women are treated in the Islamic world. As a young bride, I had been mistreated, too—but I survived and got out. I hope that telling my story will help other westerners understand and empathize with Muslim and Arab women (and men) who are being increasingly held hostage to barbarous and reactionary customs.

In retrospect, I believe that my so-called western feminism was forged in that most beautiful and treacherous of countries. Forever after, I was able to see gender apartheid anywhere, even in America.

I had married my college sweetheart, Ali, in a civil ceremony in the summer of 1961 in New York State. I was a nice Orthodox Jewish American girl; he was a nice Muslim boy from Afghanistan who had been away from home for fourteen long years while studying at private schools in Europe and America. My husband looked like Omar Sharif and was the first man I'd slept with. Even I knew that a respectable girl was supposed to marry such a man; the fact that he also happened to be a Muslim was not as strange as it might seem.

When I was five years old in Borough Park, Brooklyn, I insisted on learning Hebrew; when I was eight years old, I became a socialist-mystical Zionist and joined Hashomer Hatzair (the Young Guard), a left-wing Zionist youth organization. My mother considered this heresy and had the rabbis admonish me. I responded by joining a group that was even farther to the left. Ain Harod—my new group—envisioned Jews and Arabs living together collectively and harmoniously in the Jewish homeland, having beaten their swords into plowshares.

My Muslim father-in-law, Amir (also known as Agha Jan, or Dear Master), was an exceedingly dapper businessman. Agha Jan had also supported King Amanullah, who, in the early 1920s, had boldly unveiled Afghan women, instituted the country's first educational and health care systems, and introduced European-style trolleys in the capital city.

The king had been forced into exile in 1928 and he fled to Rome, where he died many years later. Agha Jan himself had barely escaped the hangman, but he fled closer to home, to India, followed by two wives bearing gold bricks and jewelry in baby carriages. Several years later Agha Jan returned to serve his country again.

The truth is, I did not want to get married—but I did not want to leave Ali, either. I was impatient to see the world. Ali's father would not send him money so that we might travel and would not "receive" us in Kabul if we were not married—or so Ali said. In retrospect, I don't believe Agha Jan really wanted a foreign, American, and Jewish daughter-in-law. I believe I was Ali's desperate rebellion, just as he was mine. I was flesh-and-blood proof that, for fourteen years, he'd actually been living in the twentieth century; I was his tendered declaration of independence to fight for or to sacrifice.

My plan was to meet Ali's family in Kabul, stay there a month or two, study the history of ideas at the Sorbonne in Paris for a semester, then return to Bard College in America to complete my final semester. We crossed the Atlantic and visited museums, churches, restaurants, rivers, gardens, and forests in England, France, Germany, Lebanon, and Iran. When we landed in Kabul, at least thirty members of his family, all wearing dark glasses, were there to greet us.

The airport officials smoothly confiscated my American passport.

"It's just a formality, nothing to worry about," Ali assured me. "You'll get it back later."

I never saw that passport again.

Please understand that what happened to me was as nothing compared to what routinely happened to women in Afghanistan who lived under virtual house arrest or in "purdah," seen only by close male relatives. Although King Zahir Shah had, for the second time, officially unveiled the women in 1958, most women still wore the chadari, a shroudlike garment that made them look like ghosts. Some wore scarves, gloves, and long coats.

My life was similar to that of an upper-class Afghan woman. However, I had not expected my personal freedom and access to privacy and anonymity to be so profoundly curtailed. What Muslim women accepted as a given was new and shocking for me. My experience was similar to but hardly as constrained as that which an increasing number of Arab and Muslim women face today, both in the Middle East and in Southeast Asia and North Africa. As we shall see in chapters six through eight, women who live under Islam today are being forced back in time, re-veiled, more closely monitored and more savagely punished than they were in the 1960s and 1970s.

Ali was a good man, a brave man, too, who wanted to help modernize his country. He did not consciously intend to harm me. Ali never once said that I might have to face a "period of adjustment." Perhaps he'd forgotten how things were. In the West he was just another olive-skinned "foreigner"; in Afghanistan, he was the son of a powerful father who would help him become a government minister. Ambition and loyalty demanded that Ali minimize his country's backwardness.

In Afghanistan, a few hundred families of wealth lived by modern European standards. Everyone else lived in the tenth to fourteenth centuries. And that's the way the king, his government, the mullahs, the people, and every other country on earth wanted it to remain. Western diplomats, including Americans, did not peg their foreign policies to how Afghanistan treated its women, children, the poor, or intellectuals. Even before multicultural relativism kicked in, western diplomats did not believe in "interfering." They understood that they'd be asked to leave if they did so.

The Afghanistan I knew was a prison, a police state, a feudal monarchy, a theocracy, rank with fear and paranoia. Afghanistan had never been colonized. My Afghan relatives were very proud of this fact. "Not even the British could occupy us," they told me, not once but many times. I was ultimately forced to conclude that Afghan barbarism, tyranny, and misogyny were entirely of their own making, and not attributable to colonialism or imperialism. It's what they themselves would say.

Individual Afghans (or "Afranis") were beautiful, charming, funny, humane, tender, sympathetic, enchantingly courteous, sometimes even breathtakingly honest. But Afghanistan in the 1960s was a bastion of illiteracy, poverty, and preventable and treatable diseases; yet that was not the worst of it. The overwhelming domestic and psychological misery was worse and it consisted of arranged marriages, polygamy, forced pregnancies, the chadari, domestic slavery, and, of course, purdah. Women led wholly indoor lives and socialized only with other women, usually female relatives. If they needed to see a doctor, their husband usually consulted one for them in their place. Women did not pray in mosques, but only at home, alone. Although there were some exceptions, most women were barely educated.

In 1962, when I returned to Bard College I tried to tell my classmates how important it was that America had so many free libraries, movie theaters, bookstores, universities, unveiled women, freedom of movement on the streets, freedom to leave our families of origin if we so chose, freedom from arranged marriages—and from polygamy, too. As imperfect as America may be, it was still the land of opportunity and of "life, liberty and the pursuit of happiness."

My young friends wanted only to hear fancy Hollywood fairy tales, not grim realities. They asked me: "But weren't you some kind of princess?"; "How many servants did you have?"; "Did you meet the king?" They could not understand the personal danger that had haunted every step of my grand adventure.

I felt like a Rudyard Kipling character from *The Man Who Would Be King* (only in my case, it was more like the "Foreign Bride Who Would Be Free"). My tongue seemed to have been cut out. I had no way of communicating the horror, and the truth. Perhaps I was ashamed of having endangered myself and did not want to trot out every damning detail; perhaps I was still loyal to my husband. But my American friends could not or did not want to understand what I was trying to say.

I fear that many left-dominated liberals want to remain as ignorant today as my young college friends were so long ago.

We were beatniks, about to become hippies. We assumed that the entire world was our oyster, that Americans could travel everywhere safely, that our lives would be one big on-the-road movie, that whether we stayed at all-star hotels or slummed it with revolutionary movements that our lives were somehow inviolate, protected.

At the time, the women did not think we were endangered because we were women. Even though western women who traveled abroad were sometimes raped, kidnapped, or murdered, we blocked this from consciousness. We did not want to feel constrained, and reality would have seriously limited our overwhelming need to fantasize.

We also thought that travel was an American and God-given right. Over the next four decades, I would travel all over North America and Europe and to the Caribbean, Israel, and the Far East, but my foot never again touched earth in Iran or Afghanistan or in any Islamic country in the Middle East.

Although I was obviously drawn to Islamic people and culture (I still am), I had been forced to learn how dangerous this attraction could be.

Long before al-Qaeda beheaded Daniel Pearl in Pakistan and Nicholas Berg in Iraq, and long before various "hot" wars concerning oil commenced, I understood that it was dangerous for a westerner, especially a woman, whether she was Jewish or Christian, to live in a Muslim country, even when she was under the protection of a powerful Muslim family—especially if she were.

Once a western woman marries a Muslim and lives with him in his native land, she is no longer entitled to the rights she once enjoyed in her native country. Only military mercenaries can rescue her. I have since heard many stories about western women who have married Muslim men in Europe and America and whose children were kidnapped by their fathers and kept forever after in Saudi Arabia, Jordan, Egypt, Pakistan, and Iran. The mothers were usually permitted no contact.

In Kabul, I met other foreign wives, mainly from Europe, who loved having servants but whose own freedom had been savagely curtailed. Some foreign wives who had come in the late 1940s and early 1950s had converted to Islam and wore The Thing. Foreign wives who came in the 1960s did not veil themselves, but they each told me similar stories. They had all been warned, as I had been, that whatever they did would become known, that there were eyes everywhere, that their actions could endanger their families and themselves.

Foreign wives were mistrusted; many were constantly accused of "desiring" a western life, of "dreaming" about dancing parties. Actually, private gender-integrated dancing parties were sometimes arranged, but they had to be treated like military operations. Servants had to be dismissed, family members had to be away, shades drawn, a house carefully chosen for its remote location, and so on.

Once I saw an Afghan husband fly into a rage when his foreign wife not only wore a western swimsuit to an adult co-ed swimming party but actually removed her dress and plunged into the pool! The men expected to be the only ones who would swim; their wives were meant to chat and sip drinks.

One day I was sunning myself on a private family terrace in my pink-and-purple bikini when a ruckus began below. It seemed that some men who had been building or repairing a house a mile away were able to see a near-naked woman on her own private balcony. I was forced to go indoors and ordered never to do anything like that again.

It is no accident that Osama bin Laden chose Afghanistan to train his al Qaeda suicide killers. It is one of the most inaccessible and backward countries in the world and the easiest place for a criminal to hide himself in; as such, the routine crimes perpetrated against women in the name of Islam or Islamic custom are also least visible here.

❋ ❋ ❋

Immediately upon our arrival in Kabul, my very western husband simply became another person. He did not seek me out (except at night), we were no longer a couple during the day, he no longer held my hand or kissed me in public; in fact, he barely spoke to me. Incredibly, he treated me the way his father and elder brother treated their wives: with annoyed embarrassment, coldness, distance.

For two years, Ali and I had been inseparable. He had walked me to my classes. Daily we did our homework together in the library. We talked constantly. Suddenly I had not only lost my language, my country, and my personal freedom, but also my best friend. I had absolutely no one to talk to. I was utterly alone—and yet I was never really alone.

The concept of privacy is a western one. When I would leave the common sitting room in order to read in my own bedroom, all the women and children would follow me. They'd ask: "Are you unhappy?" They had no idea what I might do alone except cry or brood. No one spent any time alone. To do so was an insult to the family. The idea that a woman might be an avid reader of books and a thinker was simply too foreign a notion.

I was strong-willed and high-spirited, and perhaps nothing would have allayed my rising fear. But surely I would have been comforted had Ali at least taken me into his confidence and explained that the social and interpersonal rules had changed, that the game was now out of his hands. He merely acted as if there were something wrong with me for expecting our relationship in Afghanistan to bear the slightest resemblance to our relationship in America.

Men did not socialize with their wives in Afghanistan. They were not meant to have anything in common with them. Most met their wives only on their wedding day, or perhaps once before that. Also, what existed between a husband and wife was meant to be private and assumed to be primarily sexual and was therefore somehow shameful.

As I show later, this situation has not changed much since then. Today women in the Islamic world are still pressured into arranged marriages; forced to veil themselves; not allowed to vote or travel without a male escort; not allowed to work at all or to work in mixed-gender settings. Worse, many are genitally mutilated in childhood and routinely beaten as daughters, sisters, and wives; some are murdered by their male relatives in honor killings and stoned to death for alleged sexual improprieties or for asserting the slightest independence. What's more, such violations of women's human rights are increasingly taking place in Europe and in North America.

Years later, when I was talking with Moroccan feminist Fatima Mernissi, she understood what I'd gone through. She said that "heterosexuality" would be a "vast improvement" for everyone in the Islamic world. According to Fatima, boys and girls do not grow up together; they are not used to being with someone of the opposite sex, there is no communication, their every contact is erotically charged—but also forbidden.

So—I had gotten married, but in doing so I had lost my husband. Something was wrong, actually *everything* was wrong, but no one but me seemed to notice it. Ali dismissed my concerns, saying "You are being overly sensitive. Nothing is the matter."

We lived with Ali's oldest brother, Abdullah, Abdullah's wife, Rabiah, and their two children, sharing a home with Ali's mother, Aishah, or "Beebee Jan" (Dear Lady). My father-in-law Agha Jan had not lived with Beebee Jan for a very long time. He lived nearby, in the same family compound, in a house that he shared with his third wife and their eight children.[1]

Perhaps my house arrest and isolation were temporary, perhaps Ali only needed to prove himself to his family. Perhaps we might soon be able to resume our private, married life, move into our own home, socialize as if we were westerners. Perhaps all I needed was patience. I was wrong. Like everyone else, Ali was under permanent surveillance. His career and livelihood would depend on whether he could prove that he was an obedient-enough Afghan son and subject. How he treated me was crucial. He had to prove that his relationship to women was every bit as Afghan as any other man's; perhaps more so, since he had arranged his own marriage to a non-Afghan, non-Muslim woman.

Westerners do not always understand that eastern men can blend into the west with ease while still remaining eastern at their core. They can "pass" for one of us but, upon returning home, will always assume their original selves. Some may call this schizophrenic; others might view this as duplicitous. From a Muslim man's point of view, it is neither; it is simply what one does in the world to remain alive and to get what one wants. It is merely personal realpolitik. The transparency and seeming lack of guile that characterizes many ordinary westerners make us seem childlike and stupid to these men with multiple cultural personalities.

Ali had not told me that his father was polygamous. In our years together, he'd never mentioned it. Then, just before we'd arrived, Ali told me that "actually" his father had two wives, but that he'd been "tricked" into marrying the second wife, with whom he only had two children—"which says everything. She's more like a family servant," Ali explained. In fact, Ali's mother Aishah had treated the second wife so badly that Agha Jan had finally moved her into her own house.

Thus, it was as if this marriage somehow did not exist or didn't "count," and that marrying in order to have an indentured servant for the first wife to kick around didn't "count" either. But there she was, the second wife, Fauzia, living in the next house over. I would visit and have tea with her. Fauzia was grateful for the gesture of respect and for the company.

But imagine my surprise when I discovered that Agha Jan actually had *three* wives. This reality was one that Ali would not or could not discuss. As I would discover, he and his brothers blamed Beebee Jan for this third marriage to Sultana, which had jeopardized their inheritance considerably; this was a risky, tabooed subject. Thus, this marriage didn't "count" because it counted all too much.

"How can you justify polygamy?" I'd ask. "It's humiliating, cruel, unfair to the wives, it dooms them to sexual celibacy and emotional solitude at a very young age and for the rest of their lives. It also sets up fearful rivalries among the half-brothers of different mothers who have lifelong quarrels over their inheritances."

When he was being eastern, Ali would say: "Don't be a silly American. You say you're a thinker—God knows, you're always reading—and I therefore expect more understanding and broadmindedness from you. Polygamy tries to give men what they need so that they will treat their wives and children in a civilized way. In the West, men are serial polygamists. They leave their first wives and set of children without looking back. *That's* barbaric. Here we try to balance things out. We do not like the earlier wives to be abandoned, impoverished, ripped from their social webs. If she is a good Muslim wife, accepts and obeys her husband's wishes, he will support her forever. She will always have her children near her, which is all that matters to a woman. Her world will remain whole."

When he was being western Ali would say: "Our country is not ready for personal freedoms. That's why I'm needed here, to help bring my poor countrymen into the twentieth century. It's my destined role and I need you to help me. Don't leave. I expect you to join me in this great task."

We spent very little time talking about the veil, the chador, chadari, burqua, ghost-sheet, bedsheet, the Thing that Afghan and Muslim women wore. About this he was slightly defensive. My eastern husband would first point out that none of the women in *his* family wore it, that upper-class women only wore the regulation gauzy scarves, long coats, and gloves; that, please recall, King Amanullah had previously unveiled the women in the early 1920s, even before Ataturk had done so in Turkey. Ali usually failed to mention that in 1958 Zahir Shah's government had had to shoot down 600 men who protested unveiling the women and that Amanullah had lost his throne for doing so.

Ali also tried to justify the Thing in other ways. He said: "The country is dusty and sometimes dangerous, and a woman is better protected in many ways by the chadari. Anyway, country women do not wear chadaris when they farm. This is largely a phenomenon of the city, and anyway it's dying out."

This was not exactly true. Afghan countrywomen almost immediately turned their faces to the nearest available wall whenever a man to whom they were not related walked by. They tended to cover their heads and faces with their scarves and to wait until the coast was clear to continue along their way. The female servants at home, all of whom were from small, rural villages, were shy, bashful, and extremely girlish. They giggled a lot and hid their faces in their scarves.

As to the veil, my western husband would say: "You are too impatient about this damn chadari. Afghan women are not stupid. Give them some time. They will eventually all adopt the more western, freeing clothing."

Had I known what would happen, would I still have gone to his homeland? I'm not sure; I certainly hope not, but perhaps nothing could have stopped me. It was written in the stars, and I was only one of many westerners for whom the call of the east proved irresistible.

Were westerners like me all searching for death? Did we simply want to stop the too-complicated and possibly fruitless march of "progress" and surrender ourselves to the past, to oblivion? Did we, the champion "doers," long for a more passive, "native" way? Was our freedom really so difficult to bear, did we want everything decided for us?

After two weeks of marathon tea-drinking and pistachio-eating sessions, my polite smile was stuck to my face. I could not really understand what people were saying, I was bored, I wanted to get out on my own and see this spectacular city, visit the markets, the museum, see the mountains close up. But it seemed I was under a very polite form of house arrest. "You'll get lost," "It's not done," "People will talk," "Tell me what you need and I'll get it for you" were some of Ali's responses. And so I began to "escape" from the house every day.

I never put on the head scarves and long coats and gloves pointedly left for me atop the bedroom bureau. I would take a deep breath, go out, stride along at a brisk, American pace. Always a female relative or servant would run after me, bearing the scarves et al. I would smile, shake my head no, and keep on going. Of course, I was also followed by a slow-moving family Mercedes. The driver would call out: "Madame, please get inside. We are worried that you will hurt yourself."

Sometimes I'd walk faster, or I'd take a bus or a *gaudi*, a horse-drawn painted cart. The buses were quite colorful, except inside, fully sheeted women sat apart from the men. The first time I saw this, I laughed out loud in disbelief and nervousness. Now I no longer remember if women sat at the back or at the front of the bus. In any event, as women moved onto the bus, men would jostle them, make sneering remarks I could not understand.

Please remember that this was 1961, before Americans took on Jim Crow segregation in the American South.

My family was right. They knew their country. Bare-faced and alone, I looked like an "uppity" Afghan woman and was thus fair game for catcalls, propositions, interminable questions, rough advances. Men would push themselves against me, knock me around a bit, laugh, joke. But I could easily have been kidnapped and held for ransom, taken to a cave, kept there for days, raped, then returned. Ali finally exploded at me and told me that this exact scenario had recently happened to the wife of an Afghan minister who had killed himself afterwards.

But not all men were interested in women on the street. Some men, their rifles slung over their shoulders (traditional Afghan men did not go out without their rifles), held hands in broad daylight. One of the pair might sport a flower behind his ear; another might be wearing lipstick or have rouged cheeks. Remember: This was long before the Stonewall riots and gay liberation took place in America. Homosexuals were still closeted in America when these Afghan men were strolling about town.

"Ali," I would say, "there are male homosexuals roving the streets of your hometown. Is this common, are they accepted? Is this Alexander the Great's living legacy?" Ali would say: "You crazy Americans are all alike. You have sex on your mind. You see it where it does not exist."

Back then, and still today, Ali remains unwilling to discuss the epidemic of homosexual pederasty in Afghanistan and other Muslim countries; the adult male preference for boys as sex and love partners; the preference for anal sex even with women—it is also a form of birth control; the extent to which sexuality is prison sex: forced, painful, and between unequals.

Bit by bit, Ali was sounding anti-American. This did not bode well for me since I was the American scapegoat. Ali had lived in Europe and America for a long time. He loved the west, but he was also marginalized and invisible there. He was not an "important man" in America; no one knew who his father or family were. And his Muslim name, olive skin, and non-Anglo Saxon, non-Mediterranean, and non-Semitic features marked him as an unusual "foreigner." Both politically and intellectually, Ali also resented American arrogance and geopolitical "meddling" and was outraged and shamed by the American and European sense of superiority to Afghans and Muslims. In addition, Ali now had to prove to his father and countrymen that he was, at heart, more Afghan than American, that he would not be importing any anti-Afghan or anti-Muslim ideas into the kingdom.

I had to be brought to heel. Ali's manhood and his future in Afghanistan depended on this.

Thus, there came a time when I was no longer allowed to slip out of the house. A male servant would prevent me from going out. The family would call Ali immediately, and he would call me to yell, threaten, plead, or shame: "Do you want to ruin my chances for us here?" Or he'd promise me jewelry or a visit to the tailor. I now understood that I needed to leave the country. I immediately presented myself at the American embassy, which was located right next door to the family compound. The embassy rented the property from my father-in-law.

"I want to go home. I'm an American citizen. I don't belong here."

"Where is your passport?"

"They took it away from me when our plane landed. But they told me that I'd get it back."

Each time the Marines would escort me back home. They told me that as the "wife of an Afghan national," I was no longer entitled to American protection.

Everything was happening all at once and far too quickly for me to understand—and the sheer physical beauty of the place was overwhelming. I bought a diary in the bazaar. I have it still; I treasure its brown leather cover and accompanying maps of Scotland and England.

> *Summer, Kabul, Afghanistan, 1961. The bazaar: a cacophony of hanging hammered silver, Swiss watches, yard goods, and sheep carcasses. Loud Indian music, the Kabul River, the Himalayan foothills—all running through, ringing round, the exquisite eggshell blue mosque, the tea shop, the ten-year-old boy bearing tea to the men in the government office.*
>
> *Child-beggars roam the streets, wearing the cosmetics of trachoma and parasitic infestations. I've seen them before, in Teheran, and Beirut. Now, in Kabul, their mothers wait for them again, behind buildings and narrowed into doorways. The children pluck at my coat buttons, my purse, my packages, they scream after my retreating figure until they sight a new quarry. One child waves his crutches, another his withered arm stumps in the air: makeshift sideshows of horror. Some passersby laugh at them, call them tricksters, devils, rich people in disguise. My relatives have warned me that only a fool—or a foreigner-would give them any money.*
>
> *Nomad caravans jingle-jangle on their way to better grazing grounds for their camel, sheep, donkeys, goats, cows, oxen, chickens. The scene is bucolic, Biblical, except for one small thing.*
>
> *Always, sheeted from head to foot, there are women: silent, moving islands in a sea of men. Ghostly apparitions, the invisible visible, the living dead in their faded shrouds, a portable purdah, the women's quarters on the move. There is nothing romantic or mysterious about women in sheets.*
>
> *The chadari is not merely a veil across the lower half of a woman's face. It is a garment that covers a woman from head to foot with only a small, latticed or webbed opening at eye and nose level which allows a woman to breathe, and see, but just barely. She is permitted no peripheral vision. She is as blindered as any dray-horse. I see women struggling to balance both their packages and their infants under their suffocating chadaris. No one stops to help them. No man can; all other women are similarly encumbered or are in chauffeured limousines. My relatives dismiss them as "poor" women who cannot afford a male servant—as if their poverty justifies their considerable public discomfort.*

It is true, Ali's sister Soraya and sister-in-law Rabiah did not wear the chadari. In fact, they navigated Kabul's mud and dust miraculously poised on fashionable high heels and wearing expensive European couture—but they did wear scarves, long coats, and gloves. I marveled at their determined dexterity, they at my wildly improper ways. (I wore walking shoes and jeans on my expeditions.)

Oh, the women and girls of Afghanistan, the women of the Muslim world. I was no feminist—but now, thinking back, I see how much I must have learned there. The first lesson I was forced to learn, although it did not become clear to me for many years, was that oppressed people can be incredibly servile to their oppressors and fairly deadly toward each other.

For example, I was quite prepared to like, even "love" my mother-in-law, Beebee Jan, who wore Turkish bo-peep pantaloon trousers beneath a long and shapeless dress and covered her shoulders and her head with large, gauzy scarves. Beebee Jan stood well under five feet. She looked twenty years older than my father-in-law, even though she was ten years his junior.

In Afghanistan, Beebee Jan's life was an enviable one. Most people there did not have servants—they *were* servants. Most people never had enough to eat, did not have indoor plumbing or their own "rooms," had never ridden in a private car, had never seen a doctor.

Still, I felt sorry for her, given that my father-in-law had stopped speaking to her about twenty years earlier and had taken two other wives. But I was not prepared for how cruelly Beebee Jan treated her female servants.

For example, she would routinely and mercilessly beat old Daw-Daw, her personal servant, who herded the family's three cows and who fetched, bent, swept, carried, did anything that Beebee Jan required. Daw-Daw worked seven days a week and was always on call. She looked at least eighty years old—which meant she might have been about fifty.

Beebee Jan would hit Daw-Daw hard with her fist or with a steel pot, a broom—with just about anything she could lay her hands on. Beebee Jan would curse Daw-Daw, too. Poor Daw-Daw would try to protect herself from the blows, but she also tried to make light of them. She had no other place to go, no family, no village. This was her only home, her fate. And Beebee Jan had promised to bury her.

The household servants were all from small villages in the countryside. They worked seventeen to eighteen hours a day, every day, and ate whatever food the family had left over. "They starve in their villages," my brother-in-law Abdullah told me. "They are lucky to have these positions." Married couples often lived apart for years when they worked for different city families.

In addition to beating Daw-Daw regularly, Beebee Jan was always fighting with the servants and threatening to fire them. The children's nursemaid, "Madar Maryam" (Maryam's mother), was a ruddy-cheeked girl from a small village, bashful, energetic, and very good-natured. Her hands were very rough. She was about twenty-two, only a year older than I was, and already she was the mother of a seven-year-old girl. She had also suffered four or five miscarriages. When we met, she was about five or six months' pregnant. Madar Maryam slept on the floor in the children's room together with her daughter, who was a mini-servant and playmate for Abdullah's children. They slept only with a thin coverlet over them.

Madar Maryam was never allowed to be idle. She was up before dawn to pick up the freshly baked bread from down the road. In addition to bathing and dressing the children, she would also play with them. She made the beds, swept the entire house on her hands and knees with a tiny straw broom, washed clothes in the stream, did the sewing, helped serve and clean up after meals. She absolutely never complained; she always had a ready smile. I would almost say that she was "happy."

At night, or when Beebee Jan went out or would take a nap, Madar Maryam would sit with me, naming the objects in the room for me in Farsi. I would show her my clothing (which was fairly modest) and it would be like a museum exhibit for her. Her eyes would grow large when she felt the soft wool of my sweaters. We hugged each other a lot. I insisted that she take one of my bulky wool sweaters to sleep in. She refused. I finally told her she could "borrow" it for the winter.

Early the next morning, Beebee Jan woke me up, yelling that Madar Maryam had stolen my sweater and must be punished. I explained that I'd practically forced it upon her. Beebee Jan then turned on me. "You idiot Yahud (Jew). You will spoil the servants. They are laughing at you. I demand that you never do anything like this again." Indeed, everyone told me that servants were not to be trusted, that they "have to be watched every minute because otherwise they'll take advantage of you, steal your food, your plates, your soap."

My act of simple generosity had nearly gotten Madar Maryam fired. When I spoke to Ali about this he and his brothers seemed disinterested, bored, even embarrassed by this discussion of household affairs. Ali explained that Beebee Jan had absolute authority over the servants and the household and there was nothing they could do about it. This was "woman's" business, not theirs. Perhaps men understood that the cruelty with which women treated their female servants gave the aggrieved women a safe outlet for their frustration and aggression.

A month went by. Madar Maryam was now about six or seven months' pregnant. One hot and sunny afternoon, as we were finishing lunch in the upstairs parlor, Madar Maryam brought up the tea. Her hand was shaking as she poured it for us. Soon, hot tears splashed over the teapot.

"What is it?," both Rabiah (my dear sister-in-law) and I asked.

She would not say a word, but she kept crying loudly and pitifully. When she got up to return the heavy tray to the downstairs kitchen, we both followed her. Beebee Jan was standing there. When she saw Madar Maryam she laughed maliciously.

"Whose child are you really carrying, you conchonee, you whore, you daughter of a whore? I have summoned your husband. I will tell him about the other man who visits you at night. Yes. I myself saw him creep out only this morning. Fat, pregnant pig. Do you like it so much that you dirty yourself with strangers? It is Allah's punishment that you have lost five children. You will lose this one too."

This was the first and last time that I saw Rabiah actually argue with her mother-in-law. It seemed that Beebee Jan had been insulting Madar Maryam all week. Her accusations were deadly dangerous; women were stoned to death for alleged adultery. That night, Madar Maryam's husband came to return her to their village. When I last saw her, Madar Maryam's face was streaked with tears. We embraced goodbye. Both Rabiah and I begged her to have her baby in the city, in the hospital. She shook her head no. (After numerous inquiries, we learned that she did give birth to a boy prematurely, about a month later.)

As I began to plan my various escapes out of Afghanistan, I would fantasize about including Madar Maryam and her daughter in my plans. I think of her still; I have never forgotten her. I still do not know her real name or where she came from.

I had wanted to see what the hospitals in Kabul were like. One day Ali took me to the Kabul Maternity Hospital. Here is what I wrote in my diary:

> The corridors and courtyards of this long, low series of wooden buildings remind me of nineteenth-century Russia—a kerchiefed woman slapping a sheet to wash, a samovar in the doctor's private waiting room. A man, wearing a turban and a long quilted coat, is pacing barefoot, back and forth. The doctor, educated in Germany, greets us first, then turns to the man and speaks brusquely, with annoyance. "You brought your wife here too late. The baby is already dead. Your wife, not long, maybe a few hours more." Turning back to us, his guests, he smiles and offers us tea. "These provincials always come when it's too late." The husband has resumed his pacing, the doctor is stirring sugar into his tea. Suddenly the husband is yelling, the doctor yelling back.
>
> Quietly, Ali translates for me. The man is refusing to pay any hospital fees because not only will he have to pay to bury both his wife and child, he will need that money to buy another wife to cook for him and take care of his other children. And where in the name of Allah did the doctor think he'd be able to get this kind of money? He had already paid for a car to transport his wife all the way from their village, which clearly was a waste of money. Why should he have to pay the doctor for killing his wife and child?
>
> I left the hospital as quickly as I could. I didn't want to hear the screams of women as we sipped our civilized tea. Now, on the way out, the smell of blood was unmistakable on some of the drying sheets.

Whenever I tried to discuss the plight of women with my relatives, the room invariably grew tense, silent, and threatening. It was a forbidden subject. The normalization of cruelty toward women was epidemic, invisible. Only I was not used to it; I neither accepted nor understood it. Thus, each time I encountered it, I was still shocked.

For example, one of the many relatives who came to see us was a tall, improbably glamorous Pathan/Pushtun from the Hindu Kush. Abdul had come all the way down to Kabul to meet his first American woman—me—and to visit with his extended family.

We sat cross-legged on the carpeted floor opposite each other. He was very grandfatherly. He let me and the children play with his homemade rifle, his bandolier, even his turban. His eyes were gentle. Everyone agreed that he was an exceptionally good, even an overly generous man. One of my brothers-in-law explained why: "When Abdul's brother died, he treated his nephews as his own sons and he married his sister-in-law. But his other wives were not happy about this marriage, so to keep family peace, he locked his latest wife away for fifteen years. He made sure she was fed. One morning she was found dead. She had hanged herself with a turban. Everyone said: Poor Abdul!"

When I lived in Kabul, not a single foreign voice was heard protesting the condition of women. On the handful of occasions I was allowed out, gin-soaked diplomats told me that it would be "immoral" to preach to Afghans about their wild-West, low-boiling-point tribal violence or about their oppression of women; these were after all, sovereign, sacred, local customs. Please note: This was how diplomats thought even before multicultural relativism became the ideology of choice for westerners.

An American diplomat put it this way: "We can't impose our moral or cultural values on these people. We can't ask them about their system of government or justice, their treatment of women, their servants, their jails. These are very sensitive, very touchy, very proud men who happen to own a piece of land that's important to us. If we aren't careful, their kids would be learning Russian—or Chinese—instead of English and German. You've got to remember, we're guests here, not conquerors."

Yes. Western diplomats had no responsibility for Afghan schoolchildren, beautiful with promise and spontaneity, who were systematically crushed, muted, shamed, and bored into hopelessness by rigid, fearful, and poorly educated teachers. This was long before mullahs came in to whip them up into hatred against infidels, the West, America and the Jews.

I humbly suggest that we have reaped the whirlwind of our non-interventionism.

Before they're ruined, Afghan children are like children everywhere: amazing, fearless—yes, and also cruel. For example, my two young brothers-in-law, Karim and Rahim, addressed me in English, carefully, emphatically, as "sister-in-law." They were the family clowns who improvised, cleverly, on Afghan society. They impersonated Afghans so caught up in greeting each other, or in gossip, that they missed appointments or were killed by enemy fire. They played bureaucrats swollen with importance and misinformation, marriage brokers, mullahs, town idiots, shopkeepers.

"Sister-in-law, listen about my teacher," Karim reminisced. The teacher, a mullah, had installed himself in a comfortable room in the house, demanded and received a servant and a huge supply of tobacco and sweets. Then he proceeded to teach young Karim the alphabet. Every day for two weeks he taught and retaught him the first letter of the Persian alphabet—alif.

"But, sister-in-law," Karim told me, "I was reading ahead secretly all the time. Then, when mullah asks me again, again, again, to tell him 'alif,' I jump up, I yell, 'Mullah, bey, bey, I know bey.'" Of course, Karim had to apologize and finish out his lessons at the mullah's pace. But so what? Karim's eyes pleaded. For once, the emperor's nakedness had been challenged.

I had been sent back to the tenth century and placed under house arrest. I understood that I was supposed to learn to accept this. But I was endangered in other ways. For example, Beebee Jan was setting me up for either illness or death. I did not know that she had stopped the servants from boiling my drinking water and washing all the fruits and vegetables. To be fair: No Afghan boiled their drinking water, and it was Beebee Jan's responsibility to make sure that, as a foreign woman, I demonstrated deference for "Afghan ways." If I failed at this, it would shame the entire family. She also did not allow the cooks to cook with anything but ghee (rancid animal fat). I was losing weight rapidly because, like most foreigners, both my nose and my stomach could not tolerate any food cooked in ghee. People who grow up on ghee love it, and food does not taste right to them without it. For foreigners, ghee-drenched food is simply inedible, unbearable. It would have been an easy accommodation to cook some rice and lamb in Crisco; the cooks sent by my father-in-law's company did this all the time for diplomatic events. They had also done so when Ali and I first arrived. Soon that kindness had been discontinued.

I was beginning to starve, I had begun to dream of food. The only food I could eat consisted of luscious (unwashed) melons, home-made yogurt, and naan (flat bread). I amassed a small store of tinned food: tuna fish, biscuits, sardines, cheeses. Beebee Jan would routinely raid my stash and throw it out. I would buy more and try to hide it in a new place.

She was also trying to convert me to Islam. Relatives told me that it would mean so much to her if she could tell "all Kabul" that she had personally converted a Jew. "Some of my best friends were Jewish," Beebee Jan told me. "The Sharbanis, do you know them? They used to live here, but once they were allowed to leave they went straight to Israel. I could never understand it. Weren't they Afghans, too?"

At the same time, my Afghan prince knew he was losing me. We fought bitterly every single night. He began to abuse me. Was he trying to make me pregnant so that I'd have to stay? I was afraid to go to bed. His eldest sister, Soraya, offered to sleep with me in our bedroom—an act of courage and kindness that I have never forgotten. She must have known what was going on. (Where are you now, dear lady?)

Yes, my husband "loved" me, but I was, after all, a woman, which meant that his honor consisted of his ability to control me. Ali was also locked into a power struggle with his father and with his culture. I was the symbol of his freedom and independence, a reminder of his life lived apart. He did not want to lose such a valuable symbol. I did not think like this at the time, but in retrospect the following scenario seems plausible: If I became pregnant, I would have had to stay. His father would have been forced to stop making things so hard for us. We might even have been allowed to move into our own house. I would have stopped "complaining"; a baby would keep me busy—and Ali would win Round 1.

I devoted all my waking time to planning an escape. I gave up on the American embassy. I stopped confiding in Ali. I began to contact foreign wives, most of whom would not or could not help me. Please understand: I could meet people only through Ali or through a relative, and I was never allowed to talk privately to anyone. All the public teahouses were for men only. I could not just drift in and strike up a conversation with a man.

There was only one western-style restaurant in Kabul at that time. I would go there, stealthily, and wait for English- or French-speaking people to arrive. Few ever did. More often Ali would suddenly turn up to "collect" me. (Obviously I was being watched; everyone was.) In any event, there were very few tourists or foreigners in Kabul, and those who were there didn't just "hang out" in public places. American and European hippies, who would later descend in droves, had not yet discovered Afghanistan's golden poppy fields.

Could I leave the house and just walk right out of Afghanistan? How could I navigate the rugged, unknown terrain? Could I find someone who would guide me across the Hindu Kush into Pakistan, or who could take me the other way round and into Uzbekistan? Could I hitch a ride with a nomad caravan; would the coochies take me? I had no money to offer them. Even if they did not turn me in, what might they do to me? Obviously, these were questions that a romantic and naive American girl would never ask; my questions showed that I fully understood where I was and what could happen to me.

Finally, finally! I found a foreign wife who was willing to help me. She was the German-born wife of the ex-mayor of Kabul. She agreed to obtain a false passport for me. I had secretly written to my parents and had called them. They had agreed to send me a money order in care of this woman. Now I only had to choose a flight, book a seat, and locate a passport I could use.

And then I fainted. Ali later said that I "went into a coma" for many hours. I do not really remember this. It seems that I and every other foreigner had come down with hepatitis that winter. Some Afghans seemed to enjoy the spectacle of westerners succumbing to such illnesses; they took it as proof of foreign "weakness" and Afghan invincibility. Afghans were long used to their native bugs; foreigners were not.

Also, illness in Kabul did not mean what it meant in New York. If a Jewish child came down with a slight fever or a cold—not to mention with a childhood illness such as measles, mumps, whooping cough, or chicken pox—she was rushed to the pediatrician or the doctor himself came rushing over. Windows were opened (or shut), medication was prescribed, one's mother mounted a vigil. Adults visited doctors and were tested on a regular basis; they also went to hospitals.

Wealthy Afghans were quick to avail themselves of the latest in European medicine—but they traveled to Europe for it; it did not exist in Kabul. For example, at that time, local hospitals did not even provide food; the family had to deliver food to the patients. There were no hospitals in the countryside. Thus, for most people, if you got sick, you accepted your fate and suffered, and then either you lived or died. It was Allah's will.

I turned yellow and became very nauseous. I threw up a lot. I was exhausted and literally could not move. After many days had passed and after much pleading, an Afghan doctor was called. He came, first had his tea, looked at me, and said: "She has what the others have." He prescribed nothing. I was, quite simply, left to my fate.

Ali continued going into town with his brothers and father. Rabiah (that saint!) would sit by my bedside and wring her hands. Beebee Jan would come in to gloat, but also to pray. With what strength I had left, I would beg for a potato or for some ghee-free rice. Once I crept downstairs on all fours (I could not walk), looking for chocolate pudding, whipped potatoes, pumpkin pie, licorice. I must have been delirious.

Nothing unique happened to me. I do not mean to complain, only to describe what the reality was. Historically, most westerners who have traveled to the east ended up with dysentery (I already had what was known as the Kabul trots), malaria, parasites, and a host of other, often lifelong diseases. It's the price one pays for the adventure.

I was lucky. I lived—and so I kept demanding to see a real American doctor. I was finally taken to the new Tom Dooley Hospital, accompanied by at least ten family members. The English-speaking doctor whispered: "Honey, you are very sick and you have to get out of here. Will they let you go? If you are strong enough to sit up and walk a bit, get on a plane, go home."

He gave me a pair of dark glasses to hide my jaundiced eyes for the plane ride. And he prescribed intravenous infusions of vitamins and nutrients. He sent a nurse to the house.

And then Beebee Jan tried to pull out the IV, and all hell broke loose. I called Agha Jan and begged him to come over.

Agha Jan was in his sixties and stood six feet tall. His black hair was thick and only flecked with gray at the temples. He had a broad, frank mustache and velvet black eyes that matched his black Italian handmade shoes. He was a devout Muslim. He did not drink alcohol, nor did he smoke. He did not permit his sons to do so in his presence. Agha Jan's grown and married children—men as well as women—all executed a cringing half-bow whenever they greeted him, as they simultaneously kissed his hand. I found this extremely disturbing and never did so.

He employed his oldest sons, who were all in their thirties, in his various businesses. He also treated them like servants. He demeaned them, laughed at them, gave them token salaries, treated them as "boys." One son, Hussein, who had been educated in England, was actually Agha Jan's chauffeur, tea-pourer, and messenger. Still, Agha Jan's sons lived in his reflected glory and were known as "important" men compared to other Afghans. His sons feared, resented, and loved him. They talked about him incessantly and competed with each other for his favors. They flushed with pleasure (or displeasure) when Agha Jan openly favored or complimented any one of them. They were jealous of him, like wives.

Here is where I learned something important about Muslim male psychology. It was clear that once a man achieves a "top-dog" position, he will hold onto it until he dies. Agha Jan was not grooming any of his sons to take his place. On the contrary. He measured his own power in terms of how completely he was able to dominate and humiliate his own sons—as well as other men. He told me several times that his sons were not "really" men. "I am still taller than any of my sons." He actually was, physically, taller than his sons. But that is not what he meant.

Women were so unimportant in terms of power that I never once saw him spend any energy trying to dominate or humiliate a woman. They were already as low as they could get. But I did see him perform various acts of kindness toward women, myself included.

Agha Jan lived like a European. Although he wore the jauntiest and most expensive of Afghan-style karakul hats, he also wore expensive, European-made suits and coats. But, the children from his second and third marriages seemed to live in another century. Their clothing was ill-fitting, mismatched, perhaps used, or shared. Agha Jan's second wife lived in a very small and simple house; her furniture was not expensive or European, nor was her bathroom.

Agha Jan's current home, with his third wife, Sultana, had one great European-style room in which he received visitors and dined. He usually ate alone, in a sitting room hushed by thick maroon carpets and thick, European-style velvet drapes. Rozia, his and Sultana's fourteen-year-old daughter, served him each dish, bowing in and out of the room, like a servant.

However, his eight children from this marriage slept in two cramped bedrooms, and the mattresses smelled of urine. The electricity was minimal. When four of these sons were twelve, thirteen, fourteen, and sixteen, he had them all circumcised at home on the same day, under fairly traumatic conditions. Ali's brothers laughed when they told me about this; it was proof that Agha Jan valued these sons less.

Here in Afghanistan I had encountered a more primitive paternal archetype, an Islamic one, in which a father is meant to literally lord it over his children with both cruelty and pleasure. He was the master of the universe as far as his family was concerned.

And now I had summoned the king, so to speak. He came. First he prayed "for my recovery." Then he asked everyone else to leave, after which he spoon-fed me milk custard. He was very tender toward me; only afterward did I come to understand that he could afford to be; my illness and probable departure meant that he had won the battle with Ali. Perhaps he did not want a dead American daughter-in-law on his hands, either. And he'd be glad to see me gone. I only spelled trouble for his family—any foreign wife would, especially one who had tried to escape so many times.

"I know about your little plan with the German woman," he said quietly. "I think it will be best if you leave with our approval on an Afghan passport which I have obtained for you. You have been granted a six-month visa for "'reasons of health.'"

And he gave it to me on the spot: #17384. (I have it still.) The Kingdom of Afghanistan passport has retained its bright orange color, just as the *nargileh* (or hubble-bubble) that I brought out with me has retained its brilliant turquoise glaze.

He also handed me a plane ticket. "We will see you off. It is better this way."

Ali raged and swore—and begged me to stay—but I remained adamant.

Thirty relatives dutifully came to see me off. Kabul was hidden in snow. I was booked on an Aeroflut that had originated in Cairo and was now on its way back to Moscow. We would stop in Tashkent first.

The minute that plane took off, a fierce joy seized me and would not let go.

I had experienced gender apartheid at its most extreme—long before the rise of the Taliban. I now understood that once an American woman marries a Muslim and lives in a Muslim country, she is a citizen of *no* country. Never again would I romanticize foreign places, people in the Third World, or marriage.

I was jaundiced and pregnant. Had Ali discovered this while I was still in Afghanistan, I would never have been allowed to leave. My medical condition would have been my death sentence.

I had an abortion. This allowed me to return to college and to complete both college and graduate school before the decade was out.

A woman dares not forget such lessons—not if she manages to survive.

※ ※ ※

Did Ali really think that I would be able to adjust to a medieval, Islamic way of life? Or that his family would ever have accepted a Jewish American love bride?

There are only two answers possible. Either he was not thinking with his brain, or he viewed me as a woman, which meant that I did not exist in my own right, that I was destined to please and obey him, and that nothing else was really important. He certainly helped shape the feminist that I was to become.

When I left Afghanistan in 1961, Ali was about to become a government minister. For the next three years he refused to agree to a divorce and in fact came to America to fight the annulment. Only now, consulting my papers, do I understand why: I did not know this, but my parents had sought the annulment on the basis of his "fraudulent" promise to convert to Judaism. Had this become public, Ali would have been ruined, or worse.

In 1979, after the Russian invasion, Ali himself escaped by crossing the Khyber Pass into Pakistan, disguised as a nomad. Since 1980, he and his wife, Jamila, and their two children, Iskandar and Leyla, have been living near me in America. Oddly, but happily, we relate as members of an extended family.

When I first met Ali, he had lustrous black hair, dark, melting eyes, long, feminine lashes—he could easily have passed for an illustration in my much-thumbed copy of Scheherazade's *Arabian Nights*. Ali's hair is white now and his health is impaired.

Every time Afghanistan is in the news, I reach for the phone and call Ali. I go to his home for a long evening of delicious Afghan food. Ali's wife is warm and charming. She once tooled around Kabul in her own sports car. When they were younger, Iskandar and Leyla used to ask me: "Phyllisjan, why did you come to Afghanistan? What were you looking for?"

More than forty-six years have passed since I first met their father, and I still don't have one right answer. I would sometimes say that I'd been in search of the lost tribes of Israel who, according to some biblical and anthropological scholars, had last been sighted there. Or I would say that I'd been in search of a tribe of Amazon warrior women who had also last been seen in the surrounding areas.

But perhaps the most important reason I went to Afghanistan was so that, post-9/11, I might be able to tell other westerners something important about what it's like for a woman and an infidel to live under Islam. In the west, my

Muslim husband was a westerner. In the east, he really was not. Ali and others like him truly have multiple cultural personalities.

Today some westerners have reluctantly begun to understand that such transculturality may have important ramifications. For example, the ruling Saudis, Egyptians, Syrians, Sudanese, and Palestinians will say one thing in English and quite another thing in Arabic. Islamists will demand religious freedom for Muslims in the west but deny it to non-Muslims in the east. Islamists will insist on veiling their women in the west but will also demand that western women dress in Muslim-appropriate fashion in the east. Muslims have flooded the west as separatist immigrants but have also systematically persecuted and exiled non-Muslims from Muslim lands. Other than the tiny state of Israel, the Middle East is now almost entirely "judenrein," free of Jews; and Christians, Hindus, animists, and Ba'hais are systematically and savagely persecuted.

Islamists are not guilty of "lying" to or "deceiving" non-Muslims. Their concept of objective truth is tempered by a warrior mentality and by loyalty to religious imperialism. "What's mine is mine, what's yours is mine, too" is the jihadic warrior's mind-set. Islamists do not play "fair," nor do they follow Robert's Rules of Order. (Actually, no one does.) But Islamists are now in accelerated jihad mode and are exercising all their transcultural options.

It is crucial that we understand this.

As I look over the correspondence between Ali and myself from 1962–1965, I see that our tale was also a tragic love story. If Ali had stayed in America, we might have had a chance. Living in Afghanistan was impossible for me and, ultimately, for him, too. If Muslims want to live in a modern, democratic world, then all things are possible. If they want to import the seventh century into Europe or North America, then we are all in terrible trouble.

The Islamists who are beheading Jews and American civilians, stoning Muslim women to death, jailing Muslim dissidents, and bombing civilians on every continent are now moving among us both in the east and in the west. I fear that the "peace and love" crowd in the west refuses to understand how Islamism endangers our values and our lives, beginning with our commitment to women's rights and human rights. As I have said, some feminist leaders and groups have publicized the atrocities against women in the Islamic world, but they have not tied it to any feminist foreign policy. Women's studies programs should have been the first to sound the alarm. They did not.

In chapter five, I explore what western women's studies professors and feminist journalists and leaders have been saying about Muslim, Arab, and Middle Eastern women and about Islamic terrorism.

Five

The One-Sided Feminist Academy

The Islamic world I fled at the end of 1961 has, almost fifty years later, pursued me to my own shores. In my opinion, unless we fight against its ideas and practices, women everywhere may increasingly be forced to live under conditions of Islamic gender apartheid. How are leading feminists handling this civilizational and planetary crisis?

I think it's fair to say that today, most of America's left-dominated intelligentsia deny, support, or underestimate Islamism and the real meaning of Islamic jihad. The Islamization of the Middle East has already occurred. Twenty-two states in the region are Islamic regimes. Israel remains the only "dhimmi" (infidel) state in the area and the only western-style democracy that practices interfaith religious tolerance; Islamic countries ban and persecute infidel religious practices. Islamism has also battled to take over North Africa and parts of West Africa and Asia, including Iran, Pakistan, Afghanistan, Chechnya, and Indonesia.

The Islamization of Europe is also well underway. This tragic circumstance is complex and is due, in part, to long-standing diplomatic and financial arrangements between the European Union and the oil-rich Arab League; European intellectuals' guilt over colonialism and to their overidentification with Third World countries; Europe's both genuine and hypocritical religious and political compassion for Third World suffering; and its long-term history of tolerance, democracy, colonialism, racism, open immigration policies, and delegation of low-paid "dirty" work to immigrants.

However, while many Muslim immigrants have indeed become "Europeans," many more have absolutely refused or been unable to do so. Muslim immigrants, including those Algerians who fought for France, did not receive decent-enough employment, housing, and educational opportunities. Bitterness and desperation set in. However, instead of dealing with the cultural and demographic destruction of their culture, Europeans have, so far, chosen to appease their non-integrated and non-integratable Muslim immigrants by stigmatizing and scapegoating Israel for daring to exist and defend itself. Many Europeans have failed to see that, to the Islamist terrorists, "Israel" is merely a code word for Europe and America.

The academic postcolonial literature is infected, as with a virus, by an across-the-board view of Palestinians as the symbol of all things noble and the Jews and Israelis as symbols of evil.

For example, Dibyesh Anand, a Tibetan doctoral candidate at the University of Bristol, England, contributed to Geeta Chowdry and Sheila Nair's anthology *Power, Postcolonialism, and International Relations: Reading race, gender, and class.* Anand's piece, titled "A Story to be Told: IR, postcolonialism, and discourse of Tibetan (trans)national identity," concerns Tibet. Nevertheless, he manages to gratuitously insult and misunderstand both the Jewish diaspora and the Dalai Lama in one, politically correct paragraph. Anand is trying to understand why the occupation of Tibet by China has drawn so little support from Third World countries. He writes:

> Here one may point to one of the paradoxes of the Tibetan situation vis-à-vis the Palestinians. While the support for Palestinians comes overwhelmingly from Third World countries, a similar support is conspicuous by its absence when it comes to the Tibetans. In fact, one often comes across references to Jewish organizations offering to support the Dalai Lama and the latter in turn expressing his desire to learn from the Jewish experience of diaspora. But we do not hear of serious efforts on the part of the Tibetan government-in-exile to form linkages with the diasporic communities like the Palestinians, who also experienced forced occupation in the recent past.

Where can one begin? Does Anand really believe that the Jewish response to thousands of years of persecution and exile (which consisted of self-supporting, nonviolent communities that developed ethical, religious, and legal bodies of knowledge) is something that the Dalai Lama should not be interested in? But that the Palestinian response to fifty-five years of exile (which mainly consists of multigenerational economic dependency, suicide killers, and fundamentalist religiosity), somehow provides a depth of knowledge worthy of the Dalai Lama?

Is Anand really suggesting that Tibetans violently reclaim their homeland? And, does he think that the Palestinians, like the Tibetans, comprise a discrete ethnic entity (they do not) or that they once had a "homeland" equivalent to that of Tibet—and not a homeland equivalent to the land now primarily occupied by Jordan, secondarily by Egypt, and to a much lesser extent, by Jewish Israel?[1]

The Palestinianization of European and North American campuses is well underway, as well. American intellectuals increasingly identify with Europeans, and they take on the role of consistently criticizing American power as the most dangerous form of colonialism. Many American intellectuals, including academic feminists, are actively propagandizing students against America and against Israel—which means that in reality they are choosing tyranny and gender apartheid over democracy and human rights for women.

This is quite dangerous. In the rush to be multiculturally correct, western feminists have betrayed their own founding principles. Many feminists who have tenure and leadership positions in women's studies programs either tend to be culturalists who are uninterested in foreign policy or they are leftists. As such, they have adopted a pro-PLO and pro-terrorist line of thinking without realizing that such positions have little to do with feminist agency.

For example: According to Professor Emeritus Leila Beckwith, the University of California at Santa Cruz has had a "steady stream of anti-Israel speakers . . . funded by the university" and sponsored by at least "ten different university departments." In February 2004, when given a first-time opportunity to "redress their bias" and sponsor author Dennis Prager, a pro-Israel speaker, "all but one [of the ten departments] refused. Subsequently, two of the ten departments "sponsored a virulently anti-Israel event, organized by the Muslim Students Association, to occur at the same time as the Prager lecture."

Prager of course questioned how academics who are committed to diversity, freedom of religion, gay rights, and women's rights could so blindly support the Palestinian Authority, which opposes all this.

According to Professor Ilan Benjamin and Hebrew language lecturer Tammi Rossman-Benjamin, both of UCSC, in April 2004, when Professor Khaleel Mohammed, a moderate Muslim, came to speak, "of the ten university departments asked to co-sponsor his talk, not one agreed to do so." Additionally, "fliers announcing his talk were systematically torn down or obscured by fliers of a Muslim student group denouncing Mohammed and disputing the legitimacy of his scholarship."

Women's studies at UCSC did not rise above the partisan politicking. On October 21, 2004, they sponsored a talk by Hedy Epstein, who compared Israel to a Nazi state and excused suicide bombings. Epstein's "credentials" include her membership in the International Solidarity Movement, which is linked to terrorist organizations such as Hamas and Islamic Jihad. According to Dr. Beckwith, Epstein did not address any women-specific issues.

However, the women's studies department refused to sponsor a talk about the same topic to be given by Nonie Darwish, a journalist and Arabic translator who spent the first thirty years of her life in Egypt and in Egypt-occupied Gaza. Darwish was sponsored by Scholars for Peace in the Middle East (I am a board member), the Santa Cruz Middle East Information Coalition, and Santa Cruz Hillel Foundation. When Darwish spoke, she did not demonize Israel. She viewed the Arab world's demonization of Israel to be a way of "turning the world's attention away from the heinous human rights violations taking place within the Arab world itself." More important, Darwish spent a "significant amount of time addressing the oppression of Muslim women and calling for reforms which would raise their status."

The clearly pro-Palestinian decisions made at UCSC are part of a systematic pattern in women's studies departments elsewhere. To further illustrate how this bias operates at UCSC, here's another example: In May 2000, women's studies at UCSC sponsored a week of events "in solidarity with the Palestinian struggle for justice." In May 2001, women's studies sponsored a video about two Palestinian women political prisoners who were "detained, tortured, mentally and physically and sexually terrorized by the Israeli occupier for their unquestioned beliefs in the moral . . . right to resist the Israeli occupier/colonizer." In March 2003, women's studies again sponsored an Israeli left peace activist who founded an organization against the "occupation of Palestine" by Israel.

According to Beckwith, in all this time, the women's studies department did not sponsor a single talk that condemned Arab violence against Israeli civilians or that addressed the grave human rights abuses in the Arab world, including the pandemic abuse of women. This kind of one-sidedness on the issue of Israel and Palestine has polluted campuses from coast to coast.

According to Beckwith, more than half of the eleven professors in women's studies at UCSC have "publicly expressed anti-Israel bias." Four, including Angela Davis, the current chair (yes, *the* Angela Davis for whom I marched outside the Women's House of Detention when she had been arrested and confined there in the early 1970s), signed a petition calling on the American government to cut off military aid to Israel and demanded that the University of California divest from Israeli companies. Professors Bettina Aptheker (the former chair of women's studies), and Helen Moglen both signed open letters calling for the withdrawal of all aid to Israel.

I have previously written about a left-wing women's studies conference that took place at the University of New Paltz in New York State in 2002. It was billed as a conference about war and peace. In fact, it focused mainly on Israel and Palestine and adopted a pro-PLO position only. Their keynote speaker was a Jewish Israeli psychiatrist named Ruchama Marton. She likened the Israelis to "batterers" in a marriage. To her, the Palestinians are the "battered wives."

She did not address the Palestinian terrorist attacks against Israeli civilians, nor did she address the Palestinian leadership's impoverishment and brainwashing of the Palestinian people. Instead, she suggested that the way to understand the complexities of the Middle East is through the prism of "marriage." In my opinion, she was both misapplying hard-won feminist knowledge about battering and rendering the specifics of Palestinian and Israeli suffering quite invisible. The inflammatory and vulgar misuse of ideas is not worthy of a supposedly independent-minded feminist.

The reality is this: Most feminist magazines, newspapers, and spokeswomen have continually, routinely, and loudly condemned Israel as a colonial, apartheid, and misogynist state and have taken the left-Stalinist position in favor of the PLO. For the last five years, many feminist and lesbian-feminist demonstrators (in anti-globalization and anti-war marches) have waved the Palestinian flag and worn Arab headdress. In the Arab world, they would not have that right, because they are wearing Arab *male* kaffiyehs. Were they marching anywhere in the Islamic world, they'd be wearing chadaris, burqas, head scarves, and veils. And if they weren't, they would be beaten, jailed, raped, possibly flogged, perhaps even stoned to death. A willful blindness to the reality of the Islamic world seems to go hand-in-hand with support for Palestine.

Although most feminists are very concerned with women's right to have an abortion, some feminists no longer seem as concerned with the "occupation" of women's non-reproductive bodies worldwide as they are with the Zionist occupation of Palestinian lands. Does the demonization of Israel help women around the world? Is the new women's studies agenda focused on helping *only* Palestinian women or *only* Islamic terrorists?

For the record, let me note that Israel is not an apartheid state. Unlike all the surrounding Muslim countries in the Middle East, Israel is the only nation that honors religious freedom and religious pluralism (at least for men), holds free and open elections, and allows minority-group members to become citizens, judges, and parliament members. While Israel is no feminist paradise, it stands head and shoulders above all the Muslim countries that surround it in terms of women's status.

In 1980, I attended the United Nations Conference for Women in Copenhagen. I was present for an important and possibly the only nongovernmental organization panel on women refugees. A North European woman was the moderator. A woman "boat person" from Vietnam spoke, as did women from Pakistan, Afghanistan, and the West Bank. Each woman was dignified, careful, and heartbreaking. The moment they finished their presentations, Soviet-trained and Arab League–backed female hooligans took over the floor.

The plight of female refugees all over the world did not interest them at all. One after the other, they delivered belligerent anti-Israel and anti-American speeches—but only on behalf of Palestinian women refugees. The pro-PLO moderator refused to call on anyone in the audience who was not on her pre-arranged list. I finally managed to persuade her to call on an Iraqi Jewish refugee, Simha Choresh, whose husband had been tortured and executed and who had herself fled for her life. The hooligans soon silenced her—but they really went crazy when an Afghan woman began to blame the Soviets for having invaded Afghanistan, which, she said, had caused unending misery for Afghan women refugees.

This took place long ago. I did not expect to see its equivalent so many years later—and in feminist academic and activist circles. Why are American and European feminists behaving as if they are Soviet-backed and Arab League–trained hooligans?

Over the last few years, researcher-activists have unearthed overwhelming, certainly credible documentation about the extent to which Arab, Muslim, and Islamist funding has supported and therefore shaped the views of the Middle East that are being taught at American universities. Anti-Zionist and pro-Palestinian conferences, courses, and professors have helped obscure the facts about human slavery and religious and gender apartheid in the Arab and Muslim world and have also minimized the real problems that Arabs and Muslims face, problems that include tyranny, illiteracy, and poverty.

For example, the Saudis have funded chairs, programs, conferences, and faculty at Columbia University, Harvard University, the University of Michigan, UCLA, and the University of California at Berkeley. Sheik Zayed bin Sultan al-Nahyan and King Fahd funded programs at the Harvard Divinity School and the University of Arkansas Middle East Studies Center. Harvard Divinity gave the funding back. Other Muslims and Arabs have funded Mideast study programs at UC Berkeley, Stanford, Georgetown, Cornell, Texas A&M, MIT, Princeton, and Rutgers. The funds have ensured that faculty and speakers are anti-American, anti-Zionist, and pro-PLO. For example, Rashid Khalidi, who accepted the Edward Said chair at Columbia University, has consistently promoted anti-American and anti-Israel ideas. Khalidi is himself a former PLO press officer and has praised terrorists such as Black September founder Abu Iyad.[2]

To the best of my knowledge, women's studies has not been directly funded by the Islamic world. Therefore, feminists should resist co-sponsoring pro-PLO hate-fests and should sponsor programs about the status of women under Islam. As we have just seen, they are not doing so.

It is my impression that, in the last decade, many feminists either consciously or unconsciously muted their critique of Arab and Muslim misogyny—as if they were, once more, fighting the Algerian war and determined not to mention Algerian fundamentalism until the French colonizers were good and gone. And every feminist knows that the women of Algeria did not get their freedom once the French were out; on the contrary, their situation afterward became perilous and terrible.

Please understand: I am not in favor of colonialism; I am in favor of feminists learning from history when it comes to women's freedom. Whether we like it or not, some of the consequences of capitalism, Christianity, and colonialism were very positive for Third World women, just as some consequences were very negative.

Some say that criticism of Israel is not anti-Semitic. In my opinion—and I have staked my reputation on this—the new anti-Semitism *is* in part, anti-Zionism. I said so in 2002 and published this view in my last book, *The New Anti-Semitism,* in July 2003. My editor repeatedly and worriedly challenged me about this; I lost countless political friendships for saying this. Zionism is not racism; however, as Judea Pearl, Daniel Pearl's father, has recently written, *anti-*Zionism is racism.

The European Union has finally recognized that not all criticism of Israel is legitimate. Our own State Department, in its first report on global anti-Semitism, has also said that it is currently important to distinguish between "legitimate criticism of Israel" and "commentary that assumes an anti-Semitic character. The demonization of Israel, or vilification of Israeli leaders, sometimes through comparisons with Nazi leaders, and through the use of Nazi symbols to caricature them, indicates an anti-Semitic bias rather than a valid criticism of policy concerning a controversial issue." Despite this, I doubt that today most feminists would agree with anything that our State Department might have to say.

As a feminist, I have also chosen to speak out for America, for its vision and practice of democracy, religious tolerance, women's rights, human rights, gay rights. The way I see it, a serious feminist cannot oppose democracy in the name of feminist utopianism. (If America and Israel are not super-perfect, then there is no difference between them and Saudi Arabia and Afghanistan.)

The left has been able to hijack women's studies due to the vacuum in foreign policy created by "cultural" feminists who now focus mainly on issues of personal and sexual lifestyle. This is no crime—but ultimately it amounts to a more minor, less altruistic vision. Anti-feminists have dubbed this "me-too feminism" and while I hate to agree, there's something to their criticism.

For example, as I have noted, women's studies courses tend to focus on the importance of sexual pleasure and the primacy of sexual identity rather than on other "primary" identities; the right to be a sex worker rather than the right not to be; freedom *from* rather than freedom *of* religion; abortion and adoption rather than biological motherhood; motherhood outside of marriage rather than motherhood within marriage; the work of women of color and of Third World women as opposed to the work of white, western women; and so on. I understand that the field of women's studies has been trying to balance women's traditional choices and to expand the dead white male canon. Nevertheless, it is now time for women's studies to include and welcome western traditional, religious, and conservative women as part of their vision.

It is also time for women's studies to rethink or at least diversify their predominantly left, multicultural, and anti-western points of view. In fact, it is essential that they do so.

In their politically correct concern about racism (a concern I certainly share), many feminist academics and leaders have hesitated to criticize misogyny abroad—lest it be seen as "racist." In the 1970s, feminists did so without guilt. By the 1990s, the feminist academy either no longer taught such work, or attacked it.

For example, Bengali feminist and postcolonial academic Gayatri Chakravorty Spivak teaches at Columbia University. Spivak has attacked the western feminist critique of non-western cultures as yet another kind of imperial humanitarianism. She has been widely quoted as viewing western feminists as no different than white men who are saving brown women from brown men, and views doing so as a racist and colonial enterprise.

Perhaps Spivak might view British attempts to end the practice of suttee (Hindu wives being forced to throw themselves on their dead husbands' funeral pyres) as similarly racist. In an interview with the editors of *The Spivak Reader,* she says that "some of the women on the pyres did actually utter . . . but even when one uttered, one was constructed by a certain kind of psychobiography, so that the utterance itself—this is another side of the argument—would have to be interpreted in the way in which we historically interpret anything." Spivak has very important points to make, but she does not make herself easy to understand.[3]

However, Spivak is correct when she argues that the "subaltern" (the oppressed, brown woman) is able to speak but that no one listens to her. She further explains: "So, 'the subaltern cannot speak,' means that even when the subaltern makes an effort to the death to speak, she is not able to be heard, and speaking and hearing complete the speech act. That's what it had meant, and anguish marked the spot."

However, many people *are* listening to Spivak, despite her hard-to-access prose. It is aggressively obscure and theoretical—and oh-so-very western. Here is just one example of what Spivak, speaking in an interview, sounds like: "It's not something like 'going in search of the primitive.' I don't know that it is an 'ever-receding horizon.' It is just a space of difference, if you like. And as for the increase in varieties of subalternity, I would say that that probably is accounted for in more orthodox theories of the feudalization of the periphery—the flip-side of capitalist development. When one begins to look at the way in which woman's position is manipulated, even within that space, there is nothing mysterious about it, as there would be about an ever-receding horizon which is always beyond our reach, and so on."[4]

Palestinian American academic Suha Sabbagh, who tends to agree with Spivak, writes in a more straightforward manner. Sabbagh also objects to the western feminist obsession with Islam's crimes against women. According to Sabbagh, such a focus depicts women as mere victims: "Whereas in past stereotypes Arab women lived only for sensual pleasure and were condemned for their wantonness, Arab women . . . are depicted as existing on the margins of society, victimized to such an extent that it defies credibility that such individuals could continue to wage the heroic daily battle that many Arab women in real life undertake to survive."

According to Sabbagh, Muslim women may voluntarily wear the hijab (head and hair covering) as a "symbol of defiance against Western policies in the region." To analyze the hijab "only as a sign of conformity to Islamic principles, and therefore a form of oppression of women, is to miss the point." Sabbagh suggests that Muslim women are rejecting western feminism because "it calls for a form of cultural conversion at a time when the West is seen by them to be a dominating force."

Like Spivak, Sabbagh views the western feminist intellectual and rhetorical penetration of women under Islam as exerting a "greater degree of domination than that actually exercised by men over women within Muslim culture." She considers such western feminist work as "clearly about establishing Western domination and not about liberating Muslim women."

I respectfully disagree with this view, although I understand why she holds it. As an Arab Muslim female intellectual, Sabbagh finds herself in a bind. If she criticizes Arab misogyny, she fears that her work will be used by the "Arab-bashing camp" against Arabs. If she minimizes Arab female suffering, she will be seen as too "complacent." She writes: "Cultural biases toward Arab women have forced Arab-American women like myself, who hold feminist views, into a defensive position. . . . And, as most Arab-Americans know, the negative images of Arabs have some serious repercussions: they condone aggressive behavior toward Arabs both in this country and in the Arab world."

The fact that Sabbagh is an academic in no way exempts her from the heightened vigilance that is visited upon all Arabs and Muslims. And her perceived and internalized sense of responsibility to the Arab or Muslim collectivity is no less than that of any other Muslim or Palestinian woman's.

What the academic Suha Sabbagh is telling us is that her ideas will be as closely scrutinized as women's hair and hair coverings are under Islam today.

Sabbagh also wants western feminists to understand that Muslim women are not merely victims, they are also political actors who address "larger" (than feminist) political issues. They are "strong" and capable of "resistance." Thus, Sabbagh objects to Palestinian leader Hanan Ashrawi's once having being "heckled" by western feminists because Ashrawi did not focus on women's oppression. Ashrawi offended because she focused exclusively on Palestinian liberation.

Fair enough. Women are also political actors; even feminists must address "larger" political realities. It is always wiser that we do so consciously.

Thus, I *do* view the Sabbagh anthology as a highly politicized—or shall I say "Palestinianized"—work. For example, although there are twenty-six Arab and

Muslim Middle Eastern, central Asian, and North African countries (if you include Iran, Pakistan, and Afghanistan), the Sabbagh anthology articles that focus on specific countries focus on only ten countries: Syria, Jordan, Yemen, Saudi Arabia, Lebanon, Egypt, Tunisia, Algeria, Kuwait—and Palestine, a country that did not exist at the time of publication in 1996.[5]

Sabbagh's anthology is made-to-order for politically correct women's studies classes. There are no fewer than six articles (including an appendix) specifically about Palestine. Thus, its focus on Palestine is six times as great as its focus on the nine other Arab countries. Consequently, there are forty-one indexed references to Palestine, compared with eighteen indexed references to Egypt, twelve indexed references to Algeria, nine indexed references to Jordan, five to Tunisia, and so on.

Why is this important? Because when feminists are "Palestinianized," they tend to unwittingly collaborate with the Arab League decision not to address the abysmal status and needs of women (and men) in every other Arab and Muslim country.

Also, amazingly, the three articles devoted to Lebanon do not mention that it was occupied by Syria and Iran, nor do they focus on the Muslim persecution of Lebanese Christians or on their consequent flight. There is one indexed reference to Israel in the Sabbagh volume. It is in an interview with Palestinian leader Hanan Ashrawi, who mentions Israel once, briefly, and negatively.

And there are no indexed references to Christianity.

One conclusion: It is not only western feminists who have "larger" political agendas.

However, Sabbagh's volume is not unique. For example, in 1991, Bouthaina Shaaban published *Both Right- and Left-Handed: Arab Women Talk About Their Lives*. The book covers Syria, Lebanon, Algeria—and Palestine. Nevertheless, the Sabbagh anthology is typical of the politically correct feminist viewpoint and the associated political biases.[6]

In the 1970s, anthologies about Arab and Muslim women included many more countries and did not overly focus on the women of Palestine; some 1990s anthologies were also more even-handed. Here I am thinking of Elizabeth Warnock Fernea and Basima Quattan Bezirgan's *Middle Eastern Muslim Women Speak* (1977); Lois Beck and Nikki R. Keddie's *Women in the Muslim World* (1978); and Nikki R. Keddie and Beth Baron's excellent anthology *Women in Middle Eastern History: Shifting Boundaries in Sex and Gender* (1991).[7]

These earlier works were not Palestinianized feminist works and, for that reason, were more inclusive. For example, in 1978, in a work that runs to almost 700 pages, Beck and Keddie have only *four* references in the index to Palestine. (The Sabbagh work is only 267 pages long and, as mentioned above, has forty-one references to Palestine.) Margot Badran and Miriam Cooke's excellent *Opening the Gates. A Century of Arab Feminist Writing* (1990) runs to 412 pages but contains only *eight* references to Palestine.[8]

Still, Sabbagh's anthology does credibly support the possibility of doing feminist work within an Islamic religious framework. Many Muslim feminists believe that the Qu'ran can potentially empower women over and against misogynist tribal customs. Such religious Muslim feminists believe that an unevolved Islam is precisely what stands in the way of Muslim women's rights and freedom. They find pro-woman sources in the Qu'ran. The work of Drs. Leila Ahmed, Fatima Mernissi, Yvonne Yazbeck Haddad, Jane I. Smith, Mervat Hatem, and Nesta Ramazani are therefore included or noted in Sabbagh's anthology.

In my view, this is an important approach. I also agree with Sabbagh on one other thing, namely that despite enormous deprivation and heartbreak, Arab and Muslim women are not merely victims. Like women everywhere, they are "players," which means they are sometimes compassionate and sometimes cruel, sometimes heroic and sometimes cowardly and reactionary.

Thus, even more important than its pro-Palestine bias, the Sabbagh anthology fails to deal with the painful psychological and economic consequences of polygamy, son preference, female phobia, gender segregation, female genital mutilation, and Arab honor killings; nor does Sabbagh explore the collaborative role that women play in such honor killings.

As we shall see, Arab and Muslim women's relationships to each other is culturally and psychologically jinxed in some rather unique ways. And Arab and Muslim women are as aggressive *toward women* as women are everywhere else; perhaps even more so.

I will deal with this more fully in the next chapter.

❋ ❋ ❋

My experience with feminist views of the Muslim world and of Israel and America is not only academic, gleaned by reading books, but is also very personal, gleaned from having led an intensely feminist political life in both the Judeo-Christian and Islamic worlds.

In the 1970s, I was friendly with Reza Baraheni, an Iranian intellectual who said he had been tortured under the Shah and who, when I met him, was the head of CAIFI—the student association against the Shah. He rushed home to Iran after Khomeini took over. He thought it was his revolution. He invited my dear friend Kate Millett to speak on International Women's Day in 1980. Iranian women wanted to march against the imposition of the veil. Kate gamely went and took her companion, the photographer Sophie Kier, along; Khomeini's thugs arrested them both. I made many phone calls on her behalf; we all did.

Thankfully, Khomeini's mullahs let Kate and Sophie go. Unbelievably, immediately thereafter, Reza started begging me to come to speak the following year. "Phyllis, you understand Islam and Muslims, you have a greater sympathy for it." I told him that I'd only come as part of an American Marine force.

Many years later, I became friendly with Rhonda al-Fatal, the wife of Dia al-Fatal, the Syrian ambassador to the United Nations. They lived in Richard Nixon's old Upper East Side townhouse, and I had a lovely dinner there. In the early 1920s, Rhonda's mother was the first woman to have unveiled herself in Lebanon. Afterward, she was placed under house arrest for a year for her own safety.

I was inspired by her mother's bravery and determination. (She had studied outside of Lebanon for years and with foreign teachers in Lebanon.) Dia's mother was Afghan-born, and he was interested in meeting the "feminist" who had lived among his mother's people.

Rhonda was a severely elegant and beautiful woman: fashionable, thin, impossibly glamorous. When she invited me to deliver a series of feminist lectures in Syria, I immediately declined. When she pressed me, I told her the truth—that I was a Jew and a passionate Zionist and was afraid of what could happen to me "by accident" in Syria; visions of trapdoors and jail cells came to mind.

She was understandably shocked and insulted. "But you would be our guest, we would be your protectors, you would stay with us in Damascus. No one would dare harm a hair on your head."

"Ah, dear lady," I said, "I am sure you're right. Consider the failing mine alone. Once I traveled with my true love to Afghanistan. He did not, would not, could not, protect me from what happened. With all due respect, and begging a thousand pardons, I would not yet risk a trip to Damascus."

In 1979, I worked for the United Nations for nearly a year. The fact that I was a white American woman, a Jew, a feminist, *and* a Zionist made my tenure there an exceedingly vulnerable one. At the time, no woman had yet been able to expose the routine sexual harassment and abuse of female employees at the UN. Indeed, at one international UN conference that I convened in Oslo, a group of feminists from Africa, Europe, North America, and South America were finally ready to challenge the director of a large UN agency for sexually harassing and abusing a number of women.

The confrontation did not take place. One North American feminist leader, Robin Morgan, appealed to everyone's hopelessly politically correct views about racism. ("How would it look for white western feminists, even if black African feminists joined them, to confront a black African man?") This is only one example among thousands in which politically correct concerns about race and ethnicity consistently trumped concerns about gender, even among feminist leaders.[9]

Morgan had been a child actress. Her theatrical skills stood her in good stead in her career as a feminist activist. I have seen Morgan cry on cue many times and feign joy in public toward someone she has vowed to destroy. She had been a leftist. She once supported Weather Underground fugitive Jane Alpert but later broke with her when it was no longer glamorous or convenient to have such a former contact. (Jane writes about this in her own autobiography).[10]

Today *Ms. Magazine,* Morgan's anthology *Sisterhood Is Global,* and its various companion institutes and action arms, including its relationship with Elly Smeal of the Feminist Majority (which now publishes *Ms. Magazine*) exemplify "the" feminist position vis-à-vis the Third World, the Middle East, and Islam. As I've noted, the position began as an essentialist one. All women were "sisters" who faced a common enemy: men or patriarchy. All women were "sisterly," and no one collaborated with patriarchy. All sisters were moral and peace-loving. Carol Gilligan's work was increasingly used to bolster this argument.

But as Third Worldism and multiculturalism gained more and more influence, especially among foundations and philanthropists, feminist essentialism adapted. It had to. Thus, while women were still all sisters, some sisters were more equal than others. Thus, brown-skinned, formerly colonized women became more equal than white-skinned, Caucasian-featured Euro-American women.

Of course, this did not happen in reality, but it did happen symbolically, rhetorically. For example, it was my impression that by the mid-1980s, many feminist-influenced mainstream foundations and feminist-owned foundations simultaneously decided to increasingly fund women of color, multicultural, and anti-racist grassroots projects; lesbians of color were favored for a while. (Of course, the foundations were mainly owned and run by white people.) There is nothing wrong with funding feminists of color or grassroots projects abroad; it is entirely commendable. However, what was being funded was the "appearance" of anti-racist political correctness. These foundations did not fund American shelters for battered women, initiatives for child support, or anti-pornography legislation with the same excitement or commitment. Equally problematic was the philanthropic failure to fund diverse and individualistic feminist thinkers and activists of any color. This meant that foundations were not funding pluralist visions for the future.

In addition, another way that white-skinned feminists could properly atone for their culture's racism was to savage Israel and America. Even as feminists tried to focus on the abysmal plight of women in the Third World, they simultaneously felt they had to "earn" the right to do so by condemning America.

Curiously enough, while feminists tend to espouse a pacifist position and oppose both violence and nationalism, they also tend to support "justified" anti-capitalist or anti-colonialist violence. Among many feminists not all nationalisms are equal. Feminists do not question the nationalism of former European colonial powers such as England, France, and Germany, nor do they challenge formerly colonized Islamic nation-states with horrifying human rights records—against women especially. Feminists *do* criticize and challenge American and Israeli nationalism. And they remain divided, contradictory, confused about the use of military power in Just Wars.

On the subject of terrorism: Many feminists have been seriously missing in action. Or they view America as the greatest terrorist power on earth. Such feminist views emanate from the academy, the media, and from international human rights groups.

For example, Amnesty International has issued many important and feminist-inspired reports on the status of women in Muslim and war-torn countries. I have read some of their work for this book. However, like so many other international and humanitarian agencies (the United Nations, Human Rights Watch, the International Red Cross, Physicians for Human Rights-Israel), Amnesty is also reflexively pro-Palestine and anti-Israel. Therefore, in their March 31, 2005, report, "Israel and the Occupied Territories: Conflict, Occupation and Patriarchy. Women Carry the Burden," they attribute the lion's share of Palestinian female suffering to the Israeli occupation.

Thus, according to their report, if Palestinian men beat or kill their wives and daughters—it's because Israel is occupying Palestinian lands, not because they are following their own Arab and Muslim codes of shame, honor, and misogyny. (Israel is not "occupying" Egypt, Saudi Arabia, or Pakistan, yet crimes against women there are epidemic.) If Palestinian men are unemployed—it's because Israel is refusing to employ them—not because the PLO, Hamas, Islamic Jihad, the al Aqsa Martyr's Brigade, and Hezbollah have all chosen to fund and launch countless terrorist attacks against Israeli civilians and, at the same time, with the possible exception of Hamas, have utterly refused to fund housing, hospitals, schools, a police force, and an economic infrastructure for the Palestinian people.

According to the Jerusalem Center for Public Affairs, the Amnesty Report focuses upon "isolated and tragic incidents that have occurred at checkpoints involving pregnant Palestinian women" but fails to contextualize the checkpoints as the temporary Israeli response to a siege of terror against its civilian population. The report also fails to mention or give any credence to the known history of how Palestinian terrorists hide both gunmen and weapons in ambulances and either dress as women or use women to smuggle explosives and other weapons into Israel.[11]

Although the word "Israel" is in the title of this report, there is no real focus on the status of or suffering of *Israeli*, Jewish, Christian, Muslim, or Palestinian women. The thirty-six page double-column, single-spaced report spends about one and a half pages (but only at the very end) listing the names of some Israeli female civilian victims of Palestinian terrorism. It does not mention Israeli women who have been wounded and disabled, often for life.

From a feminist point of view, the report fails to note that the long-lasting Islamic and jihadic hatred for both Jews and Israel has fearfully slowed the progress of Israeli feminism. If Israel is always under siege, then Israeli social, economic, religious, political, and psychological progress for women is bound to be compromised and endangered.

For years, *Ms. Magazine* and the Ms. Foundation were seen by the media as speaking for the mainstream feminist movement. The most visible leaders were and still are Gloria Steinem, Robin Morgan, Letty Cottin Pogrebin, and Marie Wilson. They are all committed feminists, authors, tireless campaign workers, and fundraisers. What, if anything, does *Ms. Magazine* or its leaders have to tell us about Islam, Palestine, Israel, anti-Semitism, and terrorism?

In the early 1970s, together with Aviva Cantor and Cheryl Moch, I tried to persuade other Jewish and non-Jewish feminists that anti-Semitism or Judeophobia was a form of racism. I suggested holding ongoing meetings about this. I was not very successful. In the early 1980s, I shared valuable information on this very subject with Letty Cottin Pogrebin, who was writing an article about anti-Semitism in the feminist movement, which she later expanded into a book. When Pogrebin's first article appeared in *Ms. Magazine,* several *Ms.* staffers approached me privately—to ask me whether I thought Pogrebin was "paranoid." I assured them that her allegations could easily be substantiated.

A number of high-profile feminists whose work I respected and with whom I had worked had deeply ambivalent, tortured, and ultimately "cold" relationships to Judaism. Andrea Dworkin (may she rest in peace) was one; Robin Morgan was another. Dworkin "got" anti-Semitism, but she was highly critical of Zionism and was also anti-religious. It's a typical Jewish position. In a novel, Dworkin once compared the Jewish God to a Nazi without mercy. In a work of nonfiction, she compared the Jewish state to a "pimp" and a "John" and viewed the Palestinians as their "prostitutes." (By the way: Great writers are allowed to take such license. I would not censor or issue a fatwa against a work simply because I disagree with it or find it offensive.)

Morgan's anti-Zionism may spring from other sources. I have no insider knowledge here, but in her memoir, *Saturday's Child,* she writes that her Jewish, Viennese-born father had abandoned her and her mother when she was born. Morgan searches for him for years and finally finds him when she is twenty. He is a gynecologist and she visits him under a pseudonym as a presumed patient. Again she is rejected by a cold, heartless, and non-paternal man. Can such personal family dynamics lead to a political position? I do not know.[12]

However, in 1989 Morgan published a book titled *The Demon Lover: The Roots of Terrorism.* It was reprinted again in 2001, post–9/11.[13] In my opinion, the book glorifies the Palestinian Authority, and romanticizes the most corrupt, scandalous, and terrorist-connected of United Nations agencies, namely the United Nations Relief and Works Agency for Palestine Refugees (UNRWA).

While this agency has provided social services to the Palestinians, it has also employed and funded terrorists and has been funded by terrorists. UNRWA has also appropriated most of the money meant for the impoverished Palestinians, whose unending misery is meant to arouse the world against the Jewish presence in the Middle East. Finally, the world has an estimated 135 million refugees. UNRWA has managed to focus the world's attention on the plight of only *one* small refugee group: the Palestinians.[14]

In 1948, an estimated 700,000 to 800,000 Arabs fled what became Israel. At the time, most would have identified themselves as Jordanians, Egyptians, Syrians, or as members of their clans and villages. An equal—or greater—number of Jews (800,000 to 900,000) fled Arab Muslim countries and were absorbed by Israel, at Israel's expense. They did not fester in refugee camps and were granted citizenship rights in Israel. One of the reasons that Palestinian refugees linger on is because not a single Arab nation-state has been willing to accept them as citizens—and because their own leaders have refused to make peace with Israel and to do the work of building a Palestinian state. Since each Palestinian woman is meant to bear at least eight to twelve children and many Palestinian men have more than one wife, by now the number of Palestinian refugees has swelled to four or five million. This includes the children, grandchildren, and great-grandchildren of the original 1948 refugees.

Now, let me take you on a feminist trip through the looking glass.

First, Morgan on UNRWA: "The entire organization won my respect for extraordinary work performed against all odds." She profusely thanks seven different UNRWA functionaries for having arranged her trip and guided her through the Palestinian "camps." Having UNRWA do this is like having the Soviet-era and KGB-controlled Intourist organize your trip to Moscow anytime between 1920 and 1980.

"Camps"? Morgan does not write "refugee neighborhoods" or "Palestinian-enforced ghettos." Rather, she uses the term "camps." Is this word chosen to remind one of "concentration camps" or "death camps"? In reality most Palestinians live in cities; some live in luxurious villas, others in dreadful poverty. They do not live in tents or cages. Throughout her chapter on the Palestinians, Morgan refers to Israel as "the Israeli Occupying Authority." Her every portrayal of Israel is theatrical and extremely negative. It captures complex reality the way a cartoon does. Morgan portrays a "violently condensed" Palestinian population in Gaza. Like the Amnesty International feminists, she does not discuss the ways in which the Palestinian leadership and the Arab League are primarily responsible for this violent condensation of Palestinian humanity. She only blames the Israelis for it all.

While some of the individual acts that Morgan describes may indeed have occurred, her presentation is without context or balance. More important, her extraordinary double standards are regrettably typical of so much feminist work. Thus, the savage misogyny in the "camps"—a misogyny that includes repetitive wife-beatings and forced impregnations (which Morgan mentions)—does not frighten Morgan as much as her dramatically heightened presentation of Jewish Jerusalem.

The British-born and American-based journalist and adventurer Jan Goodwin has written an important feminist book about women in the Muslim world: *Price of Honor: Muslim Women Lift the Veil of Silence on the Islamic World.* The book was originally published in 1994 and updated and reissued in 2003. Goodwin interviewed women in Muslim countries and in the "Israeli Occupied Territories." Goodwin is not one to hide her prejudices. The book opens with a map of the known Muslim world, and there is no Israel on it; only Gaza and the West Bank.[15]

Goodwin's interviews are powerful and moving. She is not a feminist ideologue, nor is she an academic. Thus, she describes the devastating and dangerous effects that growing Islamic fundamentalism has had on Muslim women's lives in clear and moving language. She covers the issues of veiling, polygamy, female genital mutilation, apostasy, honor killings, and the Islamist harassment of women in general and of "uppity" women in particular.

Like Morgan and Sabbagh, Goodwin does not interview Palestinian women who live in Israel proper and who are Israeli citizens (and who do not want to give up their Israeli citizenship) nor does she present a particularly sophisticated history of the persecution of Palestinian civilians by the Arab Muslim governments of the Middle East. Thus, like Morgan and the writers of the Amnesty International Report, Goodwin views most of the grievous problems of Palestinian women as mainly due to the Israeli "occupation."

For example, Goodwin links the oppression and suffering of Arab and Muslim women in nine Muslim countries mainly to Arab and Islamic misogyny—and she does so even as she depicts complicated political realities. By contrast, while she does discuss the rise of fundamentalism on the West Bank and Gaza, Goodwin attributes Palestinian women's suffering mainly to the Israeli Occupation.

Goodwin's chapter title about the women of Palestine is "Israeli-Occupied Territories: Next Year in Jerusalem." Is she suggesting that the PLO take over

Jerusalem? Or is she ironically baiting or trying to shame Jews who, for centuries, have intoned "Next year in Jerusalem" as part of their religious rituals?

Thus while Goodwin is not a *feminist* ideologue she is, however, and *anti-Zionist* ideologue. Thus, in this area her facts are often wrong or incomplete, her view one-sided, and her presentation formulaic. In a thirty-page chapter, she has only one brief paragraph in which she allows one unnamed woman to say that Arafat "talks democracy but operates as a dictatorship." The rest of her chapter is a systematic condemnation of Israel.

For example, Goodwin blames only Israeli Prime Minister Ariel Sharon for the terrible massacre of Palestinian civilians in the Sabra and Shatila refugee camps in Lebanon in 1982—and does not even mention that Christian Phalangists planned and executed the actual, retaliatory raid and that Sharon did not stop them. Goodwin also blames the Intifada of 2000 on Ariel Sharon. This is not true. Sharon's pre-authorized visit to the Temple Mount was merely the excuse given for a Palestinian Intifada that had long been planned.[16]

Goodwin also views the suicide terrorism against Israel civilians as "ultimate acts of political self-sacrifice" and as "dramatic" expressions of how "desperate the situation and the polarity between Arab and Jew have become." Goodwin—whose country, Great Britain, colonized the Arab Middle East and the known Muslim world for centuries, is relatively silent about this; instead, she focuses her attention on Israel as having "vastly superior fire power—American supplied warplanes." In her opinion, this current alliance has led "Palestinians (to become) walking weapons of terror as a means to narrow the military gap."

Goodwin claims that the Israeli military policies of self-defense have emasculated Palestinian men. Curfews keep grandiose, woman-hating, and honor- and shame-reared men at home fore long hours. Based on anecdotal evidence (studies do not exist), Goodwin believes the such men take their considerable frustrations out on women and children. Here, Goodwin quotes Suha Sabbagh, who says that the "Palestinian male, a father, the authority figure in the house, has lost all his authority." Goodwin dwells on the systematic "humiliation" of the Palestinian man by the Israelis. She writes: "Much of this belittling has taken place in front of their children and womenfolk," which in turn has "cut down" the image of the Palestinian man as the family's "hero" figure. "For Arab men, this is the same as losing their masculinity."

And here Goodwin, like so many other feminists, contradicts herself. Arab and Muslim overly vigilant paternal authority is precisely what has brutalized Arab and Muslim women. In 1992, Jean Sasson published *Princess: A True Story of Life Behind the Veil in Saudi Arabia*. The unnamed al-Saud princess (whose story Sasson tells), describes the typically cruel way in which fathers, brothers, and husbands treat their "womenfolk." Let me quote her: "The authority of a

Saudi male is unlimited; his wife and children survive only if he desires. In our homes, he is the state. . . . From an early age, the male child is taught that woman are of little value . . . the child witnesses the disdain shown his mother and sisters by his father; this leads to his scorn of all females . . . [the] women in my land are ignored by their fathers, scorned by their brothers, and abused by their husbands."[17]

Iranian-Swiss Carmen bin Laden, in her book *Inside the Kingdom,* portrays life for women under Saudi male rule similarly. Women cannot go out without a male escort and they cannot leave the house or the country without male permission and accompaniment. A daughter can be married against her will, a father can seize custody of his children and not allow their mother to ever see them again. Bin Laden writes: "I rarely met a Saudi woman who was not afraid of her husband. . . . A wife cannot do anything without her husband's permission. She cannot go out, cannot study, often cannot even eat at his table. Women in Saudi Arabia must live in obedience, in isolation, and in the fear that they may be cast out and summarily divorced."[18]

Saudi Arabia has not been "settled," "colonized," or "humiliated," by Israelis.

The absence of super-controlling woman-haters may give women some room to breathe. Indeed, Goodwin herself notes that Palestinian women have become political leaders and suicide killers not only because they are oppressed by wartime conditions but precisely because Palestinian men are increasingly absent from the home. However, like Morgan, in her zeal to endorse the Palestinian anti-Zionist narrative, she fails to challenge, in feminist terms, what it really means for Palestinian women to be forced into bearing eight to twelve children or what it means for a Palestinian child to be one among twenty to thirty siblings and half-siblings. How much positive paternal attention and love can so many children receive?

In the decade in which Morgan visited the West Bank and first wrote and published her book (the 1980s), Palestinian terrorists repeatedly attacked Israeli civilians and kibbutzim; bombed synagogues in Paris, Vienna, Brussels, and Rome; and hijacked and killed passengers on Egyptian and American airplanes. In 1985, members of the Palestine Liberation Front hijacked the Achille Lauro and threw an American Jewish tourist, the wheelchair-bound Leon Klinghoffer, over the side of the ship.

During the same decade, Islamic jihadists, all of whom had a strong pro-Palestinian agenda, also attacked America. For example, at the end of 1979, Muslim Iranians stormed the American embassy in Tehran and held 53 Americans hostage for 444 days; Muslim terrorists blew up the American embassy in Beirut, killing 63 people, including 17 Americans; Muslim terrorists, backed by Iran, blew up the American Marine barracks in Beirut, killing 241 Marines and

58 French paratroopers; Iran's Hezbollah hijacked a TWA plane, flew it to Beirut, demanded the release of 700 Arabs held in Israeli jails, killed 1 American, held 39 American passengers hostage for two weeks; and Libyan terrorists blew up Pan Am flight 103 over Lockerbie, Scotland.

In the 1990s, before Morgan wrote the new introduction and the new afterword to the post–9/11 edition of *Demon Lover*, the Islamist El Sayyid Nosair assassinated the Jewish American Rabbi Meir Kahane in New York City; an Islamist shot a young Jewish American yeshiva student on the Brooklyn Bridge; Arab Muslim terrorists, connected to the blind sheikh Omar Abdul Rahman, tried to blow up the World Trade Center in New York City; an Islamist yelling "Allahu Akbar" (God is most great) murdered 5 foreign guests dining at the Semiramis Hotel in Cairo; Arab Muslim terrorists blew up the Khobar Towers in Saudi Arabia, killing 19 American servicemen and wounding hundreds; Egyptian-based Jemaah Islamiyah terrorists shot and killed more than 60 tourists visiting the temple of Queen Hatshepsut at Luxor, Egypt; al Qaeda detonated two car bombs that destroyed the American embassies in both Dar-es-Salaam and Nairobi, killing 224 and wounding thousands; and al Qaeda bombed the USS Cole in Aden, Yemen, killing 17 American sailors.

And then al Qaeda attacked the World Trade Center and the Pentagon on September 11, 2001.

However, in her post-9/11 afterword, Morgan does not dwell on this. Instead, she continues the work of politically correct feminism. Immediately after 9/11, Morgan's main fear is that America might turn "bigoted" and become "extreme right." What concerns her and so many other feminists is not America's vulnerability but the vulnerability of Muslims in America.

In the days right after 9/11, Morgan's e-mails were widely circulated on the Internet. (I know; I received them through a number of feminist listserv groups.) These e-mails now comprise the afterword to *The Demon Lover*. Not only is Morgan worried about right-wing Christian fundamentalism; she is even more worried about the possible lynching of Muslims in America.

Morgan writes about how feminists are already "doing everything we can to avoid this kind of escalating nightmare—and a network of safe houses is already being set up to shelter and help innocent Arab or Muslim civilians who might be persecuted in the wake of this attack."

But, in all this, where is Morgan's concern for women? Or for dead American civilians? Why are feminist networks the world over presumably this concerned with protecting Muslim men who may be accused of terrorism—or who may even be terrorists? Have they all agreed to focus on racism and the civil rights of male immigrants and non-Americans in America and to forget entirely about women? What about gender and religious apartheid in the Islamic world? Has that become too politically incorrect even for feminists to say?

While Jan Goodwin's one-sided anti-Zionism is dispiriting (at least to me), to her credit, unlike some other feminists, Goodwin has the plain wit to note that Hamas has been steadily imposing Saudi-like standards on Palestinian women; that while Hamas has provided some services they have also imposed hijab and face-veils on women and have threatened and punished women who resist; that both the Palestinian Authority and Hamas are corrupt, tyrannical, and misogynist entities.

Precisely because Goodwin is a fine journalist, I must, somewhat rhetorically, ask: Is the western media obliged to espouse a strong anti-Zionist and anti-American position in order to gain entrée or maintain credibility in the Arab and Muslim world? I fear that this is the case. Of course, individual journalists may also believe the propaganda so well crafted and for so long by a lethal alliance of Islamic jihadists and European intellectuals and journalists. I fear that Goodwin may be among such individuals.

Goodwin characterizes the excessive materialism of Muslim Arab Princesses (MAPs) as akin to JAPs (i.e., Jewish American Princesses). I do not think this is a balanced or fair comparison. The wealth of the Arab oil states far exceeds the wealth of American Jews and might better be likened to the wealth of British royalty.

Goodwin utterly fails to note or discuss the persecution and oppression of non-Muslims under Islam. She does not interview Arab and non-Arab Christian women (Maronites, Copts, Phoenicians, Assyro-Chaldeans, Arameans, and so on). Nor does she interview Jews or other religious minorities who have suffered terribly under Islamic rule both in terms of gender and religion. This is scandalous but typical.

Goodwin actually reverses the truth in this particular area. Like many feminists, she attempts to present the Prophet Muhammad as kinder and fairer to women (or to his own wives), than many of his followers have been—which may actually be true.

For example, Goodwin writes that the Prophet married many women in order to forge alliances "with tribes who had been bitter enemies of Islam." Her only example given is that Muhammad married a Jew, one Safiya bint Huyay. According to Goodwin, this marriage to the "daughter of an important Jewish chief, for example, diminished Jewish opposition to the Prophet's mission."

One scarcely knows where to begin. Does Goodwin imagine this Safiya to be akin to the Jewish Queen Esther who married the King of Persia in order to save her people? Safiya is no such savior. According to scholars Bat Ye'or, Andrew Bostom, Anwar Hekmat, Ibn Ishaq, Ibn Warraq, Nancy Kobrin, Richard Landes, and W. Montgomery Watt, among others, Muhammad essentially followed a scorched earth policy where Jews and Christians were concerned.

According to Bat Ye'or in *The Dhimmi: Jews, and Christians under Islam, Islam and Dhimmitude,* and *The Decline of Eastern Christianity Under Islam: From Jihad to Dhimmitude,* Muhammad systematically attacked, exiled, ransomed, or slaughtered those Jews who refused to convert to Islam; he also confiscated their property. In 624, Muhammad did this to the Jews of Medina (the Qaynuqa), and the following year to the Jewish Nadir tribe. In 627, Muhammad attacked the Jewish tribe of the Qurayza in Medina who refused to convert. In *The Dhimmi,* Bat Ye'or writes: "Muhammad attacked and overwhelmed (the Qurayza). Trenches were then dug in the marketplace of Medina and the Jews— six to nine hundred of them, according to traditional Muslim sources—were led forth in batches and decapitated. All the menfolk perished in this way, with the exception of one convert to Islam. The Prophet then divided the women, children, houses, and chattels among the Muslims."

In a private conversation in 2003, Bat Ye'or confirmed that Safiya (whom Goodwin refers to) was taken captive by Muhammad after he slaughtered her father and husband. Safiya lived in Khaybar near an oasis. In another private communication, Dr. Andrew Bostom, author of *The Legacy of Jihad,* writes: "Safiya was the wife of Kinana whom Muhammad had tortured and then beheaded for the 'treasure' the latter possessed, before taking Kinana's widow, i.e., Safiya, as his 'bride'."

Is marrying the man who has slaughtered your husband and father Goodwin's feminist view of what constitutes peace-oriented marriage? Does her feminist critique of forced marriage apply only to Muslim women and not to Jewish or Christian women?

I am extremely saddened by such hidden biases and reversals of the truth in Goodwin's feminist work. Still, I am inclined to honor Goodwin's interviews with Arab and Muslim women elsewhere in the Middle East and central Asia.

As one-sided as Goodwin may be, she stops short of supporting or justifying polygamy or veiling. Columbia University professor, Lila Abu-Lughod, a feminist anthropologist of the Middle East, challenges us by presenting such customs in complex feminist terms. Abu-Lughod has published a number of books including *Veiled Sentiments: Honor and Poetry in Bedouin Society, Writing Women's Worlds: Bedouin Stories,* and has edited an excellent anthology, *Remaking Women: Feminism and Modernity in the Middle East.*[19]

Abu-Lughod writes clearly and powerfully. Her arguments are complex, not simplistic; her work commendably juggles multiple variables such as class, nationalism, religion, the history of colonialism and imperialism, capitalism, gender, concepts of modernity, "indigenous" Arab and Muslim feminism, as well as western feminisms. I think Abu-Lughod has been unfairly criticized as justifying or even supporting women's oppression—and in feminist terms.

Abu-Lughod draws on the work of scholars such as Leila Ahmed, Mervat Hatem, and Deniz Kandiyoti, among others, to make the following points. First, arranged marriages are not always without affection or love; second, traditional marriage and family arrangements, including polygamous arrangements, allowed women to be part of "homosocial networks that encouraged certain kinds of subversions of men's authority"; third, the adoption of hijab has many meanings and implications.

For example, according to Abu-Lughod, women may adopt hijab for many reasons. For some, it may represent a genuine religious awakening. Others may have a desire, both as Muslims and as feminists, to rescue women from male misogyny by finding religious sources and precedents for women's dignity and freedom. Historically, and still today, some women may adopt hijab as a way of opposing or rejecting secularity and certain western influences that include the sexual objectification of women. Finally, many veiled women work outside the home, often in prestigious professions and are, in many ways, "feminists."

In addition, like many other Arab and Muslim feminists and their western feminist supporters, the bitterness about historical colonialism also affects current views of western feminism. Drawing upon the work of Leila Ahmed and Marnia Lazreg, Abu-Lughod reminds us that the same British colonials who encouraged female emancipation in Egypt did so as a way of weakening local culture; at the same time, these same men were opposing female suffrage back home in England.

However, Abu-Lughod, Gayatri Spivak, and others reject the western feminist "fixation" on the veil; and in an intellectual and territorial power struggle with western academic feminists, insist that modern western feminism is, essentially, "colonial feminism." They suggest that not all roads to modernity or feminism have to be western.

But, like other academic feminists, Abu-Lughod approves of some western-based views such as postcolonialist, anti-capitalist, and postmodern feminist theory; but she opposes other western views such as a universalist doctrine of human rights. Abu-Lughod is a multiculturalist who, with western tools, wishes to defend Arab and Muslim culture.

For example, Abu-Lughod refuses to accept that western-style "companionate marriage" is necessarily good for women or in any way superior to arranged or even polygamous marriage. Indeed, many western feminists, myself included, made quite a good case in the late 1960s and early 1970s against the nuclear monogamous family in terms of the consequent or corollary female isolation, demoralization, depression, and powerlessness that it engendered. Even if women were virgins when they married, and were superlative wives and mothers, "companionate marriage" did not guarantee them lifetime support or security. On the contrary. Divorce has increased in the western world and has been economically devastating for women.

Thus, Abu-Lughod and others suggest that female relatives, including co-wives, may bond, keep each other company, share isolating and repetitive tasks, and so on. Sounds good—but neither research or personal memoirs support this theoretical possibility. Exceptions always exist but the bulk of what is known presents a far different picture of female-female relations. Many accounts portray Arab and Muslim women mistreating their female servants and slaves. They are also either directly cruel or fatefully indifferent toward impoverished and racially and religiously marginalized women in their own countries and households.

Even Abu-Lughod notes that pioneer Iranian feminist Siddiqeh Dawlatabadi "imposed on the nine-year-old daughter of her father's secretary a marriage to her seventy-year old father when he was widowed. She later ignored the girls's cries when she went into labor and thereafter, when Dawlatabadi's father died, married off the girl to someone else, taking her daughters."

Many of the Arab and Muslim memoirs by women that have been published in English in the last thirty-five years, as well as my own experience in the Islamic world, confirm that Arab and Muslim women are not exempt from universal "women's ways of being." This includes female-female aggression, competition, conformism, sexist policing, gossip, envy, and hate—as well as female-female kindness, compassion, support for resistance, and rescue from violence.

The more recent memoirs by Carmen bin Laden, Betty Mahmoody, Jean Sassoon, and Souad, as well as many memoirs from the nineteenth and twentieth centuries, tend to portray women in purdah as mainly illiterate, superstitious, apathetic, listless, passive, broken, and cruel and dangerous to each other. I would welcome Abu-Lughod's reaction to Carmen bin Laden's description of life with the Saudi princesses. Bin Laden writes: "I had the impression that none of the women ever read, except perhaps the Koran. . . . I never once saw one of my sisters-in-law pick up a book." Worse, they had nothing to do. "Their lives were so constrained—so small, and faded—that it frightened me. They never left their houses alone. They never did anything. . . . [T]he bin Laden women were like pets kept by their husbands."

The consequences of being confined were tragic. According to bin Laden, "many of the princesses lived on pills . . . [but] they never saw the light of day. They had bone density problems from the lack of sunlight and exercise, heart problems from eating too much, psychosomatic problems galore. A very large proportion of these women were depressed."

No doubt some of these women did the best they could under truly terrible circumstances; some were also kind, humorous, philosophical, and tried to do no harm. I discuss what is a complicated psychological picture more fully in the next chapter.

Dutch parliamentarian Ayaan Hirsi Ali is a Muslim feminist who has challenged crimes against humanity done in the name of Islam. I knew it was only a matter of time before the official feminist left would challenge her politics. And now it has.

Nation Magazine, through the Investigative Fund of the Nation Institute, supported the research done by author Deborah Scroggins, whose article about Ayaan Hirsi Ali it published in June 2005, titled "The Dutch-Muslim Culture War: Ayaan Hirsi Ali has Enraged Muslims with her Attacks on their Sexual Mores." Incredibly, Scroggins does not see Hirsi Ali as a hero but as a reactionary and a traitor who left the Labor Party for the "center-right" Liberal VVD Party.[20]

Thus Scroggins views Hirsi Ali as part of an anti-immigration, anti-Muslim, and anti-Islam faction that includes assassinated politician and homosexual Pim Fortuyn, assassinated filmmaker Theo van Gogh, philosopher Herman Phillipse (who "warned that Holland's Muslim community was rapidly becoming undigestible"), and the politician Geert Wilders (who argued that Muslims should "assimilate" to the more "humane" and "higher level" European culture).

Thus, Scroggins judges Hirsi Ali by the politically incorrect company she keeps; she does not judge whether Hirsi Ali is telling the truth. In addition, Scroggins condemns Hirsi Ali for describing the Prophet Muhammad as a "perverse" and "despicable" man, a "tyrant" who "married the 9-year-old daughter of his best friend." But Muhammad *did* marry a nine-year-old; this fact is true and Hirsi Ali is entitled to her opinions about it.

However, in classic left-feminist fashion, Scroggins attacks Hirsi Ali for "putting all the blame on Islam," instead of blaming "patriarchal customs"; for ignoring the work of certain Muslim feminists who have "shown that Islam's sacred texts can be interpreted in a more female-friendly way"; and for failing to focus on the "role the West has played and continues to play in assisting the rise of the Islamist movements."

Hirsi Ali's main political and intellectual crime is her refusal to rant against the West's history of colonialism and imperialism and against its ongoing racism—as if doing so will somehow lesson or effectively appease the rise of Islamism; or, as if appeasing Islamists as they blow up and behead civilians constitutes a necessary or useful action.

Scroggins actually views Hirsi Ali's passionate and feminist defense of both Muslim women and European culture as "contributing" both to the rise of Islamism—and, paradoxically, to anti-Muslim and anti-Islamic sentiment. Scroggins quotes a Muslim woman, a "self-described peace activist," who does not see Hirsi Ali as a "champion of the oppressed" but as "nothing but an Uncle Tom."

Scroggins quotes this same informant as saying that there have been "many more attacks on Dutch Muslims than on non-Muslims." She cites no sources and gives no statistics. This unsupported view is echoed elsewhere by left-dominated feminists. In fact, both the United Nations and European governments have sponsored conferences about intolerance, anti-Semitism, and Islamophobia, which have increasingly presented Muslims and Palestinians as "the new Jews." (Most recently, this happened at a conference in Cordoba, Spain, under the auspices of the European Organization for Security and Co-operation, which took place in June 2005.)

Last year, a feminist from a European country interviewed me about my Second Wave work. In the course of our discussion, she confirmed what I am saying here. (She does not want to be named.) Here is what she told me: "I thought my courses in America in women's studies would be more about women. But they were all about race and ethnicity. We keep losing women to multiculturalism. At one seminar I kept wondering why all we talked about was American imperialism, but not about women. At this particular gathering, a Palestinian feminist asked a series of angry, rhetorical questions against Israel and against Jews. Many of the American feminists were Jewish. They all kept nodding their heads in agreement with her. Then she asked what everyone thought about the fact that all the neoconservatives who are behind Bush were Jews. She kept asking this question. It took people a very long time to respond and an even longer time to say that not all the neocons were Jews."

These feminist graduate students and their professors have learned the ideological lessons of the postcolonial feminist academy and media very well. And they are not the only ones. Many feminist activists in America and elsewhere, especially members of Women in Black with whom, in the past, I have demonstrated (but only in Israel, never in Europe of America), have also learned that the feminist "position" on Islam and Muslim women has more to do with Palestine than with women or Islamic gender apartheid. Let me give you two examples.

In June 2004, I was the first pro-Israel and pro-democracy feminist guest on Pacifica's KPFK radio station in Los Angeles. After years of on-air Jew hatred and Israel bashing on KPFK, the program *Feminist Magazine,* run by a feminist collective, had taken a principled position against this unacknowledged form of racism and had invited me to discuss my views on anti-Semitism, Israel, democracy, and Islamic gender apartheid.

Tricia Roth and Melissa Chiprin bravely interviewed me. I said the kinds of things that I am saying in this book—and all hell broke loose. Even while we were still on air, the switchboard lit up with angry listeners, most of whom were Jewish left feminists. That was only the beginning. Feminist calls mounted for the censure and removal of *Feminist Magazine* from the air and from the control of the feminist collective. An online protest petition was launched that characterized what I said as "racist" and my views as "anti-feminist." The Los Angeles chapter of Women in Black made a bid to take over the collective.[21]

In October 2004, a small group of San Francisco–based feminist activists, members of both or either Women in Black and Brit Zedek (A Just Covenant), traveled to Duke University in Raleigh-Durham, North Carolina, to support the Palestine Solidarity Movement Conference that took place there.

It would be one thing if such feminists had come to protest both the systemic Palestinian abuses against women as well as the war-related burdens that Israel, acting primarily in self-defense, has visited upon both Palestinian and Israeli civilians, especially women, children, and the elderly. But they did not have a balanced or particularly feminist agenda. Although many activists were lesbians and/or pro-gay, they had not come to protest the Palestinian persecution of suspected gays in Gaza or the West Bank; nor did they seem to know that Israel has granted political asylum to Palestinian gays, including those who have been tortured and nearly killed by other Palestinians. Instead, these American feminists wore political buttons and T-shirts that read "We are all Palestinians."

In my view, their behavior was far more leftist than feminist, and far more suicidal and nihilistic than pro-peace, pro-democracy, or pro-justice. I can only hope and pray that they will become more thoughtful about these issues soon. But I doubt it. The cult-like popularity of sacred Palestinian victimhood is too great. It has cast its spell over too many good feminists.

For example, as I've noted, my colleague, author and *Ms. Magazine* cofounder Letty Cottin Pogrebin finally did sound the alarm about Jew hatred among feminists—but this was long after leading Jewish feminists had been talking about this for more than ten to twenty years. Still, to her enormous credit, Pogrebin took a risk in writing about this subject at all.

However, in the last fifteen years, Pogrebin has become more left, more sympathetic to the Palestinians, and far more critical of both Israel and of America under President Bush. She is silent on the subject of Islamic gender apartheid. Please understand, Pogrebin has the absolute right to adopt such positions. At any other moment in history, I'd possibly join her in criticizing certain Israeli and American policies. But based on my own experience in Afghanistan I could never, ever be silent about Islamic gender Apartheid.

In a recent, brief e-mail exchange, Pogrebin has apparently changed her mind about anti-Semitism among feminists. She said that she no longer encounters Jew hatred among feminists. She challenged me to give her some examples. Pogrebin is not a self-hating Jew nor is she is a faux feminist. She is—or was— a good liberal feminist with incredible energy, savvy, and the hottest Rolodex in town. If she can be influenced by leftist ideology, I must join Paul Berman in fearing for the future of liberalism.

But the spell has been woven by particularly adept spell-weavers and master linguistic reversalists.

For example, in her 2001 afterword to *Demon Lover,* Robin Morgan compares the grief and mourning of post-9/11 New Yorkers who are now "unnerved" by security checkpoints, who feel "terrified, humiliated, outraged" to her friends in the refugee camps of Gaza and the West Bank: "Palestinian women who have lived in precisely that same emotional condition for four generations." Is she actually saying that Israel has committed 9/11-like terrorist attacks against civilian Palestinians? I fear she is saying precisely this. Does she mean to have all of us identify with Palestinians and, in turn, join her in raging against Israel? I fear she does.

At the end of her 2001 letter, Morgan compares herself to a woman named Aziza, in the Gaza Strip. Although oppressed and "compressed," Aziza still manages to plant flowers. Aziza tells Morgan that the "soul needs to be fed too." And in the shadow of the demolished World Trade Center, our American, faux-Palestinian feminist bravely goes out and plants some flowers in Greenwich Village in New York City.

American and western feminists wear the keffiyah in many ways. It is a way of trying to "pass" as Third World hero victims or at least as champions of Third World victims. But, in doing so, they are leaving behind any feminist vision of universal human rights for both women and for men.

Despite Morgan's failure to look for or find them, many Israeli Jewish feminists have worked together with Israeli Arab/Palestinian feminists in an effort to help rescue girls and women targeted for honor killings. I am a member of an Israeli feminist academic and activist listserv group whose members are involved in such work. Nadera Shalhoub-Kevorkian, a member, has described "honor killings" as femicide. (The word was first coined by my colleague, Dr. Diana Russell.)

In 2001, the listserv tried to assist Nadera with her efforts to rescue a Palestinian woman whose five-year-old daughter had just been raped. The poor woman's husband had demanded that she kill the girl. When she refused, her husband, his family, *her* family, and their entire village shunned the mother. Soon the mother became seriously depressed. She had absolutely no future in that village or among Palestinians if she allowed her daughter to live. Clearly, she required money, psychiatric care, and political asylum. The Israeli feminists, both Jews and non-Jews, raised money for this purpose.

I remain haunted by this story. What would comprise a happy ending? Assuming this mother and daughter choose life over death, they cannot live as Arabs, Muslims, Palestinians, or in the West Bank; they have no home, no relatives, no culture, no past. If they "live," they must also die, both psychologically and culturally.

※ ※ ※

As I've mentioned, Lila Abu-Lughod, like other Arab and Muslim feminist academics, also finds a way to interpret the veil in positive terms. In her view, burkhas and hijab afford women some measure of "portable seclusion" in hostile public settings. That the public settings are "hostile" is indisputable. But so are private settings. As feminists, we must at least acknowledge and challenge the cultural hatred of women that forces them into both sedentary and portable seclusion. We must also call "seclusion" by its right name: imprisonment, or subordinated reality. Thus while we must acknowledge historical variables such as colonialism and genocide, in my opinion, we cannot afford to be blinded by such bitter legacies either.

For example, I am painfully aware of the genocidal persecution of Jews by Muslims, both historically and today, and historically by the Catholic Church, fascist Nazis, and totalitarian Soviets. I may therefore choose to wage only nationalist battles (which I may mischaracterize as "feminist" battles), or I may choose to confine my feminist struggles to my own tribe only—which is what I believe many feminist scholars are essentially doing (i.e., using western feminist concepts primarily to combat the specter of western colonialism. This is why they have found such safe and prestigious harbors among politically correct western academics.)

However, such postcolonial feminists may or may not be serving the cause of women's worldwide freedom, or the cause of freedom for the women in their own tribe or culture.

Abu-Lughod, like her Columbia University colleague, Gayatri Spivak, views a western-style fight for women's rights in the Muslim world as a dangerous diversion. She recommends that we continue to focus mainly on the "colonial enterprise." Why? Perhaps as a way of reminding western thinkers—heirs to the colonial adventure—that, given their ancestors' past crimes, they dare not feel "superior" to the Islamic world and above all, they dare not intervene to free Muslim prisoners from Muslim jailors, or African slaves and female sex slaves from their tormentors.

I am among a handful of both western and eastern feminists who humbly but adamantly question this approach. In fact, let me suggest that the difference between eastern (or Arab, Muslim, or Asian) feminism and western feminism has become exceedingly vague. For nearly forty years, elite Third World women have mingled with elite western women at grassroots and United Nations–sponsored conferences. The politicization of the United Nations—both its "Palestinianization" and its anti-Americanism has become *the* universal point of view for diplomats and for feminist academics and activists everywhere.

Admirable exceptions exist, such as the campaign to prevent and abolish female genital mutilation, which was first initiated by Viennese-born American Fran Hoskin in the late 1970s—she was attacked by Muslim and African feminists as a meddling colonialist for doing so—and which was subsequently undertaken by American (Alice Walker immediately comes to mind), European, and Third World feminists, sometimes in tandem and sometimes unilaterally.

But United Nations–influenced talking feminist heads are often quite removed from reality and from action. Like United Nations diplomats and heads of state, they themselves do not live like most people in their own countries do. And really, one cannot read Lila Abu-Lughod, Leila Ahmed, Suha Sabbagh, or Gayatri Spivak and distinguish their work clearly from the work of their American- and European-born feminist academic and activist counterparts. Except, of course, the western feminists are perpetually "guilty" and wish to atone for colonial and racist crimes and the eastern feminists are perpetually outraged and aggressive about the colonial racism. It's almost an S & M relationship.

But the uniformity of the feminist vision and voice represents a great loss especially because so few feminists, whether eastern or western, uphold a single standard of human rights for all. Thus, everyone is speaking the same politically correct universal language—from which a universal concept of human rights, even for women, has been utterly banished. In addition, few feminists are bringing a really "different" or truly independent way of thinking to the international or intellectual table. They have managed to disappear the troublesome, exoticized Other so that no one sounds like she's rooted in one particular place, so that anyone can sound as if she's from someplace else; from almost anywhere.

Intellectually, aesthetically, the task is to be oneself but so deeply that eventually one finds what is common to all humanity and what is absolutely unique to oneself and one's own culture. *This* kind of self- and cultural self-knowledge is both our gift to each other and the only basis upon which we may create freedom-oriented alliances.

Most academic feminists, both eastern and western, have portrayed Muslim women either as victims of profound Taliban-like misogyny (for which America and the West are solely to blame) or as freedom fighters against imperialism, colonialism, capitalism, Zionism, and apartheid. Few academics have focused on Arab and Muslim women's relationships to other women, as well as to men. Let me introduce you to some extraordinary Muslim, Arab, and Middle Eastern women. And let me use my psychological skills to make sense of what they are telling us. In the chapters that follow, I hope to open your eyes to the terrible tragedies that currently are being obscured by misguided left-feminist thinkers.

In Their Own Words

Portraits of Arab, Muslim, and Middle Eastern Women

What do Arab, Muslim, and Middle Eastern women have to say about their lives today? What do they think of western feminist views of Islamic gender apartheid? Their views vary. It is clear from my personal interviews and from the literature that some feel they have been abandoned by western feminists in the name of multicultural correctness. Others feel that western feminists do not understand them or their culture. Some think that women in the West—especially those who criticize Islamic gender and religious apartheid—are colonialists and racists.

Merry Merrell is a Syrian American feminist whom I have quoted in the Introduction; Merrell is her pseudonym. She is a poet and a clairvoyant counselor who lives in London and Boston. When Merrell first moved from America to England, she was "a raging anti-American anarchist." When she returned, she was "still an anarchist," but she had also become "a major patriot." Merry told me that she had realized that "nowhere else but in America do people have the constitutional, psychological, and spiritual rights and freedoms that we [have]. Because I love freedom, I love America, as imperfect and as in-process as it is." Merrell views Europe as "cynical" and filled with "negativity and envy."

Merell concludes: "It is vital for western feminists to say the truth about women living under Islam because of the new ways in which the Left's sympathies with the Islamist perpetrators has confused and silenced so many."

Egyptian American Nonie Darwish (a pseudonym) was raised as a Muslim. Her father, a high-ranking Egyptian officer, trained Palestinians to kill Israelis. He died in battle. Darwish and her family moved to America and became citizens. Darwish also married a Christian man—which is a capital crime under

Islam. In "Escaping Submission," Darwish writes: "I now belong to the greatest and most moral country that ever existed on the face of the earth. The U.S. Constitution and Bill of Rights [practiced in] this graceful country allowed me to practice any religion or no religion and gave me human rights I could only [have] dreamed of under Islam. I am lucky and more than lucky, I am saved. I was never discriminated against even after 9/11."

Darwish is an American patriot. She recognizes that life in America has both saved and freed her. She is not blaming America for 9/11.

Homa Arjmand is an Iranian feminist who lives in Canada. She has been leading the fight against the imposition of Shari'a (Islamic religious) law in Canada. In the fall of 2004, Arjmand delivered a speech before the University Women's Club in which she listed all the forms of oppression that Muslim women face at home—and how they follow women to their new country in the West. She said: "Unfortunately, [western] multiculturalism provides a justification for this inhuman condition. [Adopting Shari'a law in Canada forces will put the life and safety of battered immigrant women in jeopardy.]"

Merrell, Darwish, and Arjmand are voices that often have not been heard in the feminist academy and academically influenced media; that is why I have quoted them first. Although western feminists are quick to praise the heroism of dissident *Muslim* feminists, as westerners they themselves hesitate to criticize Islamic gender apartheid in their own voices and without a Muslim "chick" up front. They have been too well trained as political correctniks.

The truth is that Merrell, Darwish, and Arjmand hold minority views. Most Arab and Muslim women do not sound like them. Many view America as an evil empire controlled by Zionists; believe that western feminists have adopted a crusading and "orientalist" view of Muslim women; and believe that westerners have also wrongfully confused tribal customs (such as female genital mutilation) with Islam.

Muslim and Arab women are being ill-served by feminists who want us to believe that all women are supportive and compassionate sisters and that even barbaric cultural customs, such as amputation, stoning, and honor killings are somehow minor or due to Western racism. As I've stated previously, Arab and Muslim women have overwhelming psychological battles to wage. The fear, mistrust, and outright hatred of women in Islamic societies cannot be overstated. Many women know that at any moment they might be "honor" murdered by a male family member with the approval of their female relatives. Like men, many women also internalize their society's hatred of women and suffer from low self-esteem and feelings of unworthiness. Like men, women are sometimes exceptionally cruel toward other women.

Exceptions do exist. Some co-wives, and some mothers- and daughters-in-law get along well—especially when the mother-in-law is also her daughter-in-law's aunt, which is not uncommon. However, the prevalence and history of polygamy, coupled with the ease with which men can divorce their wives, leads to enormous female-female rivalry, jealousy, hostility, and fear. Often co-wives scapegoat each other, not their more powerful husband. First wives are known to bully and abuse second wives; second or younger wives are known to corral an older husband's time, attention, affection, and resources for herself and her children exclusively.

According to Nonie Darwish in "The Impossible Family Dynamics of Islam," the relationships among women in Muslim countries are often "strained and hostile." "There are little relationships between women outside the family or clan. There is constant fear of envy and the evil eye as well. As a child I often heard women begging their husbands after a fight not to marry another woman. 'Go ahead and have affairs,' they say, 'but please never marry another.'"

In Darwish's view, a wife is afraid that a second or third wife and her children will be considered equal under the law and will stand to inherit. Darwish believes that for this and other reasons, a woman's loyalty to her husband is undermined. Many women's primary allegiance is to their brothers, fathers, and to firstborn sons.

According to Darwish, the system actually drives a wedge between husbands and wives, as well as between women. It also turns a son into his "mother's man and defender," which often pits him in psychologically dangerous ways against his own father. Indeed, women in the Middle East "often go by their son's name, such as Om Mohammed, or mother of Mohammed." Their identity is that of "the mother of a son," not that of "Mrs. Husband." In Darwish's words, "the unit of loyalty is thus transferred from Husband and Wife to Mother and son."

It is important to note that Arab and Muslim female psychology is different in certain ways from western female psychology. For example, Muslim women do not psychologically expect to flee their families of origin and, in biblical terms, to "cleave" to their husbands. Instead, they expect to "cleave" to their brothers and firstborn son in ways that are lifelong. A normal Arab and Muslim mother expects her firstborn son to live with her forever and to remain primarily loyal to her, not to his wife. (Similar tendencies or longings may exist among western women, but they are not culturally sanctioned and are often considered pathological.) This extreme Arab and Muslim mother-son enmeshed bonding is especially charged in a culture where women are suspect and degraded and where men must constantly prove their "manly" honor.

Predictably, sadly, women also play a collaborative role in the culturally legitimized murders of girls and women in honor killings. Like men, women also enforce patriarchal customs; perhaps they are even stricter about it, since this is their one sphere of (indirect) power: namely, getting other women to toe the line and punishing them when they fail to do so.

In my interviews with Arab and Muslim women, many have confirmed that their sisters, mothers, aunts, daughters, and cousins are "brainwashed" against women. They have also told me that Arab and Muslim women have not been allowed to develop a sense of "self" (as opposed to identifying themselves mainly as members of a group) and have an underdeveloped appreciation of individual rights. Of course, one might argue—and many do—that, by comparison, many westerners are selfish individualists who are incapable of loyally sacrificing themselves for the group.

Women in the West also inhibit women's individual and psychological growth and do not support female intellectual resistance to the status quo. Western women also reward conformity and punish female dissent. Because women want approval and maternal attentiveness from other women, women can enforce conformity merely by withholding—or implicitly threatening to withhold—their approval and maternal attentiveness.

Psychologically, women also need (a number of) "best" girlfriends with whom to dyadically bond. Women need to belong to small social and ideological cliques and, like men, will do almost anything to retain such connections. Sacrificing (or minimizing) the truth is the least of it.

In the case of Arab and Muslim women, some research suggests that women collaborate in Arab honor killings by gossiping about other women. If a woman can't trust her male and female intimates to defend her from a false accusation, then the peace of mind a woman requires to develop a strong self and the psychological ability to fight for herself and for her ideas is seriously compromised.

As we have previously seen, women—all women—gossip about other women and shun them too. Gossip is a major source of female power and pleasure. Many girls and women routinely try to destroy another woman's reputation: She's a "whore," she "slept her way to the top," and so on. Perhaps this is a way of reducing some of the competition for eligible male protectors, jobs, or membership in a socially desirable clique. Some scholars say that female-driven gossip is part of what encourages or even forces men to kill the female offender on behalf of the "honor" of the family.

For example, the anthropologists Ilsa M. Glazer and Wahiba Abu Ras studied the relationship between women's gossip and family honor killings in a small village in the Gallilee, Masdar El-Nabea. A brief summary will be useful here.

Women "monitor each other's daily behavior" while the men are away. Imagine the excitement when the secluded, illiterate, and impoverished Jamila asked another girl to read the love letter she'd received! The reader talked—and the woman she'd talked to also talked. Then the village herbalist said she'd seen Jamila having sex with a young man. (Jamila said that he'd drugged her and taken her virginity.)

Luckily (or unluckily), Jamila was immediately forced to marry her rapist. She brought no dowry, no social advantage, only shame. Thus, she was flung into purdah, kept locked up, starved, beaten, and anally raped. Her mother-in-law and sister-in-law spread false rumors about her. Indeed, the unmarried sister-in-law did so because she herself was suspected of having "suspect morality" and of "not being a virgin."

Jamila's brothers were forced to kill her. Her husband soon married a "higher-status" woman. Jamila's own mother did not mourn her. Arab Israeli/Palestinian feminist groups agree that female rumors and gossip oppress and destroy women. One group has described women who "actively participate" in the "rumor system" as "faithful collaborators" who uphold the "oppressive traditions" directed against them.

As we shall see in the next chapter, one young Palestinian girl, Palestina (Tina) Isa, was murdered by her parents in the United States with the active collaboration of three of her four sisters whose fear and envy of Tina's "Americanization" turned diabolically fateful.

Again: If Muslim women are this oppressed, it is important that less oppressed western feminists at least say so. At this point, I am only suggesting that we see clearly and yearn to act morally. I am not yet suggesting that we send in the Marines to rescue them.

These stories and analyses are not meant to portray Arab and Muslim women in a poor light. All women are complex, and Arab women possess warmth, considerable charm, beauty, kindness, and incredible heroism despite often tragic fates. I maintain the warmest and most familial relationship with Ali, my former Afghan husband, his wife, and their two adult children. Ali and I do not have the same memories of our life together in Kabul, and we do not interpret what happened in the same way. Nevertheless, he is a man without a country and someone who was once very dear to me. We have not moved beyond the past because we have never thrashed it out directly. We have set it aside, we step around it, I speak the truth to his children and his wife.

I have also met and communicated with some of the leading feminists from the Arab and Islamic worlds, including Egyptians Nawal El-Sadawii, Leila Ahmed, Leyla Abu-Saif; Syrian Rhonda al-Fatal; Palestinians Nabila Espanioly and Nadera Kevorkian; Saudi Aisha al-Mana; Moroccan Fatima Mernissi; Turkish Iranian Japanese Nila Minai; Iranians Reza Baraheni, Ramesh Sepehrrad, Soona Samsami, and Benafsheh Zand-Bonazzi. I have socialized with the wives of U.N. diplomats from all over the Muslim world. I have scattered precious anecdotes about these experiences throughout this work.

But leaving academics and activists aside, what do Arab, Muslim, and Middle Eastern women have to say about the lives of girls and women under Islam?

Brigitte Gabriel is someone whose views will not be found in the Sabbagh or Abu-Lughod anthologies that I discussed in chapter five. Gabriel is a Lebanese Maronite Christian. This means that Gabriel is a descendant of the original Phoenicians who lived there long before any Arabs or Muslims invaded and occupied the region. She has dark, glossy hair, large, beautiful, almost Oriental eyes, olive skin, a ready laugh, a warm heart, and is always fashionably dressed. She is a very passionate and dramatic speaker.

Gabriel now lives in Virginia and, with her husband, Charles Tudor, runs a successful TV production company. Gabriel prepared a video for me about her life, which I have posted on my website and which you may view. Gabriel's childhood was utterly destroyed by Palestinian terrorists. She and her parents were rescued, quite literally, by Israeli soldiers and by Israeli physicians.

Gabriel confirms that most Arab and Muslim women strongly support the very culture that demeans them. Like women everywhere, they, too, have internalized patriarchal, misogynistic cultural and religious values. She says:

> Even if they are doctors and lawyers, so many Muslim women actually support an anti-woman Islam with such passion, and think we [westerners or Christians] are the ones who have it wrong. Fascinating! This is typical of so many Middle Eastern women. The biggest challenge is the brainwashed Arab and Muslim woman. Most don't have a problem with the status quo and think *we* are all sluts and that we need to be more like them to be respected. It's really sad. Women are the ones who actually support and enforce brutal anti-woman treatment and traditions. It's like the mothers who insist on their daughter's circumcision much more than the fathers.

Jean Sasson's anonymous Saudi "princess Sultana," whose story she tells in *Princess: A True Story of Life Behind the Veil in Saudi Arabia,* learns that her older sisters have all been genitally mutilated. She then has a nightmare in which she is pursued by "old women in black, razors in hand, screeching for my blood." Sultana awaken and realizes that Saudi women themselves are "a major obstacle to change." Tragically, uneducated older women were "unwittingly strengthening the men in their efforts to keep us in ignorance and seclusion."

Carmen Bin Laden found herself increasingly "frustrated, as a woman, to be surrounded by women who simply did not have the courage to resist the system." However, she saw how such women "threw all their courage" into religion. They were not submissive when it came to enforcing Islam. Bin Laden writes:

> I think that was simpler for them than fighting for their rights as human beings. Piety gave them the illusion that they had power. I think they believed that if they were strictly religious, then the men—like the other women—would respect that. It seemed to work. Religious women did get much more respect than the Westernized (women).

While in England, Merry Merrell told me that she kept inviting Muslim women to join her feminist discussions in order to "hopefully find common ground. We failed. We did not understand their inability to separate the self from the community; they did not understand the concept of individual rights." Given the ways in which so many women internalize sexism and "passively accept and justify their own mistreatment and the abuse of other women," Merrell fears that she may have "lost compassion for women who do not at least try to help themselves." However, "for the ones who try," she is "prepared to do everything."

According to a survey done in Egypt, seven out of ten women believe that female genital mutilation is justified. However, to be fair, studies done in India and in England both reveal that 50 percent of the Indian women and 33 percent of the English women surveyed believe that wife-beating is justified or acceptable. I reported this in *Woman's Inhumanity to Woman,* along with other similar examples of women's sexism and cruelty toward other women. Women routinely police girls and women into line; under Islam, such policing is heightened.

For example, in *Journey from the Land of No,* a beautifully written memoir of her life as a girl and a Jew in Khomeini's Iran, Roya Hakakian describes the indescribable "Mrs. Moghadam," the newly installed head of the Jewish girls' high school. Mrs. Moghadam tyrannizes, terrifies, and shames the Jewish girls. She asks them why Jewish fathers "deflower" their daughters and tries to convert them to Islam. However, her true passion is more Talibanesque. She informs the innocent girls that, although they do not know it, they are "diabolical," "abominable," "loathsome," "lethal," capable of "drowning everything in eternal darkness," capable of bringing the "apocalypse" by showing a single strand of hair. To Hakakian's credit, she presents a rather dangerous turn of events as a dark comedy.

Nonie Darwish agrees with such sentiments and portrayals. When Darwish left the Middle East nearly a quarter of a century ago, middle- and upper-class women in the "moderate" Arab countries all wore "modest, Western clothes." When she recently visited the Middle East, she was in for a surprise. In "The Veil: Female Form of Jihad," she writes:

> I was shocked to see almost all ordinary Moslem women covered from head to toe by their own choice, even some young girls. A large number of women chose to cover even the face. That was what one of my cousins did. She is of all things a practicing physician! She chose on her own, to wear a "Burka," her eyes covered with eye-glasses and hands with gloves in August in Egypt, when the temperatures exceed 100 degrees F.

Darwish suggests that "veiled women" in western settings might be making their own "jihadic" statements. They, too, are masked, like Ku Klux Klan members or like terrorists. Many tend to proselytize and harass other unveiled Muslim women. What other cultural dynamics might account for this kind of aggressive self-policing?

According to my interviewee, Brigitte Gabriel:

In Middle Eastern Arab culture, girls are doomed from birth. When a woman gives birth to a child, if it's a boy, the doctor will congratulate her. If it's a girl they will just hand her the piece of meat and say nothing. Thus the tragedy begins. My cousin, who lived in my town in Lebanon, was pressured by her husband into having many children. He wanted sons, she kept giving birth to daughters. When the sixth girl was born, her husband took his rifle and started shooting at God, at the sky, and cursing God. Everyone in the household was crying. He refused to talk or see his wife for a few days because it was also her fault. And we were Christians. Just imagine a Muslim Arab's reaction.

Jean Sassoon's Sultana describes how her brother was "treated like a god" and how he, in turn, persecuted and humiliated his sisters. She writes:

In a family of ten daughters and one son, fear ruled our home: fear that cruel death would claim the one living male child; fear that no other sons would follow; fear that God had cursed our home with daughters. My mother feared each pregnancy, praying for a son, dreading a daughter. . . . My mother's worst fear came true when my father took another, younger wife for the purpose of giving him more precious sons. . . . I pretended to revere my brother, but I hated him as only the oppressed can hate.

Thus, Arab and Muslim girls are not preferred, welcomed, valued, or loved in the same way that boys are. (Traditionally, this has been true in the West and is still true in Asia today.) In addition, Arab and Muslim girls are verbally abused and psychologically humiliated from a very young age—some might say "for their own good"; a humbled child is less likely to rebel, and a shamed passivity might save her life. According to Gabriel, in the Arab world, "A girl is less hugged, less kissed; less talked to, less interacted with, less played with, and less paid attention to in general. She's ignored when she's around visiting company because everyone is going googoo-gaga over the boy and she is treated like [she's] non-existent."

Thus, she is less "mothered" than her brother who, in turn, may be overly and invasively (s)mothered—but by a woman with profoundly low self-esteem and an endemic paranoia about offending or dishonoring her family.

Azar Nafisi, in her compelling and beloved memoir *Reading Lolita in Tehran*, poignantly describes the plight of her Iranian female students who have all been trained only to "memorize" and who have been persuaded "that their opinions counted for nothing." She writes: "Most of these girls have never had anyone praise them for anything. They have never been told that they are any good or that they should think independently."

Let me again stress that despite such culturally mandated abuse and deprivation, Arab and Muslim women remain miraculously kind, generous, and heroic. However, their self-esteem must still be grievously wounded. Also, they have not been taught to think of themselves as individuals first and daughters, wives, and mothers, second. This is actually a point of pride, and provides them with the only identity and safety that is possible in their culture.

Also, a Muslim and Arab woman is trained to obey a series of male dictators: the prince or king, the president, her father, her husband, her son, and her brothers. Everyone (not just women) is closely watched and judged. Conformity is exacted through shaming and punishment techniques. According to Nonie Darwish, in "Escaping Submission":

> In Islamic culture, personal freedom is not an esteemed value . . . and one is accountable to everybody for one's behavior; how you pray, how you dress, what you eat, who you befriend, in short, every minute detail of your life. Many Moslems assign to themselves the role of God in enforcing Islamic law. . . . Profound shaming is often used for people with differing views. Moslems as a group are very critical of each other. . . . As a Moslem, I found myself accountable not only to God, but to every other Moslem around me.

One might argue that all girls and women—not just in the Islamic world—go through a similar kind of indoctrination. Mentally ill and criminal parents the world over mistreat their children. Incest and child abuse exist in the West, too—*but they are not culturally sanctioned.* On the contrary, in the West, such abuse is increasingly being prosecuted and at least being viewed as negative. In the Arab Middle East and in Islamic countries, the mistreatment of girls is culturally mandated, as is the taboo against reporting and condemning it.

Gabriel pinpoints an important East-West difference. In the Arab Middle East, "girls are beaten." "Little boys grow up allowed to beat their sisters because they watch their father either beating their mothers or controlling them through intimidation and they learn by example. Boys grow up hearing their fathers tell their mothers to shut up or he will break her neck. He tells her that he will beat her if she continues talking. Boys are told to watch after the females in the family and are put in charge of their mothers and sisters even if the boy is very young. He has the authority to beat, yank, pull, boss, or do whatever he sees fit to punish any behavior that he doesn't think his father would agree with."

Thus, domestic terrorism of an extreme sort is typical. According to Merry Merrell: "Had I been raised in Syria, I would have been executed around the age of ten. At the age of seven, on being traumatized by my father's brutal treatment of my mother, I confided to my grandmother that my father was beating my mother regularly. She said nothing. But, the next day my grandfather took me into an empty room and asked me: 'What did your father do to your mother?' I said, 'He beat her.'

"I was a tiny scrawny kid afraid for my mother and trying desperately to protect her. My grandfather was a mountain. He flung his full fist at my head and punched me with such ferocity that I flew off the chair. I was in shock. My grandmother was on the other side of the door, listening. I got up and asked my grandfather, 'Why did you do that?!' He shouted, 'Don't you ever say that about your mother again!' Not then understanding how my effort to protect my mother could have been construed as a slight against her, I told my grandfather, 'If you don't want the truth, Don't ask me!' I never forgave him."

In addition, child marriages and forced marriage, male-initiated divorce, and automatic male custody of children also characterize Arab and Muslim culture. My interviewee, Sultana Wakili, is from Afghanistan. She is possibly ten years younger than I am. Her father was the village religious leader. He did not allow her to go to school past the third grade because she was not learning anything and the teachers were complaining about her. To stop the embarrassment to the family, he pulled her out of school. Sultana says: "Of course, my brothers went to school, and so did my younger sister who was born ten years after me. By that time most people let their daughters attend school. I stayed home with my mom cooking and cleaning, helping around the house. When I was thirteen years old, I got married to my aunt's nephew. Was I happy? I don't know. I was just a child. One day I was living in my parent's home and then I was married off to live with another family in Kabul. That's just the way it was."

Sultana took some sewing classes in Kabul and gave birth to her first daughter when she herself was only sixteen. After giving birth to her third daughter, when she was nineteen, her husband divorced her and did not allow her to see her two eldest daughters ever again.

"The plainest explanation is my husband wanted someone who was more sophisticated. He had finished university and was working for the Peace Corps and later UNICEF. He traded me in for a newer model. We had a home divorce because my father didn't want my name to be dragged through civil court and my name ruined forever. After the divorce, I worked as a seamstress. As a tailor, I did well. As a mother, my heart was broken being separated from my children."

Let me note that Sultana's husband is educated, sophisticated in western ways—indeed, a citizen of the world; it does not change his view of women at all. (This is what I discovered in my own Afghan sojourn and what Asne Seierstad, author of the popular *The Bookseller of Kabul,* also discovered.)

According to Brigitte Gabriel, girls learn at a young age that their "father will decide whom they will marry. There will be no negotiations and the alternative is beating." Girls are forced emotionally to marry by being told that they are "worth nothing without a man to cover their shame" (the shame that they are born girls). Gabriel says:

"In the Middle East, as a girl grows into a young lady and she starts offering the coffee to visitors in preparation for her being on the marriage market, the way she is thanked when someone takes the coffee cup is by telling her 'May God cover your shame with a groom.') That's the ultimate of her existence.

Being married and bearing children. There is no place for them to run to if they want to escape marrying someone they despise or hate. It's like a death sentence except you are alive to feel the pain for the rest of your life."

Certainly domestic violence exists everywhere, including in America. Until recently, people in America did not discuss it, and tended to blame and shun the beaten woman and to side with the batterer. However, due to selfless and pioneering Second Wave feminist work, this has begun to change in the West. This has not yet happened in the Arab Middle East and in the Muslim world. Perhaps it can, under the right conditions.

But, for now, wife-beating there is routine, predictable, normalized—and functions as a form of permanent domestic terrorism. I interviewed an ex-Palestinian terrorist who converted to Christianity. His pseudonym is Walid Shoebat. His mother is an American-born Christian who was forced to convert to Islam. Shoebat's grandfather was the muktar, village religious leader, of his West Bank village. Fifteen people lived crammed together into two rooms, although they also had a huge balcony and courtyard. He says: "Once my mother upended a backgammon board in front of my father's friends. My father immediately took a hammer and cracked her skull. I was her youngest child. I took her hand and walked with her to the nearest church where the nuns sewed up her head. There were no hospitals. My mother kept trying to escape. Whenever she got away, and she would always take her children with her, all the Shoebat men would find her, re-kidnap her, and punish her for running away."

According to Brigitte Gabriel, once a woman is married, she is the "property of the male. Her parents won't even stand by her to support her if she wants to leave the marriage because of sexual or physical abuse. A woman is beaten until she can't breathe or talk anymore. She can't tell anyone because that will be airing the family's dirty laundry in public and she will be condemned for that by more beating by the husband because she made him look bad in public."

Thus, women learn to keep their mouths shut and to "just take it." They learn to give great excuses for their scars and bruises. Gabriel says that women are routinely "raped without any regard to their physical situation. Men force sex on their wives even a few days after a C-section, sometimes tearing her stitches out without any regard. A woman is to be beaten by her brother, her father, her son, and any male relative for whatever they feel she should be punished for without any punishment for the male beater from the family members."

Such violence and prejudice is considered normal. It is not discussed.

At first, I could not understand how Arab and Muslim terrorists could so brazenly use women and children as human shields, as they did in 2002 in the battle for Fallujah, in Iraq; or how they could shoot, at point-blank range, and kill a

Jewish woman who was eight months' pregnant together with her four young daughters in Gaza. Did they hate women and children this much? Or was this culturally normative behavior? What kind of culture produces suicide killers and human bombs, glorifies mass murderers, and mandates and revenge honor-killings

According to Ellen Harris, the author of *Guarding the Secrets: Palestinian Terrorism and a Father's Murder of His Too-American Daughter,* "With or without the [1987] Intifada, the incidence of battered wives, abused children, and incest is believed to be higher in the West Bank than in the United States. Too often, families muzzle their daughters rather than dishonor their male relatives. A female's private suffering is less important than the public disgrace of her entire clan."

Harris describes a number of cases of Palestinian honor killings. For example, in 1988, a woman in a village just north of Beitin (in the West Bank, near Ramallah) was hanged in a crime of honor. All the women in town were rounded up and brought to see it. The whole town was in on it.

In 1994, a "jealous guardian of his family honor" decapitated his twenty-two-year-old pregnant sister and "paraded her head around the West Bank village of Anabta [near Nablus]." Her crime? She had been the subject of a "rumour" that accused her of having had an "extramarital affair." It did not matter whether the rumor was true or not; the allegation itself constituted a capital crime.

Finally, Harris describes the fate of a Palestinian teenager from America who went back to the "homeland, to a village near Beitin. She went jogging around the mosque in shorts and sleeveless tank tops. When she wore skirts, they were high above the knee. The old men of the village warned her three times. Three times she ignored them. Then one day she was found barely alive, her legs torn from being whipped with a hose which was still wrapped around them. To this day, no one knows who beat her; their faces were covered with checkered scarves."

According to the groundbreaking work of my colleague, Minnesota-based Arabist and psycho-analyst Dr. Nancy Kobrin, whom I have interviewed and whose work I have read, Arab culture is one in which shame and honor play decisive roles and in which the utter debasement of women is paramount. The family honor resides in its women—who, paradoxically, are already seen as inferior, contaminated, and dangerous. Human sacrifices are necessary on a regular basis to purge the group's sense of permanent shame.

In an utterly fascinating and as-yet unpublished book, which I plan to introduce, *The Sheik's New Clothes: The Psycho-analytic Roots of Islamic Suicide Terrorism,* Kobrin and her Israeli co-author, counter-terrorism expert Yoram Schweitzer, describe Arab and Muslim family and clan dynamics in which some children, both boys and girls, are orally and anally raped by male relatives; boys between the ages of seven and twelve are publicly and traumatically circumcised;

some girls are clitoridectomized; and women are seen as the source of all dishonor and treated accordingly—very, very badly.

According to Dr. Kobrin, "The little girl lives her life under a communal death threat—the honor killing." Both male and female infants and children are brought up by mothers (who are debased and traumatized women). As such, all children are forever psychologically "contaminated" by the humiliated yet all-powerful mother. Arab and Muslim boys must disassociate themselves from her in spectacularly savage ways. But, on a deep unconscious level, they may also wish to remain merged with the source of contamination—a conflict that suicide bombers may both act out and resolve when they kill but also merge their blood eternally with that of their presumably most hated enemies, the Israeli Jews.

In Kobrin's view, the Israeli Jews may actually function as substitutes or scapegoats for an even more primal hated/loved enemy: woman. Also, in Kobrin's view, widespread child sexual abuse may lead to paranoid and revenge-seeking adults.

Arno Schmitt, in his Preface to the anthology *Sexuality and Eroticism Among Males in Moslem Societies,* suggests that a Muslim boy's "often abrupt rupture" with the female domestic sphere coupled with his need to both "stand his ground (but at the same time to bow in front of his father and other men in positions of power and respect)," leads to a "precarious male identity." In Schmitt's opinion, this kind of uncertainty is often hidden under "macho behavior." From a psychoanalytic point of view, the male desire to be penetrated and the desire to be taken care of become transformed, unconsciously, into the "wish to sodomize and to appear invulnerable. The grown man remains a non-man in relation to his father."

Based on my own experience in Afghanistan (a non-Arab Muslim culture), a polygamous, patriarchal culture also leads to an infernal, fraternal competition for paternal favor and inheritance. It is brother against brother, full brothers against half-brothers, full and half-brothers against first cousins. Thus, entire families and clans can remain locked in revenge-fueled mortal combat for generations.

Carmen Bin Laden also describes the kind of fraternal bonding and rivalry that I witnessed long ago in Afghanistan. She writes that her husband, Yeslam, had a "strange relationship with his brothers. On the one hand, they were his only companions—he had no male friends to speak of. . . . So Yeslam did trust his brothers more than most people in the West trust their family. But with me, he could confide his frustrations with his clan—his brothers' petty squabbles, and their many hidden power struggles."

Clearly, only the evolution of democracy and the elevation of women can begin to change such dynamics. Western feminists, American leaders: Please note.

Homosexuality, including homosexual pederasty, is apparently as widely prevalent in Islamic societies as it was in ancient Greece. What is taboo, is admitting it.

Walid Shoebat confirmed the sexual abuse of both boys and girls in Palestinian Muslim society. "It is a strange society. Homosexuality is forbidden but if you're the penetrator, not the penetrated, it's okay. If you're a teenage boy with no hair on your legs other boys your age will pinch your butt and tease you. Once, I saw a class of clothed teenage boys sexualize their gymnastics exercises. And once, on a hiking trip, I saw a line of shepherd boys waiting for their turn to sodomize a five-year-old boy. It was unbelievable."

Shoebat's father also told him many stories about starving Arab men who would barter sex for meat from Iraqi soldiers. According to Shoebat, teenage boys prey on younger children; older male relatives prey on pre-adolescent boys and girls. They do not have intercourse with the girls since this would render them unmarriageable and bring shame upon their families.

According to a Human Rights Watch Report on Afghanistan which is cited in Amnesty International's Report on Afghanistan, warlords have been known to "routinely sexually molest young boys and to film the orgies."[1]

According to Arno Schmitt and Jehoeda Sofer in their anthology *Sexuality and Eroticism Among Males in Moslem Societies,* sex between men and boys and between men and men is quite widespread in Muslim societies in North Africa and South Asia. However, the western concept of "homosexual" or "gay" with all it's stigmatized and political implications does not exist among Muslims. Many married fathers have sex with boys and with other men. They do not think of themselves as "homosexuals." Homosexuality, especially the act of being penetrated, is forbidden and scorned in Muslim society. As Schmitt puts it:

> A man should not allow others to bugger him. Otherwise, he loses his name, his honor . . . his decisive line is not between the act kept secret and the act known by many, but only talking behind one's back and saying it in your presence, between rumours and public knowledge. . . . As long as nobody draws public attention to something everybody knows, one ignores what might disrupt important social relations.

According to Carmen Bin Laden:

> Homosexuality is forbidden in Saudi Arabia—punished by public flogging. But many men have homosexual relationships, especially when they're young, before they're married. If two men hold hands on the street, as they often do, it's not seen as sexual. . . . The habit of teenage homosexuality doesn't always go away as men age.

I have interviewed a number of American gay men who, in their youth, went in search of sexual adventures in Muslim North Africa (Morocco and Algeria).

One man reports having been gang raped by Muslim men—as a matter of course. He said that, at the time, he had not allowed himself to name what had happened to him as "rape." He did not view himself as a victim and thought that he "got what he came for." In retrospect, he changed his mind. "I was terrified by what had happened, but I felt safer by remembering it as a sexual escapade, not as a dangerous experience." Another gay man told me that the homosexuality he experienced in the Islamic world (Turkey, Iran, and Morocco) was all "prison sexuality: forced, painful, humiliating."

Some Western gay men have described, both to me and in writing, their lifelong search for young boys as sexual partners in the Muslim world, especially in Turkey and Morocco. They were the older, richer men who purchased sex from male children and adolescents who needed the money and who perhaps did not consider what they were doing to be "homosexual."

The popular novel *The Kite Runner* by Khaled Hosseini depicts Afghan Muslim boys raping another young boy. Hosseini also depicts Taliban-era commanders sexually enslaving young male orphans for orgies and sex murder. As I noted before, the men whom I saw holding hands and gazing into each other's eyes in Kabul so long ago were not considered "homosexuals."

The male sexual abuse of female children also exists everywhere; it is one of the main means of traumatizing and shaming girls into obedience and rendering them less capable of resistance or rebellion when they are grown. However, the male sexual abuse of male children—denied, never admitted—may work differently and may turn some boys into angry and predatory men.

Sexual trauma in early childhood may lead to hyper-vigilant, suspicious, often "paranoid" adults. Some may see slights or danger where none exists; others may move into dangerous situations without fear—some say in order to replay the familiar scenario one more time, but now with a hopefully different outcome. Clinical data also suggest that sex offenders in general have been physically, psychologically, or sexually abused in childhood.

Based on Nancy Kobrin's work in this area, in the Arab and Muslim world, the perceived slights, suspiciousness, "paranoia," insults to one's honor or manhood may be more excessive not only due to possible childhood trauma but also because such adult behaviors are culturally sanctioned.

From a psychological point of view, Arab Muslim women might be even less likely than their male counterparts to disconnect from the "group-ego" and to fight for an individual identity or for individual rights. If so, we must factor this into any plan to further gender equality.

Arab and Muslim boys may also be traumatized, both homosexually and psychologically, but their pride has been grossly exaggerated by close ties with a low-status, "wounded" mother and by rivalry with an all-powerful, often sadistic father. As mentioned, first-born sons never leave home. They remain at home or live nearby and grow old together with everyone whom they have ever known, including their childhood abusers. Perpetual blood revenge, even human sacrifice, might be required to "contain" such a non-resolvable set of cultural irritations and hatreds.

Most westerners do not understand honor killing or blood feuds. It *is* foreign to us. Dorchen Leidholdt, who directs legal services for battered women in New York City, told me a typical—and therefore quite extraordinary—story about her work on behalf of battered Muslim women. The batterer (and his brothers and father) not only tried to find the woman who dared run away in order to kill her; they also tried to kill her entire family back in the old country—all of whom were seen as hostages.

If one hasn't lived through something like this, it is hard to believe. Leidholdt actually worked the situation out so that no one died—no small achievement. She had some help from a local mullah and from a religious Muslim male lawyer. However, according to Leidholdt, "Both the victim and her daughter had to move into a confidential location and live in terror that their abuser and his family—as well as their own family members whom he had turned against them—would discover their location, kill their mother and abduct her daughter. Adding to the victim's distress and fear, her abuser's family continues to harass and persecute (the victim's) family members back in their home country with the help of local law enforcement authorities whom have been bought off."

I recently wrote the introduction to a very interesting volume entitled *Understanding Gender and Culture in the Helping Process: Practitioner's Narratives from Global Perspectives.* It is edited by Claire Low Rabin of Israel's Ben Gurion University. Alean Al-Krenawi and John R. Graham co-authored a chapter called: "Mental Health Practice for the Muslim Arab Population in Israel." In it, they propose the use of traditional tribal elders as mediators in a somewhat tragic-comic tale. A husband and wife had a dispute over the husband's overbearing mother. The husband sent his wife back to her father but kept their five children.

"Theirs had been an exchange marriage: where two men are married to each other's sisters. The same day that the wife's brother learned of his sister's plight, he retained sole custody of his children and sent his own wife (the first husband's sister) home to her parents. . . . Tensions rose within the two extended families."

Within twenty days, two other husbands repeated the same scenario. By now, four sets of children had been separated from their mothers, and one mother had consulted a non-Muslim, non-Arab physician who had referred her to a social worker. Luckily, the social worker was an Israeli Bedouin Arab who came from a similar-status family.

When he advised the men that, under Israeli law, they would have to return the children to their mothers, all the men visited the social worker's *family* to explain that further involvement from the social worker would create a dispute between their extended family and that of the social worker. They suggested that the social worker quit his job.

The social worker turned to four *wasits* (tribal elders) to find a solution. Together, they developed three goals: (1) to have the children all returned to their mothers; (2) to have the four women return to their husbands; (3) to "restore relations between the two families."

The wasits met with each family and listened to everyone. "Within two days of initial contact [the wasits] had personally delivered the children to their respective mothers." Whether this kind of benevolent mediation would also work in the case of an honor killing is quite doubtful. But it did work in the case of a dispute between a daughter-in-law and her mother-in-law.

Westerners must understand that Arab and Muslim families are very interconnected—first and second cousins marry, sisters are exchanged in marriage, entire villages are related by blood and by marriage. Arab and Muslim cultures are also shame-, honor-, and vengeance-based. If a woman or, for that matter, a man, breaks with this code, she or he will need nothing less than a witness protection program to remain alive. It is imperative that westerners understand this mentality if we really want to introduce concepts such as freedom and democracy into the region.

I want to close this chapter with two stories. Both are true tales; both illustrate very negative Arab and Muslim cultural patterns; both stories are also tales of redeeming heroism. Walid Shoebat, whom I've previously quoted, told me the first story.

One of Shoebat's paternal uncles, "Najib," was supposedly having an affair with "Yusuf's" wife. Yusuf was the chief of police. His revenge consisted of throwing live grenades at the Shoebat family home. Yusuf wanted to kill all fifteen family members who lived there. "My father and his immediate family all had to die because of what his brother did."

Shoebat asked me how I would resolve this feud unto death. "Imagine you are going up against the chief of police. What would you do?" I failed to come up with the ingenious plan that Najib crafted—a plan that also sheds light, in part, upon the nature of the Arab and Islamist war against the Jews and against America.

Najib persuaded the village that they had to attack, pogrom-style, a nearby Jewish community (Ramat Rachel). Once the Israelis opened fire in self-defense, most of the Arabs fled. However, the Arab attack on the Jews provided cover for what Najib had to do: He himself shot Yusuf in the back. When the Israelis, as they always did, allowed the Arabs to safely retrieve their dead, Najib proclaimed Yusuf a shahid, martyr, and buried him in his bloody clothing. This is a mark of honor.

This characterizes an Arab way of thinking. From here, it is easy to create the kinds of doctored footage and photo-opportunity journalism that dominated the 2000 intifada against the Jews. It is also a way of thinking that the liberal western media does not truly comprehend.

Yusuf's martyrdom was not enough, however; the "honor" of his family had not yet been redeemed. Another man from Yusuf's family attacked another one of Shoebat's uncles, who, in self-defense, "ripped his stomach open like a sheep." The man did not die. Shoebat's uncle, "Samir," immediately went into hiding. By this time, Shoebat was living in America and had converted to Christianity. His paternal uncles called him and asked that he pay the blood money. Shoebat did so but not until each of his uncles ("nice uncles," he says sarcastically) publicly "abandoned" Samir. "He is not my brother, I denounce and abandon him."

Only in this way was Shoebat finally able to rescue his mother. He paid the blood money and brought his long-suffering mother, her abuser, his father, and his paternal uncle to America.

Recently Shoebat's brother, a man they had previously socialized with, called Shoebat's wife. "Tell your husband that we know what he is doing against Islam. Tell him we know where he lives. Bye-bye."

"I told my wife, welcome to the Middle East, where your beloved one day can become your executioner the next day."

Shoebat is, miraculously, engaged in redefining loyalty. He has taken his mother's side and, in so doing, has broken with the shame, honor, and secrecy codes of his father's culture.

And now for another heroine. She is my friend, and her real name is Shekaiba Wakili. She was born in Kabul, Afghanistan, and grew up there in the early 1970s. She is a schoolteacher, a photographer, a wife, and a mother. Shekaiba is quite beautiful. She exudes a quiet air of seriousness, strength, and independence. In an interview, she said: "My father's family arranged a marriage for him when he was a young man. My mother is dyslexic. She walks with a limp because she fell two stories when she was six or seven. She was seen as 'damaged goods.' My father comes from an educated family. He was a graduate of Kabul University. We did not have a lot of money. My father never forgave his family for this arranged marriage with the 'damaged goods.' When I was three years old and my mother was six months' pregnant with my younger sister, my father divorced her.

"My father got custody of my older sister and me. My younger sister, who was a baby, went with my mother. Islamic law says that in any type of divorce, the wife should get two thirds of the husband's wealth. But in most 'Islamic' countries, including Afghanistan, laws are tipped in favor of the man and interpreted by the village mullahs who may not necessarily be scholars of Islamic law. You would think that a mother would have the right to see her children! All my mother got was a piece of paper saying you're divorced.

"I never had a mother. I was not allowed to see her. Sometimes my maternal grandmother used to barge into our house to see us. I hid from her. I believed that she was there to kidnap me.

"Within a year or two of his divorce, my father remarried a woman—a relative—from a prominent family. She was nonchalant about me. I was really raised by my paternal grandmother. My father started working for UNICEF in 1965. He still worked for UNICEF in 1975. When the Russians invaded, he and his wife, my stepmother, applied for visas for us all. I could not understand why. What self-interest was being served? I was ten years old at the time. My father's wife was used to a house filled with servants. As an exile in America, she would not have that. I became her servant. I did the childcare and the shopping and the cleaning and the cooking. Now I understood why they applied for a visa for me, too.

"My father was liberal when he came here but I guess America brought out the patriarchal Afghan in him. I couldn't date. I couldn't wear skirts or makeup. Couldn't go out on my own.

"They wanted to find a boy for me to get married to and I didn't want that. In my second year of college, I couldn't take the cultural conflict anymore. I announced that I was moving out. My father said, 'If you move out, then I'm going to disown you.' He disowned me. I haven't spoken to him since 1991.

"Now, he got out, but he didn't care if my mother and sister got out or not. He refused to send for them. He would not get visas for them. He knew they were living under the Taliban.

"I could not bear this. I held down three or four jobs while I went to graduate school. I began to send money home to my mother every month. Eventually I sponsored my mother. My father had listed no one as my 'mother.' My mother and I had to take DNA tests to prove our connection. My mother is here now. She is a shattered woman, but she is alive. I have put her up in an apartment nearby.

"I'm Tajik and the Tajiks are Persian, and before Islam we were part of the Zoroastrian culture, which is from the north where the poet Rumi is from. I love Rumi's poetry and feel very connected to that whole mystical tradition. But now I approach life as a Muslim. I will always be a Muslim. I will die a Muslim. My kids are going to be a quarter Jewish, a quarter Christian, and half Muslim. When they come to me, 'Oh, Mommy, somebody said Islam is a violent religion,' I've got to be able to fully explain Islam to them, because I don't want my children to learn Islam from somebody else."

And so Shekaiba, who was never mothered, found a way to heroically rescue her own mother.

Stories such as hers are more routine than one might think. Perhaps even more shocking is the reality of what Muslim women face in the West. In the next chapter I show the threat that Islamic gender apartheid poses in Europe and North America.

Seven

Islamic Gender Apartheid in the West

For centuries, both Europe and North America have functioned as beacons of hope for non-western immigrants in search of freedom and economic and educational advancement. From its inception, America has been a country of immigrants. Creating a way for culturally, ethnically, and racially diverse groups to become Americans, while preserving their separate identities is the story of America's unique genius.

Europe's history is very different. It has been composed of white Christians, both Catholics and Protestants, who have engaged in religious and nationalistic wars, periodically persecuted and exiled Europe's Jewish population, and once colonized and influenced the immediate known world, including North and South America, the Middle East, Africa, India, Asia, and Oceania (Australia and New Zealand).

Over the last forty years, Europe has welcomed a huge number of formerly colonized immigrants from Asia, the Middle East, and North Africa, many of whom are Muslims. Europe did not prepare for (or against) its own Islamization, perhaps due to a cultural sense of superiority and paradoxically its guilt over colonial-era racism. The assumption was, if any, that immigrants would want to assimilate to the European way of life. However, Muslim minorities were not really welcome in certain countries (France and England, for example), and were overly welcome in other countries (Holland, for example). Welcome or not, Muslim immigrants did not always speak a European language, were only able to do the low-paid "dirty" work, were therefore forced to live in substandard low-income housing, etc. Even if their economic and political circumstances were better in Europe than in their countries of origin, some immigrants nevertheless became resentful and bitter because in comparison to native Europeans, they were at the bottom, and as such, felt permanently humiliated. When Muslim youth committed crimes and were sent to jail, they were invariably recruited by jailed Islamists into jihadic or reactionary ways of thinking. Finally, whether for racist or multiculturally tolerant reasons, European countries did not prepare any integration-oriented educational outreach specific to Muslim immigrants. Culture clash was inevitable.

The scholar Bat Ye'or, in her important book, *Eurabia: The Euro-Arab Axis, Land of Dhimmitide, Land of Islam,* describes the pro-Arab policies that President Charles de Gaulle set into motion in 1973—treaties, conventions, laws, and a meeting of minds, whose results can no longer be easily halted. European nations adopted a pro-Arab policy because they wanted privileged access to Muslim markets and a steady flow of oil in order to achieve world preeminence. In return for this, Europe promised unlimited immigration rights to Muslims— many of whom did not truly wish to assimilate to European ways. Muslims were also allowed to hold dual citizenship. France began arming Arab dictatorships, including Iraq's Saddam Hussein and Libya's Muammar Khadafi, and stopped selling arms to Israel. According to Bat Ye'or: "In December 1969, France sold 110 Mirage jets to Libya's new dictator, Muammer al-Qaddafi [*sic*]. Beginning in the early 1970s, it became a major supplier of arms to many Arab states, while maintaining the strict boycott of Israel imposed soon after the Six-Day War. Against this backdrop, France—having developed a network of friendly relations throughout the Arab world—began to explore with Libya the concept of a Euro-Arab Dialogue (EAD)."

Simultaneously, the Arab nations engaged in "bellicose threats" against Israel and against any country in the world that dared support Israel, as they "quadrupled the oil price and cut back oil production by 5% a month" until Israel withdrew from territories it gained in 1967. According to Bat Ye'or: "'We will do like Samson, we will destroy the temple with all its occupants, including ourselves,' said Qaddafi. Saudi Arabia's King Faisal declared, 'There will not be any softening or compromise except if our demands are met without conditions . . . in no circumstances would we abandon Arab Jerusalem.' Sheik Ahmed Zaki Yamani, the Saudi oil minister, threatened that the oil producing countries could 'reduce production by 80%. How could you survive with that?'"

After the first Arab oil embargo in 1973, the European Economic Community began issuing strong pro-Palestinian and anti-Zionist statements. It also embarked on the Euro-Arab Dialogue and the Parliamentary Association for Euro-Arab Cooperation, which gladly recognized the rights of the PLO as the way in which Europe would be guaranteed "huge markets" in the Arab world.

Pro-Arab, pro-Palestinian, anti-American, and anti-Israel policies have continued to define the European Union (EU) and European Commission and to govern much of international and domestic policy for its member countries.[1] For example, despite mounting terrorist realities, Europe can no longer stop Muslim and Southeast Asian immigration. Thus, for example, the individual governments of Britain, Holland, and Germany cannot legislate against the open influx of Middle Eastern, North African, and Southeast Asian immigrants.

According to Bat Ye'or, Europe's appeasement of Islam represents a "dhimmi" psychology. "Dhimmi" refers to a person, traditionally one of the "people of the book"—that is, not only Christians and Jews but also Zoroastrians, Buddhists, Hindus, and so on. A dhimmi group is any conquered people with a religious book who require "protection" in and from an Islamic society. Historically, dhimmis were required to pay an annual head or poll tax, which was accompanied by a humiliating ceremony in which the dhimmi might receive a slap or a spit in the face. The dhimmi was required to wear identifying clothing; to step into the street to let a Muslim pass; to ride donkeys since horses were forbidden to everyone except Muslims; to dismount in the presence of a Muslim; and so on. Innumerable degradations were imposed on the dhimmi populations in Muslim lands, key among them being the extortionate annual tax, which played the dual role of enriching the Islamic state and encouraging non-Muslims to convert. In addition, Jews were required to wear yellow identifying insignia—a humiliation that was later copied by Christian European societies.

Dhimmi behavior is a way of appeasing or of avoiding, at all costs, offending Muslims or Islam, so as to avoid the usually harsh punishments that ensued whenever one insulted a Muslim or the Islamic faith. Today this kind of behavior is increasingly seen in western universities, governments, and the media, whenever people avoid "offending" Muslims, even if to do so requires that they sidestep the facts or the truth of a case.[2]

The doctrine of multiculturalism renders all criticism of such appeasement as politically incorrect and "racist."[3]

Exact immigration and population figures are impossible to find. In Bat Ye'or's opinion, this is no accident. Various estimates suggest that anywhere from 14 to 30 million Muslim immigrants may be living in Europe. In a private communication, Bat Ye'or said it was impossible to truly know how many Muslims are living in Europe today. When I pressed her for her best "guesstimate," she reluctantly said that "20 million Muslims may be living in Europe." Yet, according to her, given the pattern of clandestine immigration throughout Europe, the actual number is undoubtedly much higher. George Melloan, writing in 2005 in the *Wall Street Journal,* set the figure at "over 30 million." According to the *Washington Post,* "there are 15 million Muslims living in western Europe. Their birth rate is three times that of non-Muslims. While the Muslim population could double by 2015, the non-Muslim population is expected to shrink by 3.5 percent." According to a UPI report, "The most popular name for baby boys in Brussels is Mohammed. Studies estimate that Muslims will form the majority in the Netherlands' four largest cities by 2020 and France's Muslim population has now topped the 10 percent mark."[4]

In England, the city of Birmingham alone has seventy mosques. Many British mosque members say that they would prefer to live under Islamic religious (or

Shari'a) law—which prescribes amputation for theft and beheading and stoning to death for alleged adultery, prostitution, and conversion to any other religion. While many individual British Muslims may indeed be peaceful, some "declare open support for Osama bin Laden."[5]

Today, in Europe, advocates of an intolerant Islamic tradition fully expect and demand a western-style tolerance toward their intolerant ways and are quick to charge "discrimination" when it is not forthcoming. According to author and *New York Sun* columnist Mark Steyn, "when free speech, artistic expression, feminism, and other totems of western pluralism clash directly with the Islamic lobby, Islam more often wins."[6]

If the Muslim, Sikh, and Hindu immigrants in Europe truly wanted to become Europeans, race, class, and gender issues would remain, but there would probably be no culture and religious clashes. The modern and secular laws and customs of Europe are often rejected in favor of separate religious customs that are not only religious but are also political, educational, familial, and personal. When Islamic gender apartheid practices are challenged or prosecuted, many European Muslims say they are being "persecuted" by "racism."

One might expect immigrants or at least immigrant youths to assimilate to the dominant and more politically and economically advantageous culture; this has been the historical pattern in North America. However, the intense and recent Muslim immigration to Europe seems to follow another pattern. Immigrants who feel displaced and marginalized identify even more strongly with their native and religious culture as a way of maintaining group cohesion and a shared group psychological identity. According to the *Washington Post,* "a small but significant and vocal number of the European Muslim community are either outright hostile towards or at least ambivalent about western values." This might be contrasted with other groups that have assimilated very well in the United States. For example, Arab, Middle Eastern, Greek, Italian, and Irish Christians, as well as Jews (many of whom were initially viewed as "black,") have, over a period of time, been fully assimilated into American society; so have Japanese, Korean, and Chinese Christians and non-Christians.[7]

Some moderate and feminist Muslims have welcomed modern, western ideas and ways. But a visible and active minority have not and have also influenced the silent majority to cleave to Islamic customs in the West.

Women have become the most visible symbols and carriers of native culture, bearing the terrible burden of the past. For example, a Muslim man may be unemployed or in jail, but he may still retain his cultural, religious, and masculine identity if his wife and daughters remain in some version of purdah and all that goes with it. The symbol of women's obedience is the wearing of hijab, or the head scarf. At the same time, Muslim boys and men in Europe wear western dress.

Of course, women may wear the hijab for reasons of modesty and to express their respect for both God and family. They may do so, just as Catholic nuns or Orthodox Jewish women do, in order to set themselves apart from secular standards of behavior. Perhaps some women also feel that such garb might protect them from male sexual violence. Still, Muslim women bear a greater symbolic burden than their Muslim male counterparts and are more closely scrutinized, no matter what they do.

In chapter 6, a number of interviewees described the enormous increase in veiling in the Arab Middle East and in the Islamic world, even among educated, professional women. A similar veiled presence exists in Europe. According to a report on immigration to France: "There are no figures on this but one sees the veil commonly on the streets, and more and more one sees the Islamic *chador,* [rather than just the head scarf], which symbolizes the total segregation of women from society and their subjugation in the family."[8]

Fadela Amara, a French Muslim town counselor in Clermond Ferrand, heads the local chapter of Ni Putes, Ni Soumises (Neither Whores nor Submissive Doormats). She views the veil as an "instrument of oppression." Amara recently organized a march in Marseilles to advocate opening Islam to make it a "bit Gallic [more French] around the edges."[9]

According to Professor Walid Phares, "When women wear the headscarf (hijab), Islamic fundamentalists consider it a pillar of their influence. They can employ statistical power and project it as a maker or breaker of their growth." If women decrease their wearing of hijab because a secular European government like France has outlawed it, "the jihadists have no choice but to wage war."[10]

According to New School University provost and Professor of Anthropology Arjun Appadurai, "global culture flows" may be so disorienting that migrant communities, "assaulted by the desires and fantasies depicted by the mass media," may strive "to reproduce the family-as-microcosm of culture." In these circumstances, "the honor of women becomes . . . increasingly, a surrogate for the identity of embattled communities of males." Appadurai claims that this may produce violence against women, who become victims of men's sense of displaced identity."[11]

We know that domestic violence increases when men are under increased non-domestic stress. However, even more violence against women exists in the Islamic home countries where no stressful "geographical displacement" exists. Indeed, the very definition of Islamic culture may involve whether women (and religious minority or dhimmi groups) have been terrorized into a normalized subhuman status.

As we have also seen in chapter 6, girl-, sister-, and wife-beating are routine throughout the Arab Middle East and among Muslims. It is accepted, one does not talk about it; to do so is considered a disgrace and "dishonorable." Not only do immigrants arrive in Europe with such customs and values intact, they also continue to read home-town newspapers and watch Arab, satellite-based television.

What system of law and ethics should prevail when one religious or cultural code countenances behavior that constitutes a crime according to secular, western law? For example, Islam allows for polygamy (otherwise know as bigamy in the West). It also either allows for (as customary) or believes in (as a religious obligation): female genital mutilation, female hijab and veiling, arranged and child marriage, marital rape, daughter- and wife-battery, and honor murders. It forbids conversion, which is a capital crime.

Misogynist and anti-infidel preaching in the Arab and Muslim worlds has now been fully exported to Europe. For example, in 2004, France finally expelled Algerian-born imam Abdel Qader Bouziane, who had publicly endorsed wife-beating. (He was allowed to return after his deportation was ruled illegal). Also in 2004, Spain prosecuted and sentenced Sheik Muhammad Kamal Mustafa, the imam in Fuengirola, Costa del Sol, for publishing a book that explained that wife-beating conforms with Koranic law, or Shari'a. Steven Stalinsky, director of the Middle East Media Research Institute (MEMRI), found statements in support of wife-beating very common in the Muslim media—and available all over Europe via satellite television.[12]

In 2004, Europeans could hear Egyptian imam Sheikh Muhammad Al-Mussayar, a professor at Al-Azhar University, say: A wife deserves to be beaten who has "rebelled against her husband's advice, and [whom] abandoning in bed did not help." Syrian Sheikh Abd Al-Hamid Al-Muhajir asks: "What's better, that [a wife] gets slapped, or that she ruins her family, herself, and society?" and Egyptian Sheikh Sabri Abd Al-Rauf of Al-Azhar University says that wife-beatings should not draw blood. "The beatings are intended to instill fear . . . and to declare that [the husband] isn't satisfied with this wife."[13]

Female infanticide is still widely practiced in non-western cultures where son preference is epidemic. Female genital mutilation is both an African and a Muslim custom. While the female genital mutilation of girls is much higher in non-western countries, it is on the rise in Europe and North America.[14]

For example, according to one report, as of early 2002, "some 35,000 young women in France suffered from female genital mutilation or were at risk of being mutilated."[15] Moreover, Muslim clerics vehemently defend the practice of this brutal surgery. They consider it a primary protection against female promiscuity.

The prominent Egyptian sheikh Mustafa Al-Azhari insists that the attempt to stop female genital mutilation is a western conspiracy designed to spread promiscuity among Muslims. Surgical specialist at Al-Azhar University, Dr.

Muhammad Rif at Al-Bawwab, declares that the pleasure that women derive from the clitoris is unnatural and abnormal and leads to moral degradation.[16]

As we shall see, physicians both in Europe and North America have begun to perform modified in-hospital female genital mutilations as a progressive and humane solution to a seemingly intractable problem.

Muslim girls and women have been murdered by their fathers in Europe for "being caught with make-up in [their] purse, wearing 'revealing attire'—in other words, anything except a black serge curtain and a black pillowcase, refusing to marry the husband the family has chosen and . . . for going out with an indigenous British boy or a Lebanese Christian boy."[17] The suicide rate of Asian women in Britain is four times higher than that among the local population and other immigrant groups. When there *are* no other options, suicide is often perceived as the only escape. According to Scotland Yard homicide squad commander Andy Baker: "Those who come to police are, without question, the tip of the iceberg." Recently, a psychologist has persuaded the police to listen carefully to any young Muslim girl or woman who gets up the nerve to walk into a police station, not to inform the families, and not to try to mediate.[18]

In Holland, 60 percent of the women in women's shelters are Muslim. Muslim women have the highest suicide rate in Holland—but these suicides may actually be honor murders. In Berlin, there is a safe house for young Turkish girls to hide from family violence.[19]

If Muslim girls and women disobey their families, however slightly, they risk death. It's as brutal and simple as that. They know it; increasingly, European governments know it, too. However, politically correct intellectuals either deny that this is so or blame it on European "racism," Israeli "apartheid," and American "imperialism"—as a way of not having to deal with the problem.

Islamic honor murders are epidemic in Muslim countries everywhere. Statistics are impossible to secure, and most experts believe that the vast majority of honor murders remain unreported and unprosecuted. Nevertheless, we have some idea of the numbers.

In 1999, *one* province in Pakistan (Sindh) reported that 364 girls and women were victims of honor killings. From 1990 to 1999, the West Bank and Gaza reported 64 honor murders; however, according to a local West Bank women's group, in only a two-year period (1996–1998), 177 supposedly "natural" deaths were actually honor murders. In 1997, Egypt officially reported 52 honor murders—but recorded 843 "premeditated murders," many of which may have been honor murders. Mohammed Ba Obaid, the head of the women's studies department at San'aa University in Yemen, found 400 victims of honor murders there in 1997.[20]

Pakistan, the West Bank, Egypt, and Yemen are not European nations, but they are sources of immigration to Europe; customs, however barbaric, migrate, too. The problem in Europe is so severe that, in June 2004, the European police met in the Hague to discuss ways of dealing with it.

Western intellectuals and Islamic apologists tend to conflate Muslim honor murders with all forms of domestic violence. Writers at the Islamic website Soundvision.com suggest that honor murders are little different from the ubiquitous American murders in which a woman is killed by an abusive husband or boyfriend.[21]

However, as I have previously noted, while psychosis and criminality exist in every culture, and may also account for wife-beating and wife-killing everywhere, there are important cultural and psychological differences between a Muslim honor murder and wife-murder in the West. Muslims live in a shame and honor society that demands a human sacrifice to expiate the shame and the consequent public dishonor.

According to Nazand Begikhani, a founding member of Kurdish Women's Action Against Killing, an international group, "Honor killing is no longer limited to any national frontiers. It is happening worldwide and Britain and Europe are very much affected . . . it's not only limited to migrant communities."[22]

Among Muslims, forced, arranged marriage is the norm, as is child marriage. This is routine all over the Muslim world, and it has become "normalized" in Europe, too. Often European teenage girls are taken by their parents against their will to visit the home country, where they are forcibly married to a much older or uneducated cousin—who then becomes eligible to return to Europe with his bride and become a resident and a citizen of a European country.

According to one report, as of 2001, "some 70,000 young women in France were threatened with arranged marriage."[23] British officials have reported a large increase in the number of female British citizens forced to marry against their will.[24]

In Britain, the Home Office deals with approximately 2,050 suspected cases of forced, arranged marriages each year, most of them involving the Pakistani, Bangladeshi, and Indian communities.[25]

Of course, some women have positive things to say about arranged marriages. For example, Punjabi Harindar Grewall married a man she did not know and immigrated to England. Since the "thriving Sikh culture in south London" was also filled with arranged marriages, she felt welcome, which made it easier for her to "settle," since she had no friends.

"English people find [arranged marriage] quite shocking—how could you leave your family and country for someone you don't know that long. But in some ways, it's better because our families knew each other and our parents had done it for us and so there was more security."[26]

Well and good—as long as the woman is an adult and accepts the concept of an arranged marriage for herself and as long as the shared family values do not include grave and systematic violence toward girls and women.

Sudarshan Bhyuji, who runs a British helpline for women, reported that she handles two new cases a day of women who fled home in fear of murderous reprisals for refusing arranged marriages.

"Women genuinely fear honor killing," she said. "It is one of the first things they think about if they are considering doing something different with their lives." This "difference" is precisely what renders them vulnerable to death threats.[27]

When Muslim immigrants move to Europe or to North America, should they be allowed to live under Islamic religious (or Shari'a law) or under secular law? If a man kills his wife or daughter in an honor murder, should he be given a lighter or no sentence for "multicultural" reasons? Both Europe and North America have only just begun to wrestle with these questions. Interestingly, on one hand, Muslims are demanding the right to lead Islamic and Islamist lives in the West—and their demand is being championed by western civil rights and feminist activists. On the other hand, a small but often high-profile group of Muslim feminist dissidents and state law enforcement officials are opposing the Islamization of the West.

European countries, led by feminist and humanitarian activists, have begun to deal with this human rights crisis through a combination of social work, education, laws, and police work. This is commendable. However, the laws apply to very few girls and women—in fact, only to those who come forward seeking help.

Reliable and comprehensive statistics about gender apartheid in Europe do not yet exist. What we have, then, are stories, "cases," tragedies that either make headlines or somehow become known. For each such visible case, there are probably hundreds, even thousands more. Most Muslim girls and women do not resist or dare to complain. Those who do are amazingly heroic women whose lives are forever endangered.

For example, in 1999, a Pakistani mother and her three daughters, aged nine, thirteen, and twenty left Glasgow, Scotland, for what they believed would be a summer holiday in the Punjab. Instead, the girls' father, Abdul Haq, beat, drugged, and starved them all and then married Nazia, his thirteen-year-old daughter, and Rifat, his twenty-year-old daughter, to older, uneducated men whom they had never seen before. Rifat had been a university student in the biosciences. Haq also confiscated their passports.

With the help of a British Member of Parliament (MP), a reporter found Nazia and interviewed her. She described "being tied to the bed for sex. When [she said] 'I don't like you,' [her husband] just used to batter me. He used to slap me and pull my hair and punch me and then he would do it. He used to say, 'You are my wife and you will do what you are told.'"

The story is very complicated and long but does have a partially happy ending. Ultimately both girls were rescued. The governments of England and Pakistan cooperated. The Pakistani government allowed Nazia to return to Scotland because a Pakistani judge determined that she was legally underage for marriage both in Pakistan and in England. However, Rifat became pregnant and fell in love with her uneducated husband and lobbied for him to join her in Scotland.

For his efforts, the brave and determined Mohammed Sarwar, Britain's first Muslim MP, who helped spearhead the rescue campaign, was ostracized by the Pakistani communities in Pakistan and Scotland and sued by Abdul Haq in both countries for defamation. The defamation suit in Scotland was dismissed.[28]

Western standards of right and wrong and of what constitutes heroism and villainy are not the same as eastern or Muslim standards. There are so many examples of this; let me share only a few stories from several continents.

In 1999, in a high-profile case in Pakistan, twenty eight-year-old Samia Imran was shot to death in her feminist lawyer's office for initiating divorce proceedings from a violent husband, who was also her first cousin. Samia's parents were wealthy. Her father, Ghulam Sarwar, was the president of the Peshawar Chamber of Commerce; her mother, Sultana, was a gynecologist. They prided themselves on being modern and liberal.

Thus, they told Samia that she could leave her husband and return to school; they even had a hand in banning her husband from the home. However, Samia's parents were adamant: Whatever she did, she could never, ever get divorced. This meant that, at twenty-eight, Samia would have had to resign herself to a life without intimate companionship. (An affair would be out of the question.) Samia told others that she feared her parents "would kill her" if she disobeyed them.

Bravely, but in retrospect, tragically, Samia decided to initiate divorce proceedings. She made an appointment with two leading feminist lawyers, Hina Jilani and Asma Jahangir. Within five minutes of Samia's entering their offices, her mother came in, accompanied by a hired hit man who shot Samia to death. Unbelievably, Samia's paternal uncle was there, too. The hit man proceeded to kidnap at gunpoint a woman, Shahtaj Qizalbash, who worked in the law office building.[29]

Following a bad Bollywood script, Sultana, the hit man, the uncle, and their captive all shared a taxi and rushed to give Samia's father, Ghulam Sarwar, the good news. They said: "The work has been done." According to the International Jurors Commission, the killer was later shot dead by a policeman when he took Qizalbash hostage after the murder. Hilna Jilani lodged a First Information Report in which she identified the victim's killer, father, mother, and uncle. But although the police finally obtained warrants for the arrest of the accused, no one was arrested and Samia Imran's family were allowed to leave Lahore.[30]

Many Pakistanis were not angry that the Sarwars had murdered their own daughter. On the contrary. Violent demonstrations broke out *against her feminist lawyers*—whom the police and the courts refused to protect. The two feminist lawyers received death threats from religious extremists. Imran's family organized a meeting of the Peshawar Chamber of Commerce which supported the murder and issued fatwas denouncing the lawyers. Members of Pakistan's upper house in Parliament demanded that the two women lawyers be punished.[31]

Samia's father considers himself a "liberal." He is also a realist. He is not in a position "to change society. Everyone must have honor."

These customs and attitudes are imported to Europe—as is the naiveté and/or heroism of dissident Muslim girls and women.

For example, in 1998, Fadime Sahindal became a cause célèbre in Sweden when she went to court to halt her father and brother's threats of "rape and murder." Although a Kurdish Muslim, Fadime was also a Swedish citizen who lived in Sweden and who wanted to lead a Swedish way of life. Her father, Rahmi Sahindal, was fined and received a suspended jail sentence. At the time, Fadime said: "All of this is based on my parents' fear of Swedish society. They can't read and have difficulty in understanding Sweden. They are surrounded by their own people and a satellite dish that lets them see Turkish television. I don't know how many times I've told my mother that Swedish girls are not whores, but her reply is simply, 'Don't you think I can see with my own eyes?'"[32]

After bringing her father to court, Fadime was continually harassed by family members who were outraged that she had decided to pursue a higher education and had chosen a white Swedish boyfriend. Eventually Fadime had to live under an assumed name. Then, tragically, her boyfriend was killed in an allegedly unrelated car accident.

In January 2002, Rahmi Sahindal, fifty-six, finally found and shot his daughter Fadime to death in cold blood. He pleaded guilty to the murder and was jailed for life. At the trial, he said that Fadime had "humiliated him by discussing family issues in public." The Kurdish community in Sweden did not condemn him. A spokesman for that community said that Kurdish women in Sweden were "lost." "If a girl goes out with a boy without being married then she's a whore" said Kamaran Shwan, chairman of the Kurdish Association in Malmo.[33]

Here's another story. In 1996, Hatin Surucu, a fifteen-year-old Turkish German citizen, was forcibly married to her cousin in Turkey. In 1999, she returned to Berlin, where she had been born, together with her son. Hatin broke with her family, refused to wear the Muslim head scarf, and lived with her child in a hostel. She had recently completed training as an electrical engineer. She said she "simply wanted to live her life." Hatin lodged frequent complaints with the Berlin police about her brothers' threats to kill her.

On February 7, 2005, Hatin made her way to a bus stop in the main Oberlandgarten Strasse in Berlin. Minutes later, a volley of pistol shots hit her; she died choking on her own blood. A bus driver discovered the body and called the police. Hatin's three brothers, aged eighteen to twenty-five, were arrested and formally charged with the murder. They pleaded not guilty. As of this writing, they are still awaiting trial.

It is important to note that in a Berlin *high school* class discussion about her murder, teenage Turkish male Muslim students said that Hatin "had only herself to blame" and that she "deserved what she got—the whore lived like a German." Their age is important because one might expect younger Muslims to express more European views; obviously, this is not the case. Their age is also important because families often choose underage males to carry out an honor murder.[34]

Juvenile prison director Marius Fiedler confirmed that the families often carefully plot the murders, with help from the women. He said: "Usually the patriarch selects the youngest son to carry out the crime because he knows that judges in Germany don't usually give the maximum sentence of ten years to a minor for manslaughter." Most such murderers come from rural Turkey and Lebanon and show absolutely no regret for what they have done—even when they have killed a favorite sister. According to Fiedler: "Instead, they're honored and feel like martyrs for having been chosen to carry out the crime."[35]

Sadly, Hatin Surucu's 2005 murder was the sixth suspected honor murder in *four months* in Berlin's Muslim community of 200,000. The five other Muslim women killed in that period of time were murdered by their husbands or partners because they had "insulted" the family honor. One woman was strangled; another drowned in a bath. In a third case, a twenty-one-year-old Turkish woman who had been forcibly married to her cousin was stabbed to death on the street by her husband in front of their three-year-old daughter.[36]

Karl Mollenhauer, a Berlin police psychologist, blamed Islamic religious leaders and German authorities for failing to address the problem. "We have silently allowed a parallel society to develop because of fears that we would sow hatred by talking openly about its injustices . . . . Police fail to intervene because they do not want to be called racists. The women have paid the price for this," he said.

According to Jamie Glazov in *FrontPage Magazine,* Germany needs to decide whether it wants to "remain a united social construct or allow itself to become balkanized internally . . . . If they do not have the will to enforce German law in Muslim communities, they will have begun the process by which civil wars start. In the meantime, the primary victims of German [political correctness] will continue to be Muslim women, at the hands of their own families."[37]

Serap Cileli, a German-born Turkish woman who finds homes for women threatened by honor murders, said: "Germans criticise me for being anti-foreigner. At the same time, many Turks say I am fouling my own nest. . . . Official claims that the majority of Turks are well integrated here are pure eyewash."[38]

Seyran Ates, a Turkish German lawyer in Berlin, also blames the courts. "Certain judges consider social and cultural pressure or traditions to be mitigating circumstances. This is absolutely unacceptable."[39]

European citizens are at grave risk, and the governments must do something; perhaps they must do something more. For example, as noted, the suicide rate for Muslim women living in Holland is five times higher than that of non-Muslims. Either Muslim girls and women are really being driven to kill themselves or, as parliamentarian Hirsi Ali believes, some of these suicides are really honor murders. She castigates the Dutch government for having "believed [that] tolerance required respecting different cultures and traditions." Such tolerance has condemned girls and women—who are Dutch citizens—to torture and death.[40]

In November 2003, in Amsterdam, Maja Bradaric, a sixteen-year-old schoolgirl of Muslim Bosnian descent, became a member of an Internet website to "hunt" for boyfriends. She called herself "Sweety." Responding on the website to the choice "life or death," she said: "Life, of course." In response to the question: "What will be your last words before you die?" the girl answered: "I don't want to die yet."

Poor Maja did not get her wish. Within weeks of her first Internet explorations, someone set her body on fire and killed her. At first, it was suspected that the girl was killed by her eighteen-year-old nephew, a Bosnian Muslim immigrant in Holland. However, the Dutch authorities refused to call the crime an honor killing.[41]

According to a 2005 article, the appeals court in Arnheim sentenced twenty-year-old Ferdi O., of Nijmegen, to twelve years in jail for his role in Maja's murder. O. had appealed an earlier ruling and claimed that he participated in the killing but only because he was afraid of Goran M., who was the main suspect. Goran M. had been sentenced to ten years in jail and psychiatric detention. Another Goran, known as Goran P., was jailed for five years because he was present at the murder but did nothing to prevent it.[42]

Muslim girls and women are being killed all over Europe for showing any interest, however innocent or however appropriately western, in a boy, especially a non-Muslim boy. In 1998, in Greece, an Iraqi man allegedly shoved his sister into the sea as she fled from a train that was returning to Iraq. He claimed she had formed a sexual relationship with a non-Muslim boy. This obliged him to kill her.[43]

Most such honor murders are "hot," vicious, gruesome, and angry. In psychoanalytic terms, they are primal, sadistically infantile, and suspiciously sexual. Girls and women are not shot or stabbed once but many times.

For example, on October 12, 2002, in England, Abdalla Yones "stabbed his 16 year old daughter, Heshu, 11 times and cut her throat" after she began seeing a

Christian boy.[44] Yones then cut his own throat; he survived. Interestingly, at first Yones had claimed that members of al-Qaeda had broken into his flat, murdered Heshu, and then attacked him. Only under questioning did Yones finally admit to the murder. Commander Andy Baker said: "After hacking his daughter to death, Mr. Yones has attempted every defense, from psychiatric and diminished responsibility to extreme provocation, in order to save his own skin." Nevertheless, Scotland Yard described Heshu's killing as a brutal honor killing that was "appalling" and had nothing honorable about it. Yones was sentenced to life in prison.[45]

In 2003, also in England, twenty-one-year-old Sahjda Bibi was getting dressed for her wedding when "her male cousin burst into the house, knifed her 22 times and left her dying on the floor covered with blood, in her wedding dress." Her cousin, a father of three, was offended that Sahjda was not marrying another first cousin and because she'd chosen a divorced man as her spouse-to-be. Rafaqat Hussein, whom police believe carried out the murder, was then helped to flee the house and the country by another cousin, Tafarak Hussein. An international manhunt ensued. Two months later Rafaquat Hussein was caught reentering the United Kingdom on a flight from Dubai. Both Hussein cousins were tried and convicted of murder. Detective Inspector Adrian Atherley said: "It was [a] completely callous and cowardly attack . . . there is no honor in this . . . if people commit these sorts of crimes they can't hide behind their religion or culture."[46]

One possibly atypical case in Marseilles, France, continues to haunt me. In 2003, Tunisian-born Ghofrane Haddaoui, twenty-three, was about to be married. Two boys stoned her to death because she *refused* to have sex with them. This might have been her fate had she *accepted* their advances. They literally smashed her skull in with rocks.[47] The savagery of such woman-hatred is both surreal and commonplace.

More often, it is those Muslim girls and women who try to lead European lives whose lives are endangered forever.

For example, in 1986, when she was two years old, Iranian-born Aylar Lie came to Norway and was raised by Norwegian foster parents. In 2004, when she was twenty years old, Aylar was disqualified as a Miss Norway contestant because her past as a porn star was revealed. She immediately received death threats from Iranians and Muslims whom she did not know. "I really fear for my life now," she said. "I have received a crystal clear message that there are people who want to kill me."

Aylar said she was being hunted by extremist Muslims who claimed she had disgraced their people and their religion. Her lawyer, Hanne Gredal, sent the violent threats to the police, who gave Aylar a violence alarm. Due to the threats and the unrelenting media coverage, Aylar fled Norway to an undisclosed location. She admits that she now "has nerve problems. I know someone is after me,

I keep looking over my shoulder." Aylar does not understand why she, an "ordinary girl," has to "die" simply because she did something "stupid earlier in life."

Aylar is aware that there have been other honor murders in Scandinavia. Only a month before she fled, an Iranian father had strangled his eighteen-year-old daughter in Oslo in a "culture clash." Aylar made the following defiant yet commonsense observation: "Very many Muslim women want their freedom— and extremist Muslims have to respect that! That is the price they have to pay in order to live in a free country like Norway."[48]

Meanwhile, Aylar must live in hiding, on the run, cut off from contact with her family. She is not alone. Europe is filled with similar high-profile cases.

For example, in 2004, in Belgium, Mimount Bousakla, a thirty-two-year-old senator of Moroccan origin, criticized a Muslim group for failing to condemn the murder of filmmaker Theo van Gogh. She received a telephone call threatening her with "ritual slaughter." In 2002, Bousakla wrote a book, *Couscous with Belgian Fries,* which criticized forced marriages and the subjugation of Muslim women. She continues to function as a senator, but is cautious about going out at night. A Belgian convert to Islam was recently arrested for threatening her.[49] He was sentenced to six months in prison and fined 500 euros.[50]

Or there's the case of Sabbatina James in Austria. Like Bousakla, Sabbatina also wrote a book: *Sabatina: From Islam to Christianity—A Death Sentence.* Sabbatina lives with round-the-clock protection based on threats to her life made by her own family. Born to a Muslim family in Pakistan, James immigrated to Austria when she was ten years old. Her mother flatly rejected the "immoral" Austrian culture. When Sabbatina became interested in Christianity, she was immediately sent back to Pakistan to an Islamic madrassa (religious school). Only when she agreed to marry her cousin was Sabbatina allowed back to Austria.

But upon returning, Sabbatina turned to Christianity for its doctrines of love and forgiveness and for its attitude toward women. "There were no commandments that said women were put on this earth to serve men," she said. Austrian author Guenther Ahmed Rusznak, who had also converted from Islam to Catholicism, unsuccessfully tried to arbitrate between Sabbatina and her father. "Ninety-nine percent of the Islamic Community here in Linz condemn this girl, calling her a whore," he said. "This is ghastly."

In 2003, Sabbatina said: "The fear is still there. The fear that my parents could murder me under the laws of Sharia." Indeed, [my] father plans to fly [my] grandfather from Pakistan to carry out [my] death sentence. He told [me]: 'Your grandfather is already an old man and will die soon. It wouldn't bother him to spend time in an Austrian jail.'"[51]

It's important to understand that once the family feud is on, it never quits; extended family members continue to play a part in the harassment and murder scenario: forever, or for as long as it takes. The Muslim family intent on an honor murder will remain in hot and everlasting pursuit.

Western jurisprudence may or may not be able to contain such "normal" family criminality. Or perhaps only western jurisprudence can—but at great expense to the average citizen. Pro bono or state-subsidized lawyers, judges, police officers, social workers, physicians, shelters, and witness protection programs, are all required. This places a tremendous burden on the European state.

For example, British Pakistani "Zena Chaudhuri" (not her real name) has been fleeing her relatives and living in hiding somewhere in England since 1993.

Zena knew she was supposed to marry Bilal, a relative in Pakistan, whom she found uncouth, domineering, and spiteful. Bilal's brother was already married to Zena's sister, whom he beat regularly. Zena's potential brother-in-law threatened Zena with the same treatment. And then Zena fell in love with a white Englishman named "Jack Briggs," who was one of her brother Karim's friends. When Zena's passport suddenly disappeared, she suspected she would soon be whisked off to Kashmir and forced to marry Bilal.

In January 1993, Zena escaped from her family's Yorkshire home and married Jack. She also phoned her family to let them know she was safe. Karim told his sister that the family had already hired a bounty hunter. He himself swore to track and kill them. "I'm going to make it my life's mission to find you," he said. You're both going to end up in bin liners."

Three men smashed windows and broke down the door at the home of Jack's mother. They told her that one of them was "the man who's going to murder your son." Jack's sister received a call, promising to "chop up" her children.

Zena's brothers went to the police and falsely claimed that she'd stolen £9,000 from her family. In this way they found out Zena's address. Luckily, the police actually arrested Zena and she spent a night in jail. After this, Zena and Jack were both listed on Britain's national register as "sensitive" and given new identities, passports, national insurance numbers, and medical cards.

But these new identities came without educational, employment, or character credentials. Employment and housing have remained difficult for Zena and Jack. They have moved thirty times in the last twelve years. They assume they are still in danger. "We are dealing with intelligent, resourceful people, who fully believe that what they are doing is justified," said Jack, who, like Zena, is in poor physical and psychological health. Wouldn't you be—if you had to live with a permanent death threat, had been betrayed by your family (Zena) or could never see your relatives again (Jack), could never manage to find good enough employment or housing, and could never reveal your true identities to any new friends and neighbors?[52]

And this constitutes a relatively "happy" ending. There are some others.

For example, in 2003, a twenty-year-old British woman, Neelum Aziz, was duped by her father and brothers into visiting Pakistan to explore her ethnic roots. Once there, her passport was confiscated, and she was taken captive, beaten, and forced to marry her cousin. The British High Commission filed suit on her behalf. Amazingly, a Pakistani judge, in a precedent-making decision, ruled that a "forced marriage does not make her living with her alleged husband legal or proper." Aziz was allowed to return to England.[53]

In 2004, an eighteen-year-old Turkish woman, "Jasmin," who was also a German citizen, narrowly escaped an arranged marriage to a wealthy Pakistani man who wanted to gain German residency and citizenship. Her parents stalked her at work. They threatened to kill her if she did not leave her job and agree to the marriage. A supervisor hid her for a week. Her parents cased the building. Co-workers did not call the police. (Since Jasmin was a minor, the police might have turned her over to her parents.) Friends helped her sneak out through the garage and escape to a shelter in Berlin. Jasmin said: "I'm not going to get married to somebody that I don't know just because of my parents. I never even saw a picture."[54]

Jasmin escaped the arranged marriage, but she has lost her entire family and her freedom as well. Were she to surface and return to her family, she risks being murdered for her refusal.

Even with the best intentions, European and feminist resources are barely equal to the task of saving girls and women from being killed in honor murders. Murea Bohmecke works with Terres des Femmes in Germany, an organization that protects women and has begun a campaign to educate Europeans about honor murders. She says: "There are no concrete statistics available, but unofficial estimates are considered to be high." According to Bohmecke, most of Germany's honor-related crimes happen within the Turkish population, the largest foreign group. "Many of them have been living here for years, speak perfect German and are well integrated. But they often call only after the violence has escalated."

Bohmecke cited an example of a girl in her mid-twenties from Lebanon. "The girl was hiding from her family when she approached us. One of her sisters was murdered by her father and brother several years ago in Germany for having had an extramarital affair, and now her second sister was being held by her parents in an unknown place and was to be forcibly married off. She wanted us to find her. But we couldn't do much except give up a missing ad, and then the police insisted the girl get in touch with them personally. But, of course, she couldn't because she had gone underground and was scared of being discovered."[55]

British police have begun to insist that murderers should not use the notion of "honor" to secure a mitigated sentence. "We don't think honor should be a mitigating factor," said one officer. "In quite a lot of these cases there is a lot of pre-planning that goes on." Forced marriages are of particular interest, and the British police also work with airlines to keep tabs on any family returning to their homeland with a one-way ticket for a daughter. This might suggest a forced marriage—or worse.[56]

In December 2004, the Swedish government hosted what was described as the biggest-ever international conference on honor-related violence.[57]

Shahrzad Mojab, writing for the Association for Middle East Studies, asks: "On what grounds can Europe respect a culture that endorses extreme violence against girls and women? To do so is to exert another form of racism." Mojab castigates those governments that spend huge sums on military spending but nothing on shelters for battered women.[58]

European feminists say that the law often puts culture ahead of the safety of women. Communities say their culture is sacrosanct, inalienable. But, according to Diana Nammi, who runs the International Campaign Against Honour Killings, excessive tolerance for peculiar minority practices is tantamount to putting culture ahead of women's lives. "Many of these women bring 'shame' to the family if they even wear make-up or smoke or go out to the cinema," Nammi says. "Respect for minority culture puts lots of women's lives in danger and they suffer."[59]

Seyran Ates, a Turkish lawyer in Berlin, confirms that the problem is deep-rooted. Ates said that she was shot herself by Turkish extremists when she was a student and that the only way to fight the practice of gender apartheid is to launch information campaigns in schools, starting with girls at a very young age.[60]

Today Dutch parliamentarian Ayaan Hirsi Ali is probably the best-known dissident European Muslim feminist. She knows what it's like to live under African and Saudi Arabian Sunni Islam and under Iranian Shiite Islam. When she was five years old, Hirsi Ali was ritually "circumcised" in Somalia by her grandmother. Hirsi Ali was born in Somalia but lived with her father in exile in Saudi Arabia, Ethiopia, and Kenya. In Nairobi, she attended an Iranian Shiite School for Girls. In an interview by Christopher Caldwell in the *New York Times,* Hirsi Ali says: "We were no longer taking part in sports, we were not laughing anymore, we were not visiting each other anymore. We were praying five times a day. We were reading the Koran. And suddenly we hated Israel with a passion. We didn't even know where Israel was . . . I had never seen an Israeli, but we hated them because it was 'Muslim' to hate them."[61]

When Hirsi Ali was twenty-three, her father arranged her marriage to a cousin whom she did not know. They were married in Kenya. On their way to live in Canada, Hirsi Ali ran away and applied for political asylum in Holland. By the time she was thirty-two, Hirsi Ali was delivering speeches in political clubs. She said that "what Islam needed was not understanding from others but its own Voltaire." She criticized Islam for its "backward" treatment of women. The Dutch multiculturalists were outraged; so were the Muslims. Since then, Hirsi Ali has convinced some Dutch multiculturalists that it is politically incorrect to tolerate "women who live like slaves under their noses."

Hirsi Ali suggested that Theo van Gogh make the film *Submission;* she also wrote the script. According to Christopher Caldwell, after van Gogh was assassinated, Hirsi Ali left the country for a while. She "insisted on going to either Israel or the United States. "Those are the only places where people will understand what happened on November 2."

Hirsi Ali still receives death threats. She has been sued by Muslims who are offended by the "blasphemous and offensive" language in her book, *The Cage of Virgins.* Hirsi Ali sleeps very little and has no real social life. Caldwell describes her existential reality rather eloquently. He writes: "Hers is a big heroic life that moves her fellow citizens but now gets lived mostly in locked rooms and bulletproof cars. She leads a life partly above other Dutch people as a national symbol—and partly below them, as a prisoner. She is a democracy campaigner for whom the role of an ordinary democratic citizen is off-limits, an egalitarian for whom equal treatment is turning out to be an elusive and maybe impossible thing."

❊ ❊ ❊

Could Islamist gender apartheid actually take root on American soil? I don't think so—but on the other hand, in some ways it already has.

For example, on November 5, 1989, in St. Louis, Missouri, sixteen-year-old Palestina ("Tina") Isa was murdered by her parents for the crime of becoming too "American." Her Brazilian-born mother, Maria, her father's second wife, held her down for twenty minutes while her father, Zein Isa, a West Bank Palestinian and a member of the Palestinian Abu Nidal terrorist group, viciously stabbed her again and again until she died.

Ellen Harris wrote an extraordinary account of Tina's murder, *Guarding the Secrets: Palestinian Terrorism and a Father's Murder of His Too-American Daughter.*[62] According to Harris, the forensic pathologist "found thirteen wounds, six of them mortal. The worst one plunged into her chest wall, breaking her sternum and ribs and piercing her heart. A second gash ripped her left lung. Her liver had been slashed five times, four fatally." Her breasts had been punctured seven times.

Tina's murder was a classic honor murder—and it took place in the heartland of America. Because it did, Tina's parents were tried and ultimately convicted. However, they expressed no remorse. They did not think they had done anything wrong. They blamed Tina's death on the girl herself. Her father insisted that he had "stabbed his daughter in self-defense, that she had so shamed him, that he had to commit a crime to restore his honor."

Zein Isa wanted "revenge." He said: "The glass, when it becomes dirty and broken, is there any way to repair it? Is there a way to cleanse my name? . . . . For me, this one has become a burned woman, a nigger's whore. There is no way to cleanse her, except the red color [blood] that cleanses her." Isa kept telling the police that Tina "deserved it, that she attacked me."

The couple believed that Tina had forced them to kill her. Although they beat her continually and seriously, the girl still would not give up her dreams; no matter what, she kept smiling and hoping. She also continued to excel in school, she refused to end her (sexually innocent) friendship with an African American boy, and she refused to adopt her family's wild hatred of African Americans. She "adored American holidays" and even passed out Christmas cards to her Christian friends. As Harris puts it: "A girl without a country, she adopted America. She desperately wanted to belong somewhere."

Tina once ran away from home, and she once called the child abuse hotline. Tragically, the worker, who agreed with Tina's family that Palestinian "culture" demanded such strict treatment of girls and women, did nothing.

Tina was treated "like dirt" and like a full-time servant by her family. She worked long hours in the family store, and she baby-sat for her sisters. She never complained. She always tried to please them. But, as Harris notes, "as many American teenagers do, the more her parents restricted her, the more Tina resisted. And the more she fought back, the more punitive they became." For example, Tina was beaten for wearing headphones while she stocked shelves in the family store.

However, when Tina finally became convinced that her family was indeed planning to kill her, she got a part-time job elsewhere in the hope that she could save enough money to move out. When Tina returned home after her first evening of work, her parents killed her.

According to Harris, three of Tina's envious and unhappily married sisters kept nagging their father to "do" something about the "nigger-loving whore." One half-sister, Faiza Darwish, demanded blood vengeance: "A person should shoot her and throw her into the sea." A second sister, Soraia, plotted with her parents about how to kill Tina. Soraia "faced a domestic tyrant and a loveless marriage." She could not abide Tina's potential happiness or freedom. Soraia said: "This one doesn't deserve to live one year on the face of the earth."

A third sister, Mona, unhappy and abused both by her in-laws and her husband in an arranged marriage, could not bear Tina's becoming "Americanized." Mona was also convinced that if Tina got away, Mona would never be able to arrange respectable marriages for her own small daughters. Thus, at a school conference, Mona matter-of-factly described Tina as "a whore and a tramp. If she were my daughter, I would kill her." Mona also berated her father "for not taking a tougher stand with Tina."

Only one sister, Feyrouz, and Feyrouz's husband, had opposed Tina's honor murder. However, after Tina's murder, Feyrouz fled back to the West Bank as a way of refusing to testify against her family. "You can't extradite a witness from the West Bank," a law enforcement official explained.

Tina had committed another sin: She had refused to travel with her father as his "cover" on some terrorist missions. To Zein Isa and other Abu Nidal terrorists, this meant that she might expose the cell. Palestinian terrorists would not find it hard to believe that any girl or woman who asserted the slightest independence (or indifference to their needs) presented a clear and present danger.

Chances are the Isas would have gotten away with Tina's murder if the FBI had not been taping the Isa's phone line and home due to their suspicions of Zein Isas's involvement with the Abu Nidal terrorist group. Thus, the FBI had Tina's murder on tape. Once the jury heard the heartbreaking tape, conviction was inevitable.

The U.S. State Department had classified the Abu Nidal group as the most "vicious terrorist group in the world." On Christmas Eve of 1985, they were responsible for the simultaneous attacks at the El Al counters in the airports in Rome and Vienna, in which 18 people died and 101 were injured. In 1986, they attacked an Israeli bus on the West Bank and killed the driver; they also attacked a group of Sephardic Jews as they prayed in a synagogue in Istanbul, machine-gunning 22 worshippers to death and then killing themselves.

It is important to note that Tina was not rescued by the American educational or child protective systems. Adults saw that Tina was being seriously abused at home. She was bruised; she often wore dark glasses, looked weary, and seemed beaten down; she even said that her family was going to kill her. Tina also confided in one of her school counselors and placed an anonymous call to the child abuse hotline. A child abuse worker made a home visit but did nothing to protect her. Instead, the case worker agreed with the Isas that "kids weren't being brought up the way they had been." He also said that he was "reluctant to cross cultural lines."[63]

This reluctance endangers all those who live in America, who may be American citizens or who may wish to integrate into an American way of life.

Would more multicultural "sensitivity" have saved Tina's life? I think not. But some serious education about the crimes committed in Allah's name (backed up by swift and effective law enforcement) might have.

In order to truly understand the Isas and to gauge the danger that Tina was in, the non-Muslim American adults in Tina's life would have to have read a book that did not yet exist: *Burned Alive,* by "Souad," which was only published in 2003.[64] Souad's voice is that of one who has returned from the dead.

Souad was born in 1957 or 1958, before Israel won disputed territories in the 1967 war that was waged against her by Arabs. Souad describes Palestinian village life on the West Bank as Zein Isa must have known it.

Souad, her mother, her sisters, and most other girls and women in her (unnamed) village were threatened, cursed, thrashed, severely beaten, and verbally humiliated on a daily basis. In addition, the boys and men all wore shoes; the girls and women all went barefoot—pebbles and thorns tore into their feet every minute. The boys and men in a household each had the right to his own bathwater; the girls and women all shared the same water for washing. The boys went to school; the girls did not, and they began backbreaking domestic and agricultural labor when they were eight or nine years old. Boys went to the movies; girls did not. When Souad's brother got married, his wedding celebration was far more lavish than her sister's was.

Souad has no memory of ever celebrating her birthday, playing games, or taking a holiday vacation. Her life, she writes, was more that of "a small animal that eats, works as fast as possible, sleeps, and is beaten."

Most traumatized people repress and try to forget the near murders and actual murders they have witnessed or have themselves endured. Only dimly, and after a long period of time, does Souad dare to remember that she saw her beloved brother inexplicably strangle one of their sisters; saw her mother suffocate seven unwanted newborn girls; and that she saw various girls in the village murdered.

Souad and others like her have absolutely no escape except that of death—or marriage. However, for girls and women, marriage often means being beaten by their husbands instead of by their fathers; in addition, their brothers and male cousins will continue to monitor their female kin's behavior. In Souad's case, a neighbor had asked for her hand in marriage. Her father had refused the offer; he was waiting for his eldest daughter to be married first and she had had no offers. At seventeen, Souad was still an illiterate, barefoot peasant who led a medieval sequestered life—except that she was also surrounded by men who wore western dress, drove cars, attended university, and worked in cities. Her potential fiancée was just such a man. He accosted Souad in a field secretly. They met three times. He promised to marry her—and then proceeded to deflower, impregnate, and abandon her to her inevitable fate.

Her parents decided that she had to die and delegated the task to their son-in-law, who set her on fire. Her agony was unimaginable. Souad did not die immediately and was therefore removed to a hospital, where the doctors and nurses purposely neglected her. When she still did not die, her mother came and tried to poison her. The hospital finally barred her. Souad was rescued by a Swiss humanitarian worker, assisted by a male Palestinian physician. Souad miraculously lived.

Years later, Souad was persuaded to speak out. But her tragic fate is shared today by other Muslim (and Palestinian) women in the Middle East and by those who live in America and Canada.[65]

Souad's story, and others like it, should be required reading for every social worker and police officer in Europe and North America. I would especially like feminists to read the book and to examine their own multicultural perspective and pro-Palestinian views with the facts of her life in mind. There are other honoer killings in our midst as well.

For example, on January 8, 1999, in Cleveland, Ohio, after attending mosque services with her parents, another Palestinian woman, Methal Dayem, was murdered in what prosecutors termed an "honor killing" because she had turned her back on her culture. She had refused to marry her cousin, dared to attend college (Cleveland State University), planned to become an elementary school teacher, drove her own car, and was "too independent." Her sister told police that two of her cousins, Musa Saleh and Yezen Dayem, followed Methal to school and to work. She was shot four times and died choking on her own blood. No money was taken nor was she sexually assaulted. The police arrested these two cousins.[65]

A judge threw out an aggravated murder charge against Saleh, who remained in jail because of pending burglary and witness intimidation charges. Perhaps the prosecutors did not fully understand what they were up against. Thus, they granted Musa Saleh immunity on the pending charges in the mistaken hope that he would testify against Yezen Dayem. In addition, the fact that potential jurors had heard the phrase "honor killing" was deemed "prejudicial," "inflammatory," and "anti-Arab" to the defendant, Yezen Dayem, whose lawyer promptly requested and received a non-jury bench trial.

Leaders of the Ohio Muslim and Arab communities denounced the prosecutors' "honor killing" theory as a "cultural slur based on an outmoded medieval custom." In my opinion, they engaged in what is known as taqiyya, (dissimulation, disinformation), which is recommended Islamic practice when engaged in battle with the infidel.

When they were originally charged, prosecutor Carmen Marino had said: "What these two did was shoot a woman in the back of the head. They believe that their religious beliefs supersede our law." His comments led many of the thirty Arab Americans in the courtroom to simultaneously "clear their throats in an effort to try to drown him out." Sam Quasem, an Arab American activist, said: "The Muslim religion does not preach to kill a woman. If that's not racism, I don't know what is."

Circumstantial evidence pointed to Musah Saleh and Yezen Dayem's guilt: A video showed Dayem's car near the murder site; cell phone records revealed that whoever used his phone placed a call within minutes from a location not far from the murder site; the entire cultural context strongly suggests an honor killing. However, detectives found a pair of ski gloves covered with gunshot residue in the victim's car. Who placed it there, when, or why, remains unknown. Nevertheless, because the DNA evidence retrieved from the gloves did not match the DNA of either of Methal's cousins, the second and presiding judge, Thomas Pokorny, found that this constituted "reasonable doubt." He therefore acquitted and freed Yezen Dayem. However, according to Amanda Garrett of the *Cleveland Plain Dealer,* Methal Dayem's mother, sister, and aunt were "devastated" by the verdict. Methal's sister, Nebal Ali, shouted 'You will not get away from Allah. Allah will punish you.'" Afterward, both she and Methal's mother 'rushed' at Yezen Dayem's family . . . shouting 'Murderer' and a string of vulgarities."

In 1999, in St. Clairsville, Ohio, Dr. Nawaz Ahmed, forty-four, a computer scientist, former Pakistani Air Force pilot, and physician, slaughtered his wife, Dr. Lubaina Bhatti Ahmed, thirty-nine, a general practitioner and internist, her father, Abdul Majid Bhatti, her sister, Ruhie Ahmad, and her niece, Nasira Ahmad. Ahmed cut their throats and fled to New York where he was apprehended trying to board a plane back to Pakistan. Bhatti's father had come from Canada and her sister had come from California to lend Bhatti moral support and to testify on her behalf in the last stages of her divorce hearing. The couple had two young sons.

Theirs was an arranged marriage. Ahmed physically and psychologically abused his wife from the moment they were married. Bhatti eventually began filing complaints with the police when they lived in West Virginia; ultimately, she got orders or protections against her husband in Ohio. Because she was terrified of him, she delayed divorce proceedings.

Ahmed moved away to Columbus, Ohio. Bhatti's lawyer, Grace Hoffman, said that Bhatti "was afraid of him but she never thought he would kill her." Bhatti was tired of the "physical and emotional torture."

Battered women are at great risk when they initiate divorce proceedings or insist on separating from their batterer-parasite. This is one of the reasons battered women hesitate to do so. What marks this as an honor killing, and not just a typical case of domestic violence is the grisly and ritual method of murder and the fact that Ahmed slaughtered Bhatti's entire family because they dared to support her in the matter of a divorce. Ahmed was sentenced to death but his execution was stayed in November 2004.[66]

America remains a country of immigrants. However, not as many Muslims live in the United States as live in Europe. One estimate puts America's Arab and Muslim population as anywhere between 1.2 million and 8 million.[67] In addition, many Arabs who live here are Christians mainly from Lebanon and they do not consider themselves Arabs. They have a higher-than-average per capita income, and have often fled Islamist terrorism and despotism.[68]

On 9/11, al Qaeda came to call. Finally, some Americans understood that they had to wake up. Some Americans no longer believe that America has done all that it can and must do to defend itself; others feel that America has gone too far to defend itself from terrorist enemies.

America does not yet *seem* to have Europe's problem with a large, hostile, and non-assimilated Muslim immigrant population. However, various Islamic cultural practices and hard-core beliefs have arrived. In fact, as I have argued, jihad has been openly declared against our universities—which, in classic dhimmi fashion, have become appeasingly Palestinianized.

In addition, Muslim Americans have become increasingly vigilant, litigious, and publicity savvy. Many are trying to use American law to impose Shari'a law on Muslim Americans. For example, according to an article written by Daveed Gartenstein-Ross, Ali Khan, a law professor at Washburn University in Kansas, suggests in the *Cumberland Law Review* that Islam is a form of intellectual property, whose Muslim "trustees" have vowed to protect their faith's "knowledge-based assets." As such, Islam allows its adherents "the right to integrity"—that is, according to Gartenstein-Ross, Muslims should be able to safeguard the faith from reform or, as Khan puts it, "from innovations, repudiation, internal disrespect, and external assaults."

According to Gartenstein-Ross, in Khan's view, apostasy is therefore punishable under U.S. law, (Khan doesn't say how), since it aims to dishonor Islam's protected knowledge. In Gartenstein-Ross's words, Khan views "the murtad (apostate) [as] akin to a corporate insider who discloses the secrets he has undertaken to protect." He (or she) "is akin to a state official who turns traitor and joins the ranks of the enemy. . . . All legal systems punish insiders who breach their trusts; Islam punishes murtaddun [apostasy] too, sometimes severely." Gartenstein-Ross finds Khan's views "outlandish." However, Gartenstein-Ross is troubled by the fact that Khan "was able to use an American law review as a soapbox from which to advocate the licensed punishments of apostates, and that his grossly illiberal views were never rebutted in its pages."[69]

Author and columnist, Daniel Pipes, has been brilliantly and aggressively documenting jihadic activities for more than a decade. In his view, American politicians and law enforcement have been reluctant to see religious terrorism as such.

For example, the 1990 murder of Rabbi Meir Kahane by the Islamist El Sayyid Nosair; the 1994 murder of Aaron Halberstam by Rashid Baz on the Brooklyn Bridge; the 1997 murder of a Jewish man and his companion by a Palestinian at the Empire State Building; the purposeful 1999 crash of Egypt Air 990, which killed 217 people; the 2002 Los Angeles airport murders at the El Al counter; the 2002 intentional crash of a small plane into a Tampa high-rise building by a bin Laden supporter—were all initially dismissed as deeds committed by individual maniacs or as personal disputes. Pipes concludes that "police, prosecutors, and politicians, shy away from stark realities . . . those who refuse to recognize the enemy cannot defeat him. To pretend terrorism is not occurring nearly guarantees that it will recur."[70]

Most recently, Pipes has asked whether Muslim Americans are now courting "special privileges." This includes: "Setting up a government advisory board uniquely for Muslims in America; permitting Muslim-only living quarters or events in America and Great Britain; setting aside a municipal swimming pool for women only, as in France; allowing a prisoner the unheard-of-right to avoid strip-searches in New York State; changing noise laws to broadcast the adhan, or call to prayer, in Michigan; prohibiting families from sending pork or pork by-products to American soldiers serving in Iraq; requiring that female American soldiers in Saudi Arabia wear American government-issued abayas or head-to-foot robes."

According to Pipes, "the key distinction is whether Muslim-American aspirations fit into an existing framework or not." If Muslim Americans accept that they are one among many other religious groups, then they are certainly entitled to those religious privileges shared by all. However, if Muslims aspire to dominate or to "overturn" the Constitution, that is not acceptable.[71]

In Pipes' opinion, Muslim Americans have the right to wear beards and head scarves, to found Muslim cemeteries, and take certain Muslim holidays off from school and work. I agree. But, in my opinion, Muslims in the West should *not* have the right to face-veil their girls and women; practice female genital mutilation; arrange forced marriages; or commit crimes such as polygamy, wife-beating, child abuse, and shame-based honor murders.

We have just seen that honor murders take place in America. Their perpetrators are sometimes punished (Tina Isa's parents were convicted as was Dr. Lubaina Ahmed's husband); sometimes they aren't.

I doubt that most feminists ever knew about the honor killings of Tina Isa, Methal Dayem, or Dr. Lubaina Ahmed. Before I began work on this book, I had never considered the possibility that Islamic gender apartheid had already reached North American shores. I was only aware of the inability, on the part of many Muslim Americans, to tolerate any criticism of their culture and religion. For example, I knew that an organized Muslim group, the Council on American Islamic Relations (CAIR), in Cincinnati, Ohio, had managed to shut down the play that a friend of mine, Glyn O'Malley, had been commissioned to write. The subject was about the first Palestinian female suicide bomber.

In 2003, O'Malley's play, *Paradise,* was awarded the Lazarus New Play Prize by Cincinnati's Playhouse-in-the-Park. When the theatre attempted to mount the play, a firestorm of controversy erupted. It dramatized the story of the March

2002 suicide bombing carried out by eighteen-year-old Ayat al-Akhras, a young woman living in Dehaishe, near Bethlehem, that killed (among others) seventeen-year-old Israeli Rachel Levy, out shopping for a Sabbath dinner. The Islamist CAIR claimed the play was disrespectful of Islam and forced its cancellation in the first stage of production. Afterward, the play had public readings in several U.S. cities. In 2004, O'Malley was nominated for PEN America's Newman's Own First Amendment Award for his defense of freedom of expression for all writers. The play was finally produced at New York's Kirk Theater in March 2005 and will open outside New York at New Theater in Coral Gables, Florida, in February 2006.[72]

In 2000, a year and a half after Methal Dayem was murdered in Cleveland, thirty-three-year-old Pakistani Shahpara Sayeed was burned alive by her husband, Mohammed Haroon, a taxi driver, in Chicago. Various Muslim groups quickly pointed out that domestic violence occurred in all faith communities or was due to "a fit of violence that nobody yet fully understands." Nevertheless, Haroon was arrested. The case was closed when he died of AIDS in a Cook County jail.[73]

In Jersey City, New Jersey, Ali Hassan, a Muslim from Guyana, had been fighting with his wife, Marlyn, a Hindu, about converting to Islam. She refused to do so. On July 29, 2002, Hassan stabbed Marlyn, who was pregnant with twins, to death. Hassan also killed Marlyn's thirty-year-old sister, Sharon, and their fifty-year-old mother, Bernadette Seajatan. According to the Associated Press, a fugitive warrant for the arrest of Ali Hassan was issued by the Hudson County prosecutor's office. After receiving a phone tip that Hassan was attempting to flee to Canada, Canadians removed Hassan from a Greyhound bus and turned him over to the Buffalo, New York, police.[74]

On April 15, 2004, in Scottsville, New York, Turkish Muslim Ismail Peltek slaughtered his thirty-nine-year-old wife, Hatice Peltek. She died of repeated stab wounds and hammer blows to the head. Peltek also assaulted his twenty-two-year-old and four-year-old daughters and fractured both their skulls. He told police that he did so because his brother had molested his wife and twenty-two-year-old daughter: "I was concerned that my family honor was taken." He had also subjected his youngest daughter to a gynecological exam, which, in and of itself, had also stained the family honor. When asked, in Turkish, Peltek confirmed that to regain his honor, he could only kill his female relatives, but not his "male family."[75]

Similar issues exist in Canada, where the Muslim population is estimated at about 750,000 people. Between 1991 and 2001, the Muslim population in Canada doubled.[76]

Let me mention two recent Canadian honor murders.

In 1995, on a visit to the Punjab, Jaswinder (Jassi) Kaur, a Muslim Canadian woman, fell in love—but with the wrong man. Although Sukhwinder Singh was also a Pakistani Muslim, he was her economic inferior. Nevertheless, their relationship flourished, and they were secretly married in 1999. She returned to British Columbia and started the paperwork to bring her husband to Canada. What happened next bears all the markings of an honor murder. The Pakistani police received a fax from Jassi's family informing them that Sukhwinder had "forcibly raped and kidnapped their daughter." The police launched a manhunt for him, and Jassi ran away from home and flew to Pakistan "on borrowed money" in order to exonerate her husband.

Two months later, Jassi and Sukhwinder were kidnapped and beaten by a gang of men who left Sukhwinder for dead; he survived. They took Jassi to a nearby farmhouse where phone records reveal that she received a phone call from her mother, Malkit Kaur. Jassi's body was found in a ditch the following morning. Her throat had been slashed by a sword. The police arrested, tried, and convicted three of the contract killers; eight members of Jassi's maternal family remain out on bail. As of 2005, the Pakistani police are a few steps closer to extraditing Jassi's mother from Canada to stand trial.[77]

In 1999, Muhammed Khan battered and then butchered his five-year-old daughter Farah to death. He cut her throat, then dismembered and disposed of her body parts. He suspected that she was not his biological child. At first, he told police that the child had committed suicide! In 2005, in Toronto, a jury convicted him of first-degree murder. Farah's stepmother, who assisted him and who may herself have been a battered wife, was convicted of second-degree murder.[78]

I could describe more such cases, equally horrifying. From these examples, it's again clear that shame-based honor murders are not the same as western domestic violence and that Islamic gender apartheid is not the same as western gender inequality.

But something else has happened in Canada that is of great importance. A Canadian judge ruled that Muslims in the province of Ontario may apply Shari'a law in domestic and civil disputes. The judge did not devise a mechanism whereby an impartial third-party could rule on whether such Shari'a decisions will or will not be in accordance with Canadian law. What this means is that Muslim girls and women will be as trapped in Canada as they are in Muslim countries. Most Muslim immigrant women are not familiar with their rights under the Canadian Charter of Rights and Freedom and will most likely abide by a Shari'a court ruling.[79]

Homa Arjomand is an Iranian exile who lives in Canada and is the director of the Campaign Against Shari'a Court in Canada. On January 19, 2005, she submitted a petition opposing Ontario's imposition of Shari'a law to the Canadian members of Parliament. It was signed by seventy-three organizations and by many prominent individuals. The petition states: "The initiators of the Shari'a Court in Canada have Islamic states' support. Their goals harm our society as a whole. . . . If they succeed . . . the violation and oppression on the women and children in so-called Muslim 'communities' will be legalized."[80]

Although the judge refers to "Muslim principles," according to Alia Hogben, the executive director of the Canadian Council of Muslim Women, "there is no one, codified agreed upon law on which this statement of Muslim principles could be based." Canadian feminist groups believe that the judge was "hoodwinked" by Islamists and have vowed to "go to the barricades."[81]

Mumtaz Ali is one of the Canadian Islamists in favor of Shari'a law. On the website of the Canadian Society of Muslims, he affirms that "apostates must 'choose between Islam and the sword'" and argues that if "Canada is to be true to its own Charter of Rights and Freedoms, it must allow the country's Muslim community to punish those of its members who renounce or traduce their faith." In his view, failing to incorporate Islamic law as concerns apostasy and blasphemy would constitute "a flagrant breach of equality rights. . . . Failing to interpret the guaranteed rights and freedoms of Muslims in accordance with the true spirit of multiculturalism results in the effective denial of the fundamental philosophy of the Canadian constitution. This is a tragic departure from that cherished 'tolerance' which is the distinguishing quality of a cultured people."[82]

In the frustrating absence of studies and statistics, I interviewed a number of lawyers who specialize in defending immigrant women in cases of domestic violence in the United States. Let me close this chapter by sharing two stories in depth.

In the late 1990s, an arranged marriage took place in a Middle Eastern country I have been asked not to name. The husband became increasingly obsessed with fundamentalism—and with the possibility that his own mother was a "whore." We might consider him mentally ill; in his culture, he was only seen as righteously strict. This psychiatrically challenged fundamentalist left the Middle East and brought his young wife and two young children to live in the Midwest. However, he did not adopt an American lifestyle. Instead, he demanded that his wife cover herself from head to toe. His wife tried hard to please him, but nothing worked. He beat her savagely. Suddenly he decided that his wife had been having an affair and must be punished. Therefore, he tortured her for twelve hours. He tied her up, tore off her clothes, heated a drill bit, and cut and burned her body so that no man would ever desire her again.

This is frightening enough. More frightening: His brothers and their wives happened to stop by, saw the torture in process, stopped him temporarily—but then they all left. He continued the torture, which eventually put his wife into a coma. Because he committed this crime in America, not in the Middle East, he was arrested and convicted. Of course, his family—including the mother he reviled—pressured his wife not to assist the prosecution.

When he was in jail, this criminal continued to threaten and harass his ex-wife, who had remarried. He also sent a copy of a false taped confession he'd extracted from her under torture to *her brothers* back in the old country. This was equivalent to her death sentence. Her lawyers told me, "Several of her brothers and male cousins convened a meeting to plot her death and then ordered their mother to bring her back so that they could kill her. When the mother came to her daughter's aid and refused to bring her back to be killed, she was threatened with death too. Both mother and daughter had to go into hiding." Simultaneously, her former husband's relatives started threatening not only her new husband, but also his family back in the old country.

At this point, federal authorities granted political asylum to the battered wife, her mother, and to an older half brother who refused to join his brothers in the plot.

Frequently, in order to keep a woman from being murdered in the Middle East, she is jailed for her own safety. This is done in Jordan, and it's what the Dutch did, temporarily, with Ayaan Hirsi Ali. In America, a potential honor killing victim may have to be put into a witness protection program. According to Dorchen Leidholdt, a lawyer who has represented a number of battered Muslim women in New York City: "It is harder in America for parents to maintain control of children than in Europe. It's harder to maintain a closed community here. In the north of England, Pakistanis live as if they were still living in Pakistan."

Leidholdt does not believe that a European-style Islamization can happen in America. In fact, she has worked with imams on programs about domestic violence that took place in mosques, and she has worked with religious Muslim lawyers who are opposed to wife and child abuse.

While I know many sophisticated, educated, westernized, and progressive Muslims on both American coasts, including radical feminists and pro-democracy feminists, I still believe that what has happened in Europe can happen here if we make Europe's mistakes and welcome a large influx of Muslim immigrants in too-short a period of time without a huge educational and employment initiative in place to absorb them—especially if such future citizens do not want to learn to speak English or become Americanized, and if they were uneducated, even illiterate, in their own countries.

The heartbreak and danger of what I'm saying is this: Many women in flight from Islamic persecution may be uneducated and illiterate. Already the excellent work of Robert Spencer (Jihad Watch), Daniel Pipes, Maria Sliwa, Ibn Warraq, and others is quite persuasive about the Islamic intention to practice religious separatism and religious apartheid on American soil and to use the American legal system to help them do so. We have already seen versions of Islamic gender apartheid on American soil, ranging from honor killings, to female genital mutilation, to veiling, to separatist education.[83]

On the other hand, if Muslim immigrants do not congregate in large, closed communities as they do all over Europe, especially in England and France, and if we insist that all Muslim students learn English and are schooled in American democracy, even if they also attend an Islamic religious school, then I agree with Leidholdt: It will be difficult to stop the assimilation of the younger generation of Muslims. One of the problems that Holland made, for example, was to "encourage students to speak Turkish, Arabic, or Berber in primary schools rather than Dutch." They did so in order to be multi-culturally tolerant. They have reaped the whirlwind.

Leidholdt told me about a tragic yet fascinating case involving some South Asian Muslims in the United States that she was able to resolve with the help of a friendly imam and a young male Muslim lawyer. A Muslim woman could no longer take her husband's beatings; she fled to a shelter for battered women. The woman's older brother came here to kill her. Leidholdt explained: "Her brother was required to protect his younger siblings. They were in danger because their older sister had fled a marriage, filed for divorce, and was living with strangers. We were very concerned because we knew that one of her female cousins had recently been murdered in an honor killing back home. We met with her brother. I could not have talked him out of it without the help of my colleague, a religious Muslim lawyer."

The West—Europe, America, and Canada—have in some ways both refused to and yet have been forced to begin to understand the nature of international Islamic terrorism. In addition, the West has both resisted yet been forced to begin to understand the nature of Islamic *domestic* terrorism.

For example, America, Canada, and various European countries have criminalized female genital mutilation and provided political asylum for girls and women in flight from it and who are at risk in other ways specific to Islam (and to other religious and secular despotisms). America, Canada, and Europe have also protected high-profile Muslim dissidents and have hidden Muslim women who are in danger of being honor-murdered by their families.

What kind of foreign and domestic policies might the West consider adopting toward Islamic gender apartheid? I would like to discuss this in chapter eight.

Eight

Toward a New Feminism

The women's stories throughout this book are important for a host of reasons. In the absence of comprehensive and reliable studies and statistics, their stories are crucial to our understanding of what Islamic gender apartheid is and what it does. These stories should evoke our compassion and compel westerners in general and feminists in particular to wrestle with the issue of women's global freedom. Most academic feminists are ignoring the challenge in favor of other causes. I hope that reading these stories will open your minds and hearts. As jihadists advance their war against us, more and more women will suffer the consequences of our not fighting back.

The stories of Muslim women's and men's heroic resistance should humble us in the more privileged West and persuade women to rethink their multicultural yet isolationist positions.

For example, according to what Professor Leanna Keith told me, on August 30, 1945, on his flight to Tokyo to accept Japan's surrender, General Douglas MacArthur handwrote his agenda as follows: "First destroy the military power. Punish war criminals. Build the structure of representative government. Modernize the constitution. Hold free elections. Enfranchise the women. Release the political prisoners. Liberate the farmers. Establish a free labor movement. Encourage a free economy. Abolish police oppression. Develop a free and responsible press. Liberalize education. Decentralize political power. Separate the church from the state."

MacArthur's list might well apply to the Arab and Muslim world of today. But, I am neither a military historian nor an expert in the relationship between constitutional law and individual freedom. Thus, my policy-related analysis is that of a psychologist. If we want to jump-start democracy and modernity in the Islamic world; if we especially want to stop the most extreme violence against women and humanity that is so out of control in that world, then it is important to understand the psychology of the peoples involved—theirs, and ours, as well.

There are five points or areas of concern that I want to discuss with relation to democratic initiatives in the Arab, Muslim, and Middle Eastern world.

1. The psychological relationship between voting, gender, and democracy.

2. Humanity's psychological tendency to deny or minimize evil and to scapegoat vulnerable parties (women, Jews) when people are afraid and feel they cannot control their destiny.

3. The psychological relationship (or non-relationship) between ideological thinking and the truth. What kind of diplomatic actions can people take to stop femicide if they refuse to see it in the first place?

4. The psychological (and feminist) tendency to deny or minimize that woman's inhumanity to woman exists both in the West and among Arab, Muslim and Middle Eastern women.

5. The psychological nature of patriotism (or anti-patriotism) among feminists and intellectuals.

Some say that being able to vote is the sign and symbol of democracy. They may be right. From a psychological point of view, democracy also requires voters, especially female voters, who are informed, feel free to vote their conscience, and know how to think independently. Ideally, this means that a voter should not automatically be influenced by the views or desires of others, even if those others are her parents, husband, or religious and political leaders.

For example, if suffrage is granted to people who have never before voted or lived in freedom, they may vote to uphold the rights of their oppressors; or they may not. Many (but not all) seriously abused women have low self-esteem and do not always have the psychological strength to rebel against their abusers. They sometimes do. But as the authors Bin Laden, Darwish, Sasson, and Souad make clear, psychological rebellion is particularly difficult for traumatized Arab and Muslim women.

As we have seen, many Muslim women, whether they are traumatized or not, are just as religiously fanatic as men are and they police other women in aggressive, often vicious ways. This concept is true everywhere and is not specific to Muslim women. Women are not simple victims. Like men, they also internalize sexist values.

Thus, some Iraqi women have, post-Saddam Hussein, vigorously campaigned for and voted to uphold Shari'a law.[1] In my view, women have every right to exercise their religious freedom. Some feminists insist that those Muslim women who adopt hijab do so out of modesty and in order to obey God, not men. Their point is well taken. However, religious men and women should not have the right to force their religious practices on other adults. A secular constitution would try to preserve both such rights. An Islamic constitution is not likely to do so.

Thus, merely casting a vote does not necessarily mean that one has voted independently or in one's own self-interest. To do so requires that the voter have a self-concept, as well as a group concept of identity. Further, she would need to be educated to believe that loyalty to herself (as well as loyalty to her family, clan, or tribe) is also an honorable and positive choice. Specific training in how to think independently and in how to maintain an independent opinion when it differs from those held by one's peers and authorities would also be required.

As we have seen, women in the West, including feminist academics and activists, may also need such training. I have not recently seen much tolerance for divergent views or voting choices among educated feminists in America. As we have seen in chapter 3, I was "purged" from a left-feminist listserv group because I wrote that I would be voting for President Bush. Many Muslims abhor and fear the kind of western-style "individualism" and independence in which many westerners take pride. In addition, if the new Muslim female voters do not feel safe to vote their individual conscience, they simply will not do so. Thus, even though the Muslim Middle East is apparently on fire with "voting fever," voters may end up voting for totalitarian, theocratic, and misogynist leaders. It's what they are used to.

Secular, democratic life is foreign to the Arab and Muslim world. Muslims are used to obeying one brutal leader. A Muslim father dominates his family in autocratic and often brutal ways. He often lives more comfortably and has more freedom than his wives and children do; indeed, this distance is a measure of his honor and power. He is nevertheless feared, hated, obeyed, and abjectly adored by his sons, daughters, and wives. This kind of family life may be the psychological template for the relationship between many Muslim people and their political rulers.

My second psychological point is about the nature and power of denial. As we have seen, domestically terrorized women are often permanently traumatized. Like Souad, they may even "forget" that they have been beaten or nearly murdered or that they have seen other girls and women beaten and murdered. This kind of denial also exists collectively in terms of people "forgetting" or minimizing the crimes which their leaders have committed.

Western feminists have denied the danger of Islamic gender apartheid. Western governments have also denied the danger of Islamic jihad for a long time. They have viewed various acts of terrorism as the isolated acts of individual maniacs and not as part of a pattern. For example, police the world over often have denied that serial killers are targeting prostitutes because they are *women*.

I was tangentially involved in a case known as the Montreal Massacre. On December 6, 1989, Marc Lepine entered the engineering school at the University of Montreal and gunned down fourteen women and wounded fifteen others. Lepine, who had been rejected by both the Canadian Army and the engineering school at the University of Montreal, said in his suicide note that he was after "the feminist viragos" who had ruined his life.

The Canadian police saw this as the isolated act of a madman, not as part of a patriarchal conspiracy; this is to be expected. But they also failed to understand the importance of certain biographical and childhood factors. For example, Lepine was born Gamile Rodrigue Gharbi to an Algerian Muslim father and a French Canadian mother who had formerly been a nun. Lepine's father, Liess Gharbi, physically and psychologically brutalized both his son and his wife. He probably taught his son that women are chattel property who deserve to be beaten even when they are obedient—perhaps murdered when they are not. What is important to note is that Gharbi/Lepine scapegoated women for the considerable crimes of his father.

In my 1978 book, *About Men,* I posited that the paternal abandonment of and cruelty toward sons may be a crucial component in mother- and woman-hating (women are scapegoated for the crimes of men). Dr. Nancy Kobrin, in her unpublished book about Islamic suicide terrorism, *The Sheikh's New Clothes: Al Qaeda's Suicide Terrorism and What It's All About,* posits that the absolute degradation of Arab and Muslim women by a shame-and-honor society means that sons must perpetually rid themselves of the "contamination" that contact with women represents; and that sons must psychologically abandon their mothers—which they may experience as being abandoned *by* their mothers. Many sons are trained to mistrust, police, batter, and sometimes murder their female kin. Kobrin believes that such psychological dynamics may play a crucial role in the genesis of Islamic terrorism. She writes: "These terrorists harbor a profound fear of being abandoned, which is so great that they must commit in one instant both suicide and mass murder in order to fend off the fear of dependency and abandonment. They literally regress in fantasy and action to that period in early childhood when they were held in the arms of their mothers."

While I agree with Kobrin, I also want to point out that the exceedingly wealthy male masterminds of suicide terrorism usually do not themselves undertake such missions nor do they send their biological sons into suicide martyrdom. They appeal to young men who are not necessarily impoverished or uneducated but who may be starved for a protective alliance with a benevolent father figure—precisely because one does not exist in reality.

Although many other disciplines and bodies of knowledge must be brought to bear on our understanding of Islamic suicide terrorism, I also suggest that foreign policy analysts consider the psychological variables in any long-term educational programs which target the Islamic world.

Many people also deny international and domestic terrorism for another reason. People feel safer if they think that other people are mainly good, not bad, and that they are also rational beings. The idea that people may be evil (or may commit evil) is genuinely frightening, often paralyzing. Thus, good people do too little to end the genocides until it is far too late. According to Lance Morrow, in his excellent book *Evil: An Investigation,* "It is in rich Western democracies that the denial of evil is strongest."

Third, most people tend to think that other people are like they are. Of course, most people barely know themselves—but no matter. What this means is that westerners tend to resist knowledge of Arabs and Muslims whom they have already romanticized, exoticized, justified, and so on. Politically correct westerners have another reason for not looking too closely at the realities of the Muslim world; they fear that to do so might be seen as "racist."

We can no longer afford to look away. Westerners must finally understand that it's the Wild West Plus in the Arab and Muslim world; that the violence against all children, but especially against girls and women, is surreal and pitiless. I am not sure what we can do to end this violence, but denying its existence will lead nowhere.

I have said that the stories I've told in this book are overwhelming. Sadly, they are typical; there are even more nightmarish, true stories to tell. The Arab and Muslim world are places where horrifying things can and do happen. While crimes against humanity are perpetrated everywhere, each culture may perpetrate such crimes in culturally distinct ways. Allow me three more such true Muslim culture stories as a way of raising certain questions that belong to this chapter.

In July 2001, in Hassi Messaoud, Algeria, a mob of three hundred men conducted a three-day pogrom against thirty-nine economically impoverished Algerian women who had been imported to work from another province. These women, the sole support of entire extended families, now worked as cleaning personnel and secretaries for foreign oil companies. In his Friday sermon, Imam Amar Taleb described these women as "immoral" and called on his male congregants to launch a "jihad against the Evil" and to "chase the women fornicators out of the area." Shouting "Allah Houwa Akbar" (God is the highest), the men went to war against the women.

The women, including three young virgins, were tortured, stabbed, mutilated, gang raped, buried alive, and murdered. Their houses were looted and set on fire. Male mobs launched similar pogroms at two other locations, targeting the houses of single women and shops owned by women, especially hairdressing salons. The police had to lock up ninety-five women to protect them from the rampaging men; hundreds more begged to be incarcerated, but there was no more room.

Incredibly, the survivors brought charges. Three and a half years later, on December 15, 2004, a hearing was finally held. Most of the women did not come to court. They lived too far away and could not afford to travel; they no longer believed that justice would prevail; they had been either threatened by the families of the perpetrators or offered much needed money to stay away.

Three women did come to court: Fatiha, Rahmouna, and Nadia. Even their lawyers did not show up. The women testified for more than four hours. As they spoke, their tormentors mocked them. Fatiha had traveled a long way to testify. She wanted to "show them that it is for the perpetrators to be full of shame, not me. How could I pardon someone who sodomized me with a broomstick and who cut my breasts? How can Nadia pardon the man who tortured . . . then raped her? How can Rahmouna forget that youngsters the age of her own children cut her sex (mutilated her genitals)?"

Rahmouna, the mother of three, has never recovered. She wanders from town to town with her children. She says: "Sometimes I have destructive ideas that push me to go blow myself like a kamikaze at the Tribunal of Hessai Messaoud. Anyhow, these criminals have murdered in me any hope of life. All [that] is left for me is death and taking with me in death all those who have participated in my torture." (Please note, she is not talking about murdering innocent civilians. She is talking only about murdering her torturers—and she is talking only, she is not doing it.)

In their January-February 2005 newsletter, Amnesty International/Algeria Groups Network reported that twenty-six men (out of three hundred) were sentenced from three to twenty years imprisonment for the attacks on the women in Hassi Messaoud. This is nothing short of a miracle. But I fear that such femicide will still continue to happen.[2]

How do you educate a lynch mob? If you jail them, will they have a change of heart and mind in prison, where they will be associating with other criminals much like themselves? If you execute them, will their punishment educate others who share their woman-hating views? Will breaking off diplomatic relations with Algeria or imposing economic sanctions educate Algerian imams, mobs, and paramilitary organizations to stop kidnapping, gang raping, and lynching girls and women—and shooting the intellectuals, too? If we economically pressure or reward the Algerian government, will it be able to reeducate a population that approves of lynch mobs and whose hatred of women is horrifying?

I ask because I do not think that the usual diplomatic sanctions will work, and I am not sure what will. Perhaps the same media (radio, television, and the Internet), that has amplified the mosque-based Islamic hate propaganda may be used to teach an opposite lesson about tolerance and human rights. I am in favor of undertaking such ventures although they may or may not bear quick fruit. Such ongoing programs and the requisite technology will cost substantial sums. We will need to strategize collective ways of bearing the economic burden.

Poverty is relative; so is greed. People in every country live quite differently, in financial terms, from one another. World poverty, disease, illiteracy, and unemployment are all urgent priorities. But, if we, as a world community, fail to deal with the force of Islamic terrorism, which includes religious and gender apartheid, we will all be increasingly endangered by it. The barbaric nature of Islamic woman-hatred is impossible to overstate.

For example, on March 11, 2002, in Mecca, Saudi Arabia, the religious police (the Commission for the Promotion of Virtue and Prevention of Vice) physically prevented twelve- to fifteen-year-old schoolgirls from leaving a blazing school building, because they were not wearing their head scarves and abayas. They literally beat the young girls and forced them to re-enter the burning building—and they beat male Civil Defense members who were trying to rescue the girls. Fourteen to sixteen girls (reports vary) died in the fire.

What diplomatic or even educational initiatives will work when grown men have such murderous rage toward twelve-year-old girls?

However, the Saudi interior minister, Prince Naif, said he would investigate the matter and would ask those responsible to pay blood money to the families of the girls who perished and compensation to the injured. Prominent Saudis also called for a "reassessment of the religious police." A Saudi civil report concluded that "people claiming to be in the religious police hampered rescue efforts and prevented the evacuation of students."

This is a small first step. But much more is needed. From a psychological point of view, I know that it is almost impossible to penetrate a closed system of thought or a closed society. So, how can we in the West influence the Saudi princes in the matter of gender apartheid? By continuing to do business with them—or by refusing to do so? By going to war against them, imposing economic sanctions, working within an Islamic framework to elevate the status of women, bringing criminals to justice in an international criminal court? I do not yet have one answer. I *do* know that if we are not thinking at this level, nothing can change.[3]

Please allow me to share one last example of what, and how much, must be changed in the Islamic world in terms of Muslim attitudes toward and treatment of women.

Saira Shah is the author of an exquisitely written memoir, *The Storyteller's Daughter.* She is a British Afghan journalist and filmmaker, whose film *Beneath the Veil* documented the tragedy of women's lives under the Taliban. On a return trip to Afghanistan, Shah describes a Dantean scene in a hospital—in reality, a charnel house. Suddenly, her heart goes out to an Afghan mujahid who is bleeding from a head wound.

I lurch upon him, and say in Persian: "Brother how are you? Can I help you? What is your name?"

His face contorts with anger. "You do not know my name—but I know yours. You are Saira Shah, you have written lies about my commander, and if I have an opportunity, I will kill you."

His wound is pouring blood, he is dazed, he is nearly dead; but his hatred is still alive. The shock of it hits me like a physical blow, and I reel backwards into the masses of the injured and dying.

On his deathbed, this man is filled with murderous hate for the woman who has just expressed compassion towards him.

What is it, exactly, that diplomats or soldiers or even mullahs and imams can do to change this man's attitudes toward women, especially toward an independent woman who has publicly exposed his commander as a misogynist?

Woman-hating has been bred over a lifetime and down the centuries. Sons see their fathers beat and humiliate their mothers; they learn to do likewise. Islam as a religion might be able to discourage such behaviors; if it did so forcefully, it might have a very positive influence. However, Islam as a religion has also amplified and supported the most savage hatred of women.

After a series of violent demonstrations in which 300,000 religious fundamentalists called for her death, feminist author and physician Taslima Nasrin was forced to flee her native Bangladesh. She has lived in Sweden in hiding for more than a decade. In her view, there is no difference between "Islam and Islamic fundamentalists." In an interview she says: "Some liberals always defend Islam and blame fundamentalists for creating problems. But Islam itself oppresses women. Islam itself doesn't permit democracy, and violates human rights. . . . I don't agree with those who think that the conflict is simply between two religions, namely Christianity and Islam. Nor do I think that this is a conflict between East and West. To me, the key conflict is between irrational blind faith and rational logical minds. Or between modernity and anti-modernity."

Thus, some Muslim feminists are ardent secularists while others are ardently religious. I suspect that most Muslims are religious, not secular, and that most are *not* feminists. Therefore, reformers may have to support pro-woman forces within Islam as well as forces for secular democracy within the Islamic world.

Over the years, I have been a domestic violence researcher and activist. I have also been a therapist and have worked with and testified for battered women. Domestic violence exists everywhere. But, as we have seen, the Islamic world has its own unique version. It is my impression that the intimate, moment-by-moment terrorization of girls and women within and by their own families might be more widespread and normalized within the Islamic and non-western world than it is in Europe or North America.[4]

Batterers typically justify their battering as a form of self-defense. They view themselves as the victims. Lance Morrow, in *Evil: An Investigation,* asks how the Serbs kept on with their genocidal ethnic- and gender-cleansing programs in the face of the "world's condemnation." He answers his own question: "They found a remarkable solution. They felt sorry for themselves . . . they declared themselves the injured party. An artful, disgraceful display of jujitsu. . . . Regarding oneself as an innocent victim betrayed prepared the way for justifying virtually any act of retaliation."

My fourth psychological point concerns the cruelty of women toward each other in the Arab and Muslim world. Denying or minimizing this factor will not help free the Muslim world from tyranny. Despite western feminist ideals about "sisterhood," and despite the fact that women may share a common biological and social fate, female-female kindness, cooperation, or solidarity does not always exist.[5]

We might be able to create educational and ethical programs if we acknowledge, not deny, that woman's inhumanity to woman really exists. Understanding this has important policy implications; namely, we cannot assume that women will necessarily support women's rights or that men will necessarily oppose them. It is important to educate men about women's rights for two reasons: (1) because it is the right thing to do, and (2) because many women will follow a male lead on this question.

Let me pause here for a moment to make something clear. I am not saying that love, family feelings, happiness, poetry, or friendship in Arab and Muslim society do not exist; obviously they do. Prick them, they will bleed; Arabs and Muslims are human beings. Muslims are not necessarily the problem; jihadic and reactionary Islam is. I *am* also saying that Arabs and Muslims do not enjoy civil, secular, modern, or democratic societies. They have few legal rights, no freedom, and few economic opportunities. Sanctioned blood feuds, honor killings, and lynchings do not constittute modern concepts of justice.

This brings me to my fifth point. I would like to say something about American feminists and the psychology of patriotism. It is time for feminists to rethink our relationship both to America and to nationalism.

Why do feminists and progressives accept and even respect the fact that other people are loyal to their tribes and nation-states but despise such feelings among Americans as backward and dangerous? Why do they criticize America so obsessively for its failure to perfectionistically live up to our own high standards and yet remain so quiet about the absence of *any* standards and about the systematic violation of human rights in non-western countries?

Why are many American feminists so understanding about why Muslim women might "choose" to veil themselves, accept arranged and polygamous marriages, or undergo genital mutilation—but denigrate American women who "choose" to be stay-at-home mothers or who become soldiers whose bravery and self-sacrifice may lead to greater freedom for women and men elsewhere? Why do many American feminists view America's freedoms as sometimes meant for Americans only ("We can't impose our cultural standards on others") and at other times, insist that everyone else on earth is entitled to American rights—especially those whom we have captured in a jihadic and terrorist war they have declared against us?

I am not sure that feminist academics, activists, and civil libertarians are right to fight so hard for the rights of captured Muslim male warriors to be tried as if they were American citizens and not prisoners of war. Interestingly, according to a 2002 Pew Research Center Report, 72 percent of men favored a military tribunal for non-citizens as opposed to 58 percent of women. (Perhaps women are more compassionate toward men, even those charged with jihadic terrorism, than men are toward each other, or than women are toward other women). In my opinion, feminists ought to fight as hard for the rights of women, who live under Islam to be treated as if they were American citizens—as they are fighting for the right of Guantanamo's inmates to be so treated.

I have not heard one American feminist rant against the French over their sordid oil-for-food deal in Iraq or because they militarily invaded their former Ivory Coast colony. Did you? Nor did I hear any feminists rail against the jihad that non-assimilated Muslim immigrants in France have declared against France's highly assimilated Jews—and, increasingly, against the "white French."

I did not hear one American feminist complain bitterly about France's having sent a military jet to transport the dying Arafat the terrorist to the best hospital in Paris. And even when Arafat's financial greed could no longer be denied, I did not hear a single American feminist or progressive condemn Arafat and his Paris-based high-spending wife, Suha, for stealing billions of dollars meant to feed the starving Palestinian people and for squirreling the ill-gotten loot away, presumably in French bank accounts.

To the best of my knowledge, feminists did not single France out for condemnation. (To this day, only Israel has been singled out as responsible for the suffering of the Palestinian people.) Feminists are not obsessed with France's many failings—or, rather, they do not question France's right to exist because of them. But, many do question both America's and Israel's right to exist and to defend themselves because neither country is . . . perfect.

Whenever I have described how unassimilated French North African Muslims have been mistreating the assimilated Jews of Paris, many feminists shrug or throw up their hands helplessly, as if to say: "They are humiliated animals, what can you expect?" Or "Given Ariel Sharon's policies, what can you expect?" Both responses are racist.

One of the reasons that the Democrats may have lost the last American presidential election is because they were perceived as unpatriotic. I am not saying that Democrats *are* unpatriotic—only that from one point of view, they may be perceived as such. Democrats are liberals (increasingly left-dominated liberals), which means they think of themselves as internationalists who oppose "narrow" nationalisms, especially their own. I favor thinking of ourselves as citizens of the world and therefore as having transnational moral obligations—but I also favor pride in our own culture and a pro- rather than an obsessively anti-American perspective.

Is patriotism a thoroughly reactionary and selfish emotion—or is it a noble and altruistic one? Is patriotism an ideal or an emotion that only formerly colonized and European peoples are entitled to feel—or is it a sentiment that Americans and Israelis are also permitted to enjoy? Is patriotism an empty symbol that tyrants and oligarchs merely manipulate for their own evil ends, or can patriotism also embody the finest values and dreams of a people? Does patriotism impede all global progress, or does it have a crucial role to play in the twenty-first century?

There are, of course, different definitions of patriotism. Some people believe that the truest patriot is she who is loyal to the entire world—or to the impoverished, suffering peoples of the world—over and above her loyalty to her own countrymen and women or to their (corrupt) political leaders. This way of thinking is idealistic and therefore unrealistic and potentially dangerous. It assumes that both human nature and culture can be vastly improved by human beings in possession of the right social program; that such a program can rid the world of inequality; and that violent, permanent revolution is justified in order to accomplish this end.

Others believe that human beings cannot love "everyone," that anyone who says they are loyal to billions of unknown people is probably incapable of more intimate and less symbolic loyalties.

Is the most "patriotic" American someone who loudly and obsessively criticizes America—but not its enemies—when America is under siege and at war?

Some American patriots would argue that doing so is a quintessentially "American" virtue, that true Americans expect the best of America and do not stop demanding it merely because we are at war. There is something to this argument, but I would prefer criticism to be less polarizing, less purist, more balanced, and more civil.

Nationalism was once a radical and progressive idea. It inspired people to overthrow monarchies and to transcend their narrow loyalties to their own families and clans. In a sense, nationalism may allow people to feel altruistic toward and responsible for a larger number of people. From this point of view, nationalism is not intrinsically evil or even selfish. Would we have had an American

Revolution if we had not begun to think of ourselves as "Americans" as opposed to "British Virginians" or "British New Yorkers"? According to Israeli American author Hillel Halkin: "Without nationalism there would have been no American revolution, no French revolution, no end to the great empires that tyrannized immense populations—the tsarist empire, the Ottoman empire, the Soviet Empire. It was the concept of the nation-state, an embellishment upon the city-state of ancient Greece, that made the idea of a democratic society possible, for only in a society with a common language, common interests, and a common identity, could one imagine a common people deciding its own fate."

Just as most Euro-style American feminists currently despise nationalism and patriotism, they also assume that internationalism is intrinsically good. Yet it may not always be so. Actually, some institutions that they oppose the most are international in scope: imperialism, capitalism, and patriarchal religions. But feminists also tend to support the United Nations, which, in my view, represents a toxic and ineffective internationalism. Today we also have international jihadic terrorism that threatens innocent civilians everywhere.

To the extent to which American feminists are rebelling against misogynist practices, they will be the first to condemn their own patriarchal nation-state and religion. After all, American women are still not included in the Constitution, the Equal Rights Amendment did not pass, and women's reproductive rights remain under severe siege.

Most American feminists are critical of America because they see it as a powerful country that has failed its moral mandate on behalf of women, children, and the most vulnerable in America and has failed the needs of countless others in Third World countries. There is something to this critique, it has merit; still, it is unacceptably perfectionistic and lacks perspective.

Many American feminists equate America with the Enron and Abu Ghraib scandals—and not with its extraordinary commitment to passing legislation against the trafficking of girls and women, both worldwide and domestically; its military bravery on behalf of freedom in Afghanistan and Iraq; its decision to monitor global anti-Semitism and its almost immediate action against the prisoner abuse in Abu Ghraib. Many American feminists also want contradictory things; no surprise, they are only human. Thus, many feminists want Big Daddy and right-wing America "out" of Iraq, and "out" of their beds and their heads. However, psychologically, feminists also want this same Big Daddy to be publicly humiliated, perhaps impoverished, but still to fix the whole world.

Feminists have been well taught to feel ashamed of America and guilty for the alleged "crimes" America has committed against people both here and in other countries. This is another reason that many feminists forgive gross misogyny abroad.

We must rethink our feminist multiculturalism. Author Taslima Nasrin implores us to do so, saying:

> Some authors in the West are coming forward in support of the fundamentalists. They are trying to argue that not all customs in vogue in the third world countries are harmful for women. They find a sort of stability and social peace in the oriental world. They think that even the harems are not necessarily bad for women, because they provide a degree of autonomy and independence!
>
> May I humbly observe that all this is a plain hoax.
>
> In fact the fight is more urgent in the East, because most of the women have neither any education nor any economic independence. If modern secular education is good for western women why should the eastern women be deprived of it? The peace that some authors visualize in the Eastern countries is, clearly, the peace of the grave.

There are also moments in history when loyalty to one's own tribe or nation-state is both rational, but might also benefit non-nationals, as well. In my view, at this moment in time, loyalty to America means loyalty to a vision of a freer world, one not demoralized by Islamic totalitarianism and gender and religious apartheid. In my view, an American and western vision of individual freedom and freedom from tyranny is now our shining legacy to the entire world.

Obviously, people can have multiple loyalties. Although I am loyal to universal feminist ideals, I am also an American patriot. However imperfect, I love this country. I would not live anywhere else; not now, and never again.

❋ ❋ ❋

In the matter of Bosnia and to a lesser extent in the matter of Rwanda, many feminists did note and did protest the savage mistreatment of the female civilian populations. Some American feminists brought lawsuits on behalf of the raped women; some funded or personally helped with rape crisis counseling. I was supposed to testify about rape trauma syndrome before the war crimes tribunal in the matter of Bosnia, but the tribunal did not have the money to continue its work or to protect those who testified from being killed by those whom they were accusing.

Perhaps feminists are (unconsciously) ashamed that they have been so ineffective in stopping the larger, more horrifying sexual abuse of girls and women; perhaps we are seeing a "scapegoat" phenomena: Feminists can't eliminate rapists, gender cleansing, or gender apartheid, but can vent their frustrated rage on a far more acceptable, symbolic target, namely, America. Even feminists will be listened to respectfully in most academic and media circles when and if they attack America or Israel. Less attention is paid to feminist statements about women's freedom.

And thus, precisely because they are *not* paying attention to feminist business, feminists are overly engaged in "hating" America.

As I was completing this book, I accepted a dinner invitation from two long-time feminist friends whom I had not seen since 9/11. I was unexpectedly treated to a tirade. Scarcely in my chair, one friend emphatically, immediately intoned: "Today, we are the Nazis. Our government thinks it can invade sovereign space at will. How dare it do so? We will pay dearly for this."

She assumed I would automatically agree with her. It was the end of a long hard day and I did not want to fight—but I would not return our era's equivalent of the "Heil Hitler" salute. Wearily, warily, I said: "Do you believe that America has no responsibility beyond its own borders? Are we right to have done too little in the matter of Bosnia, and nothing to have stopped the mass rapes and genocide in Sudan and Rwanda?"

I was merely asking difficult questions. But, I had not condemned America. Failing to do so was apparently still a treasonous act among my old crowd. My second friend stared, glared, and raised her voice. "Why don't we help raped women right here, or work on ourselves? Violence is never the solution. We have to evolve the world's consciousness in non-violent ways. We have to let people work out their own destinies."

However, the anti-violence speaker had begun to shout. Heads turned in the restaurant. As she continued yelling, the first woman started a filibuster about how right-wing American Christians are far more dangerous than right-wing Muslims in Iraq, Afghanistan, and Saudi Arabia. Thus, one was shouting, the other wouldn't shut up. The dinner was no longer civilized.

I asked: "Would you have argued against stopping Hitler?"

Both said: "Hitler was different, Muslims are not like Hitler, we are. And you have been taken over by the right wing." Dialogue was impossible, their minds were utterly closed, it was like talking to racists in the 1950s. I wished them well and left. No American soldier deserves to die to protect these two.

There are more reflective and less combative ways to have this same conversation. For example, my dear friend, anthropologist Barbara Joans, tells me that while she supports Israel's and America's right to exist and opposes Islamic jihad, she is still a "cultural relativist." She says: "The position of women in most areas is horrendous. But, they are not our cultures. What do we do? Can we police the world? Will that help? Do we have the right to change another culture?"

We talk, calmly, respectfully. The questions are huge. We do not have the answers. We are in search of them.

Am I in favor of interventionist and military solutions to every problem? No, I am not. But some problems cannot be solved in any other way. If a woman is being beaten or held hostage either one intervenes and rescues her or one does not. Pacifists (who are themselves rarely in harm's way) are willing to sacrifice those who are being tortured in order to lecture the non-torturers about the virtues of non-violence. Like my friends, many anti-war pacifists say they are willing to wait hundreds of years for humanity to "evolve."

But Gandhi and Martin Luther King, Jr. put their bodies in harm's way *non-violently* to accomplish their noble ends. Today's pacifists did not go up against the Taliban or al-Qaeda. True, humanitarian workers have risked their lives in order to deliver goods and services to civilians trapped in war-zones but they did not surround Saddam Hussein's, Yasser Arafat's, or Osama bin Laden's homes or bunkers singing songs of non-violence addressed to *them*. Nor, in the name of pacifism, did they start riding the Jerusalem buses to protect civilians.

Is President Bush waging the very best war against terrorism in Afghanistan and Iraq? Probably not—but who could? By definition, war is Hell. Were it up to me—and it's not—I would suggest that only standing armies should fight other standing armies and that they should all do so in one, far-distant country so that the world's civilians may remain out of harm's way.

But batterers, torturers, slavers, despots, and terrorists specialize in persecuting and destroying the vulnerable. The question remains: How long do we—the good people—allow them to do so? How much blood must they shed before we are willing to risk our own lives to stop them for another century? How much of our own blood are we willing to shed to do so? Who gets to decide?

As I tried to ask my friends: Is it good enough to do nothing, to hide behind the corrupt non-interventionism of the United Nations?

Over the years, I and every other feminist leader grew accustomed to being attacked by other feminists. At first, the attacks concerned being (unjustly) articulate, ambitious, accomplished, or famous; this happened to every feminist "star"—and there were "stars" in every town and circle. Clearly, the "trashers"—the word feminists coined for such ad feminem attacks—felt less endowed by nature and character; group attacks were their revenge. These useful idiots served to toughen me up for the combat that was to occur between feminists about issues such as pornography, prostitution, surrogacy, and women's custody rights, and between feminists and a largely anti-feminist world.

Second Wave feminists did not support their thinkers and leaders; that is an understatement. In my opinion, those few feminists around whom cults once formed were ill-served by them. However, in the late 1960s and throughout the 1970s, feminists did enjoy salon-like societies which sustained and connected us. Politics, protest, culture, night-life, social-life, career information were all merged into an endless moveable feast. Most of us could not sustain this level of excitement, civility, and *society*. But a small reminder of it still goes a long way.

For example, after I was "purged" from that left-feminist listserv group, it meant a lot to me that Barbara Seamen reached out to me to make sure that I would not feel isolated.

And, earlier in 2004, the philosopher and environmentalist Linda Clarke and her domestic partner, retired teacher and musician Joan Casamo, came to visit. They had heard the rumors about my voting for President Bush. They did not demand that I change my vote. They sincerely wanted to understand my thinking. (These two righteous Gentiles had also tendered their support, both privately and socially, as I dealt with the issues of anti-Semitism and anti-Zionism among feminists and intellectuals.)

Linda and Joan viewed my battle against racism and totalitarianism as valorous. Since they are grand party-givers, they had a vision that our dear friend Kate Millett and I would be able to model respectful, attentive, open-hearted listening across greatly polarized ideological divides, both socially and perhaps publicly.

They recently helped Kate host a dinner party so that a small group could hear what I was saying. Present were College of Staten Island president, Marlene Springer, several retired educators, including Eleanor Pam, harpist Myra Kovary, and the lawyer with whom I live. After serious and giddy expressions of delight in each other's company—some of us go back to 1968—the Great Experiment began.

In her most thrilling and dramatic "whiskey voice," Kate said that the detention of prisoners in Guantanamo, as well as the scandal of Abu Ghraib, is horrifying, unacceptable, and that the Bush regime is the Evil Empire. She almost began to filibuster—but Linda pulled her back with eye contact.

My lawyer coolly remarked that at least we have a judicial process in America, granted, one that often works too slowly, but one that responded very quickly in the matter of Abu Ghraib. Overall, the American system of checks and balances is well positioned to deal with oligarchies.

Everyone agreed. This bought some time.

I reminded Kate that the jihadists are an even bigger problem than what's happening at Guantanamo. Based on her published work, the entire world knows that Kate is claustrophobic and identifies with torture victims everywhere. I understood that she was psychologically as well as politically threatened and outraged by the Abu Ghraib photographed realities. Gently, I said: "Israeli civilians have been living in smaller and smaller boxes, both psychologically and physically, for the last five years. The Iranians just whipped and stoned to death a nineteen-year-old Iranian girl whose mother had sold her into prostitution when she was eight and whose life had been a horrific series of abuses. So many women living under Islam are living in literal boxes and cages. They have no judicial process in place, we have no way of rescuing them, the men who are torturing them are coming for us next—unless we are willing to fight back."

Everyone nodded. There was no small talk; no one even cleared her throat.

"What about the government's attempt to abolish our civil liberties?" someone asked.

I agreed this could be dangerous—and everyone sighed in relief. But I continued. "The danger of tolerating the intolerant overly much in the West is that they will use our virtues and strengths against us and will increasingly try to impose intolerant ways upon our society. We have to strategically balance our concept of civil liberties against our right to live, and to live as westerners in a western-style democracy."

This idea was greeted by a thoughtful silence—not by the usual attacks.

The university president comes from the South. She cautioned me against trusting "right-wing Christians." She said she'd grown up among them and they would do anything to get their way.

I agreed that fundamentalism was dangerous—and I do—but this also allowed me an opening which I immediately took. "Today, many secular leftists, including academic and activist feminists, are fundamentalists, too. They refuse to grasp the realities of terrorism or jihad because the reality challenges their left ideology. And many conservative intellectuals are far more tolerant and libertarian than we are."

The university president agreed. A sad silence ensued. Some women sighed.

You must understand that in such feminist circles, these sighs, as well as the entire conversation thus far, was heretical.

We were talking, not fighting; listening, not pontificating. My secular feminist pals were gladly and lovingly consorting with a known American patriot and Zionist. From this point of view, the dinner party was already a glorious success.

As Donna Hughes and I wrote in our 2004 *Washington Post* Op-Ed piece: "Islamist fundamentalism and al-Qaeda terrorism threatens women all over the world. Wherever they have gained power, Islamists have denied women their essential humanity and dignity. Islamic fundamentalism is not a conservative religion but a fascist political movement bent on world domination."

As I have said, the polarization of public thought in the West concerns me. Such polarization leads to the inability of thinking people to work together on one issue unless they agree with each other on every other issue. We are all further endangered when intellectuals become intolerant ideologues.

I agree with author Paul Berman who, on October 4, 2004, in a joint lecture with Michael Ignatieff in New York City, said: "The larger war is that of ideas. We should be appealing to Muslims trapped by tyranny. Our success depends on our ability to express this."

We need our intellectuals, including *feminist* intellectuals, at the ready. In *Terror and Liberalism,* Berman called for a non-cynical "third force" in foreign policy. He envisioned this as a "force devoted to a politics of human rights and especially women's rights, across the Muslim world; a politics of ethnic and religious tolerance; a politics against racism and anti-Semitism, no matter how inconvenient that might seem to the Egyptian media and the House of Saud . . . a politics of authentic solidarity for the Muslim world . . . a politics, in a word, of liberalism, a 'new birth of freedom'—the kind of thing that could be glimpsed, in its early stages, in the liberation of Kabul."

In March 2005, Ramesh Sepehrrad of the National Committee of Women for a Democratic Iran (NCWDI) honored me by asking me to join her and other dissident Iranian and Afghan women on a panel that took place at the United Nations. Thirty-five-year-old Ramesh was the moderator. Two dissident film crews, one from Iran, another from Afghanistan, filmed our evening.

About eight women in hijab sat in a menacing bloc in the audience. They were official representatives of the Iranian government. Ramesh stood up and pointed at their leader. She said: "We know who you are. Tell the mullahs back in Tehran what you heard here. Tell them that women will overthrow their corrupt regime, that women will bring them down." I was thunderstruck by her cool bravery. As she spoke, Ramesh's colleague, Soona Samsani, stood up and began taking their photos. Clearly, the government officials did not want their photos taken. At a signal from their leader, all eight left.

According to the NCWDI, "Iran is still the largest prison (in the world) for women." In a comprehensive and alarming 2005 report prepared for the 49th session of the Commission on the Status of Women in New York, NCWDI challenged a brazen Tehran government which claimed that the regime had made significant "achievement and progress on women's rights and empowerment." On the contrary, according to NCWDI, since 1979, tens of thousands of women have been tortured and executed in Iran. The report concluded that:

> A regime like Tehran that uses rape and sexual slavery as weapons against women, stones women to death, and has the highest number of female executions in the world should not be allowed to get its hands on nuclear weapons. The Iranian regime is a state sponsor of terrorism and violence against women. Therefore, the struggle of the Iranian women against this regime is extremely important in the field of international peace and security.[6]

These are the kind of feminists whom western feminists and academics need to support. To do so, we need the kind of "moral clarity" that Natan Sharansky and Ron Dermer write about in *The Case for Democracy.*

The authors note that those who live in fear must find the "inner strength to confront evil," while those who live in a world of freedom must find the "moral clarity to see evil." Without "moral clarity," sympathy for the weak "can also be placed in the service of evil and manipulated by tyrants." They suggest that "we must move beyond Left and Right and begin to think again about right and wrong."

As I've previously noted, Sharansky and Dermer then propose that the free world, inspired by America, begin to peg its foreign policy to a country's *domestic* record on human rights. Thus, if the "Saudi regime wants American protection, it will have to change its draconian emigration policies and improve its record on women's rights."

In addition to moral clarity, let me suggest that we also need intellectual clarity, intellectual independence, and non-ideological thinking.

And, I am finding it among the upper echelons of American government, not among most feminist academics, journalists, and activists. For example, I am very proud that President Bush appointed Condoleezza Rice, an African American woman, as our Secretary of State. I am ashamed that left-dominated feminists have failed to celebrate this achievement or to reach out to Rice and offer their support. I am amazed and pleased by what Secretary Rice said to the leaders of Egypt and Saudi Arabia in 2005. She spoke about the importance of allowing women to vote and about the dangers of poverty and tyranny. But she also talked about a new kind of American foreign policy, one that will "no longer pursue stability at the expense of democracy." In her Cairo speech, Rice praised Anwar Sadat for making peace with Israel. And, she said:

"For sixty years, my country, the United States, pursued stability at the expense of democracy in this region here in the Middle East—and we achieved neither. Now, we are taking a different course. We are supporting the democratic aspirations of all people . . . the right to speak freely. The right to associate. The right to worship as you wish. The freedom to educate your children—boys and girls. And freedom from the midnight knock of the secret police."[7]

In a separate address to the American Israel Public Affairs Committee, also in 2005, Secretary Rice was more specific. She hailed the Kuwaiti Legislature's decision to grant women the right to vote; the mass movement in Lebanon that ousted the Syrian occupiers and held elections; the incredible bravery of Iraqi citizens "who defied threats of murder to vote in free elections" and so on. She also said:

> Some in the Arab media have even asked why the only democracies in the Middle East are found in the "occupied lands" of Iraq and the Palestinian territories. What an incredible thought . . . the Palestinian Authority must advance democratic reform and it must dismantle terrorist networks in its society. Arab states must end incitement in their media, cut off all support for terrorism and extremist education, and establish normal relations with Israel.[8]

Secretary Rice is setting quite a standard. But, in addition, in terms of foreign policy initiatives, *New York Times* columnist David Brooks believes that little will change unless—or until—intelligence community analysts are "sent to training academies where they study Thucydides, Tolstoy, and Churchill to get a broad understanding of the full range of human behavior." He writes: "I'll believe the system has been reformed when policy makers are presented with competing reports, signed by individual thinkers, and are no longer presented with anonymous, bureaucratically homogenized, bulleted points that pretend to be the product of scientific consensus."

According to Saudi author Wajiha Al-Huweida, "All Arab countries, without exception, harbor covert animosity and open discrimination against women." Al-Huweida denounces the view of women as "impure" and "immoral." She says flat out that "cats and dogs in the developed world have more rights than Arab women."

Tunisian author and researcher Dr. Munjiyah Al-Sawaihi writes that as she "looks beyond the horizon," all she can see is "the tightening of the noose around the [Arab and Islamic] woman." She calls for Arab intellectuals to address this problem "courageously and with strong resolve" and not to sidestep it out of "fear of reactionary forces."

I wholeheartedly agree with her. As Jews say: "Hineni [I am here]." My book is here. I hope it will be of some assistance in this enormous struggle for women's and humanity's freedom.

Notes

Introduction

1. Kay. S. Hymowitz admirably made some of these points but she did not write as a feminist leader or to a feminist audience. I hope to do so. Hymowitz, Kay S. "Why Feminism Is AWOL on Islam," *City Journal* (Winter 2003).

Chapter One

1. This point was first made by Harvard professor Ruth Wisse on a panel about anti-Semitism we were both on and which took place in Montreal in 2004.
2. Noah Liben, "Anti-Semitism and Discrimination: Case Analyses," no. 1, Jerusalem Center for Public Affairs, April 13, 2005, http://www.jcpa.org/phas/phas-liben–05.htm, accessed 4/13/2005.
3. David Horowitz, "Bowling Green Barbarians," *FrontPageMagazine.com,* April 4, 2005 and "An Ill-Bred Professor and a Bad Situation," *FrontPage Magazine,* Apr. 25, 2005.
4. The 1995 *American Enterprise* (TAE) study reported that its "Cornell sample showed 171 Democrats, 7 Republicans, and 21 professors registered as independents or in other (mostly left-wing) parties. The Stanford professors broke out this way: 163 Democrats, 17 Republicans, and 6 independent/other." Karl Zinsmeister, "Diversity on Campus? There Is None," *American Enterprise Institute,* Dec. 13, 2004.
5. The 2002 study by David Horowitz and TAE compared lists of tenured or tenure-track professors (in economics, English, history, philosophy, political science, and sociology) with voter registration lists. They found that faculty voted 10 to 1 for Democrats. They described this as a "grossly unbalanced, politically shaped selection process in the hiring of college faculty."
6. Daniel B. Klein and Andrew Western, "How Many Democrats per Republican at UC–Berkeley and Stanford? Voter Registration Data Across 23 Academic Departments," 2004. Forthcoming *Academic Questions.* http://lsb.scu.edu/dklein/voter/default.htm, accessed 06/27/05.
7. The 2005 Klein and Stern study was based on questionnaire respondents who were members of six nation-wide social science and humanities associations: American Anthropology Association, American Economics Association, American Historical Association, American Society for Political and Legal Philosophy, American Political Science Association, and American Sociological Association. http://lsb.scu.edu/~dklein/voter/default.htm, as accessed 6/27/05.
8. Stanley Rothman, Robert S. Lichter, and Neil Nevitte, "Politics and Professional Advancement Among College Faculty," *The Forum* 3 (1), Article 2, http://www.bepress.com/forum/vol3/iss1/art2, accessed 4/15/2005.

In the study, the most "liberal" departments across the board are the humanities (81 percent) and the social sciences (75 percent). Self-described "liberals" outnumbered "conservatives" even among engineering faculty (51 percent to 19 percent) and business faculty (49 percent to 39 percent).

This is not the same as self-identifying as a "Democrat" or a "Republican." Indeed, only 50 percent of the faculty members surveyed identified themselves as Democrats and 11 percent as Republicans.

The self-described "liberals" are, strongly or somewhat, in favor of abortion rights (84 percent); believe homosexuality is acceptable (67 percent); and want more environmental protection, "even if it raises prices or costs jobs" (88 percent). What's more, the study found, 65 percent want the government to ensure full employment, a stance to the left of the Democratic Party.

According to Robert Lichter, "even broad-minded people gravitate toward other people like themselves. That's why you need diversity, not just of race and gender but also, maybe especially, of ideas and perspective."

It is important to note that 72 percent of all full-time faculty are male and only 28 percent are female.

9. The 2000 study, "Losing America's Memory: Historical Illiteracy in the 21st Century," was conducted by the ROPA organization for the American Council of Trustees and Alumni. Among the fifty-five top universities sampled were the California Institute of Technology, Harvard, MIT, Yale, Stanford, Duke, John Hopkins, University of Pennsylvania, and Columbia. Among the top national liberal arts colleges sampled were Swarthmore, Amherst, Williams, Wellesley, Haverford, Middlebury, Pomona, Carleton, Bowdoin, and Wesleyan.

10. The 2002 study was conducted by Zogby International for the National Association of Scholars. It consisted of a random sample of 401 college and university seniors. The authors write: "The 2002 college seniors did better than the 1955 high school graduates on seven questions and worse on eight. Compared with the 1955 college graduates, the 2002 college seniors did better on two and worse on thirteen questions."

11. Only a small number of people in both samples (17 to 32 percent) volunteered that they had a favorite author. For example, in the 1946 sample, only a single (different) person said that Charles Dickens, John Steinbeck, Leo Tolstoy, and Ernest Hemingway were their favorite authors. Five people chose Shakespeare and Somerset Maugham. In the 2002 sample, ten people voluntarily mentioned Ernest Hemingway, seven mentioned Edgar Allen Poe, and two mentioned W. E. B. DuBois and Kurt Vonnegut. One each mentioned Milan Kundera, Henry Miller, J. D. Salinger, Shakespeare, Tolstoy, and Tennessee Williams. The NAS study determined what constitutes "highbrow" or "canonical" works versus "popular" or "lowbrow" works.

12. Battered women who kill in self-defense ultimately do so because no one else will stop the torture or save them. Most battered women are killed when they attempt to leave. Most have no place to go, no safe haven. If they run, they risk losing their jobs and the very children they may be trying to protect. In my opinion, the fact that some battered women kill their batterers when they *can,* when their batterer is unarmed or resting, must be understood, not used to prosecute them. The legal rules that apply among men for justifiable homicide assumes contenders who are of equal height, weight, and training. Most battered women are at least fifty to one hundred pounds lighter and a foot shorter than their batterers; they are not karate experts nor have they had military or weapons training. Perhaps a batterer has just beaten his hostage for the hundredth time for trying to escape, perhaps he has also just announced, in a matter-of-fact way, that he's made up his mind, he's going to kill her right after he takes a short nap/bath/phone call. He puts the

gun on the table, laughing. He knows that she's too afraid to use it. He turns his back. . . . Finally, even she believes that he really *is* going to kill her. She miraculously decides to save her own life. Call it a desperate, one-time "preemptive" action.

Saying so does not mean that I believe that homicidal suicide bombers are also entitled to "preemptive" actions against civilians as a form of self-defense.[0]

13. I am no Anne Frank. I no longer believe that leftists are capable of the slightest social civility when faced with truths with which they strongly disagree.

Chapter Three

1. At the time, Pollitt also tore into me over a communication that I had sent to another listserv group about that American feminist involvement in fund-raising for Afghan women. My piece had somehow come to her attention—and she proceeded to share and challenge it on this listserv group. Pollitt herself was writing about RAWA (the Revolutionary Association for the Women of Afghanistan) for *The Nation*, and was sponsoring or promoting a benefit for them. Laudable perhaps—but I wondered whether American feminists were profiting more from the exposure of the Taliban than Afghan women were. I also wondered whether RAWA's primarily secular agenda had any chance of succeeding in Afghanistan. Pollitt attacked me on the HIA listserv group for making these points in an article that I had sent to another listserv group and had not been meant for her or for anyone else on the HIA listserv group to see. Ironically, years later, *Ms. Magazine* and Feminist Majority activists revised their view of RAWA and removed them entirely from the summary of activism on behalf of Afghan women.

2. This listserv group had a number of frequent, active "talkers," a number of intermittent "talkers," and a number of "non-talkers." According to one membership list there were about 50–60 members on this listserv. I have no way of knowing whether this number is accurate. But my point here is that I knew most of the talkers either well, or less well, but for a long period of time, ranging from 5–35 or more years. None of the sixteen or more listserv members whom I had known very well or for a long time ever came to my defense online.

They include novelist and poet Marge Piercy, who used to dedicate poetry to me, with whom I was in a consciousness raising group in the early 1970s, and who was once my friend; Professor Roxanne Dunbar-Ortiz who once stayed with me overnight and whom I had introduced to the listserv group; Professor Naomi Weisstein, with whom I co-founded the Association for Women in Psychology in 1969; Naomi's husband, radical left historian Professor Jesse Lemisch, with whom I'd had some unpleasant dealings—mainly on this listserv group; my former lawyer, Justice Emily Jane Goodman, with whom I once co-authored a book, and who had recently rushed up to embrace me when I spoke about anti-Semitism at a meeting of the Jewish Lawyers and Judges of New York City; former professor and historian, Ruth Rosen, who had quoted me at length in her work about the Second Wave movement, both about feminist-era "trashing" and about "woman's inhumanity to woman"; Professor Ros Baxandall, who earlier turned to me for a letter of recommendation to help her obtain her distinguished professorship; Professor Barbara Winslow, who had thanked me for my work when we met a number of times; feminist author, Louise Bernikow, with whom I go back to the early 1970s; my friend and feminist ally, the health writer and activist, Barbara Seaman, with whom I co-founded the National Women's Health Network in 1974; Laura Murra (Laura X), whom I have known since the late 1960s and who was herself routinely savaged by the highly aggressive Pollitt; Third Wave feminist author and lecturer, Jennifer Baumgardner, who together with

Amy Richards attacked my book *Letters to a Young Feminist* in the pages of her work *Manifesta: Young Women, Feminism, and the Future* and with whom I have subsequently dined and reconciled; Sonia Robbins Jaffee, feminist editor and activist, whom I've met over the years, most lately in the company of Ros Baxandall at a party for the great feminist author Sheila Rowbottham; Bea Kreloff, who was in my feminist Passover seder group from 1975 on and for whom I taught a workshop in Assisi in the late 1990s; Merle Hoffman, whom I've known for eighteen years and who published the feminist magazine *On the Issues*, where I served as editor at large for more than a decade; Linda Stein, an artist whose work I supported and whom I met in the 1990s. I have known other listserv members over the years too but not as well. I have been on panels with them, marched by their sides in demonstrations, and so on.

It was my impression that frequent, active "talkers" included Katha Pollitt, Sonia Robbin Jaffee, Roxanne Dunbar-Ortiz, Carol Hanisch, Ros Baxandall, Jennifer Baumgardner, Laura Murra, Judith Ezekiel (whom I have never met), and Barbara Winslow; intermittent "talkers" included Judge Emily Jane Goodman, Marge Piercy, Naomi and Jesse Lemisch, Ruth Rosen, Barbara Seaman, Louise Bernikow, Merle Hoffman, Bea Kreloff, and Linda Stein. One can never be entirely sure whether every member actually reads every posting.

My point: The active intolerance of the left feminists was cruel and disappointing. The silence on the part of the less vocal bystanders was equally disappointing. Perhaps they were not reading the e-mails. Perhaps they were—but simply chose not to get involved. Non-involvement or neutrality when intolerance is on the march does not equal "goodness."

3. Socrates was also accused of "heresy" because, according to Plato, Socrates "does not believe in the gods of the state but has other new divinities of his own." A jury, composed of 501 Athenian citizens, found him guilty and condemned him to death by poison.

4. The monk Giordano Bruno was tried and condemned by the Catholic church as an anti-Catholic materialist, pantheist, scientist, and stoicist. These beliefs constituted "heresy." Bruno was jailed for seven terrible years, forced to recant (which he did, many times over, until he stopped doing so), and then burned at the stake at the steps of St. Peter's.

5. The Catholic Inquisition banned Galileo Galilei's work and tried and convicted him of heresy. His crime? He claimed that the earth revolved around the sun and was not stationary. He was not only condemned to lifelong imprisonment (mercifully, at home), but he was also forced to publicly recant his views. He recited and signed a "formal abjuration" in which he "cursed and detested (his) said errors and heresies . . . contrary to the Holy Catholic Church." Thereafter, Galileo was closely watched by officers of the Inquisition and had to smuggle subsequent writings out of Italy to be published in Holland.

Chapter Five

1. Geeta Chowdry and Nair, Sheila, *Power. Postcolonialism, and International Relations. Reading Race Gender and Class* (New York: Routledge, 2004). In this anthology, J. Marshall Beier, an assistant professor of political science at McMaster University and co-author of a book published by Oxford University Press, writes about "the near total neglect of Indigenous peoples" in the study of international relations. He may have a point—but once again, his point of reference is this: He asks what marks the difference between the statelessness of "Indigenous American peoples" and, you guessed it, that of "the Palestinians or the Kurds."

2. Alex Alexiev, Testimony before the U.S. Senate Subcommittee on Terrorism, Technology, and Homeland Security, "Wahhabism: State-Sponsored Extremism Worldwide," June 26, 2003, http://www.centerforsecuritypolicy.org/index.jsp?section=static&page=

alexievtestimony, accessed 5/4/2005;Alan Cooperman, "Harvard Will Refund Sheik's $2.5 Million Gift," *Washington Post,* July 27, 2004, http://www.washingtonpost.com/wp-syn/articles/A19223–2004Jul27.html, accessed 5/4/2005; Adam Daifallah, "Funding a Professor of Hate," *New York Sun,* July 28, 2003; Candace De Russy, "Saudi Spending Jag on American Campuses," NAS, July18, 2003, http://www.nas.org/forum_blogger/forum_archives/2003_07_13_nasof_arch, accessed 5/4/2005; Amina El-bendary, "Not All Academic," *Al-Ahram,* Oct. 17, 2002, http://weekly.ahram.org.eg/2002/608/bol.htm, accessed 5/4/2005; Kevin J. Feeney, "Harvard Seeks Mideast Specialists," *Harvard Crimson,* Dec. 8, 2004, http://www.the-crimson.com/article.aspx?ref=504945, accessed 5/4/2005; Rachel Fish, "A Troubling Gift: Will Harvard Take $2.5 Million from a Man Tied to Holocaust Denial?" *Opinion Journal,* June 6, 2003, http://www.opinonjournal.com/taste/?id=11000, accessed 5/4/2005.

Jacob Gershman, "Saudis Funded Columbia Program at Institute that Trained Teach-ers," *New York Sun,* Mar. 10, 2005; Eric J. Greenberg, "Harvard Chair Mess Is Anything but Divine," *The Jewish Week,* May 30, 2003, http://www.thejewishweek.com/news/newscontent.php3?artid=7986, accessed 5/4/2005.

Sandhya Jain, "Saudi Halo Over US Academia," *Pioneer,* May 4, 2004, http://www.hvk.org/articles/0504/15.html, accessed 5/4/2005; Lee Kaplan, "The Saudi Fifth Column on Our Nation's Campuses," *FrontPageMagazine.com,* April 5, 2004; Mar-tin Kramer, "Saudi Oil Money Puffs Middle East Centers," *MartinKramer.org,* April 8, 2003, http://www.martinkramer.org/pages/899529, accessed 5/5/2005; Alyssa A. Lap-pen, "Enemy with a Human Face," *FrontPageMagazine.com,* September 2, 2003; http://www.frontpagemag.com/Articles/Printable.asp?ID=9564, accessed 5/3/2005.

Matthew Levitt, Testimony before the Senate Judiciary Subcommittee on Terrorism, Technology, and Homeland Security, "Subversion from Within: Saudi Funding of Islamic Extremist Groups Undermining U. S. Interests and the War on Terror from Within the United States," Sept. 10, 2003, http://www.washingtoninstitute.org/templateC07.php?CID=13, accessed 5/4/2005; Steven A. McDonald, "HDS Hires Islamic Studies Prof: Harvard Recruits Islamic Studies and Muslim Law Professor to Di-vinity Faculty," *Harvard Crimson,* March 21, 2005, http://www.thecrimson.com/arti-cle.aspx?ref=506635, accessed 5/4/2005.

Jennifer Mishory, "Meeting to Address Possible Suspension of Islamic Studies Graduate Program," *Daily Bruin,* Nov. 19, 2004, http://www.dailybruin.ucla.edu/news/aricles.asp?id=31023, accessed 5/4/2005; Daniel Pipes, "Harvard Celebrates Middle East Studies," *DanielPipes.org,* Aug. 9, 2004, http://www.danielpipes.org/blog/302, ac-cessed 5/4/2005; Steven Plaut, "Berkeley's War Against Israel," *FrontPageMagazine.com,* Mar. 7, 2005, http://www.frontpagemag.com/Articles/Readarticle.asp?ID=17270, ac-cessed 5/4/2005; Steven Plaut, "Taking Orders from Arafat," *FrontPageMagazine.com,* June 29, 2004, http://frontpagemag.com/Articles/Printable.asp?ID=14006, accessed 5/3/2005; Rachel Pomerance, " Can College Faculty Save Israel's Image?" *Jewish Tele-graphic Agency,* May 19, 2004; Rachel Pomerance, "Cal Accused of Taking Saudi Money with Al-Qaida Ties," *Jewish Telegraphic Agency,* http://www.jewishsf.com/content/2–0-/module/displaystory/story_id/20312/edition_id/414/format/html/displaystory.html, ac-cessed 5/4/2005; Steve Sexton and Ben Barron, "Saudi Terrorists Fund Berkeley Center," Aug. 27, 2003, http://www.calpatriot.org/September03/saudi.html, accessed 5/4/2005.

Ben Shapiro, "King Fahd's Plan to Conquer America," *Townhall.com,* Dec. 20, 2002, http://www.townhall.com/columnists/benshapiro, accessed 5/4/2005; staff Editorial, "Balance and Khalidi," *New York Sun,* Feb. 25, 2005; staff Editorial, "Columbia's Fun-der," *New York Sun,* Aug. 27, 2004, http://daily.nysun.com/standard/ShowStoryTem-plate.asp?Path=NYS/2004/08/27&ID=Ar01004&Section=Editorial_and_Opinion,

accessed 5/4/2005; worldNetDaily, "War on Terror: UC Berkeley Benefactors tied to 9–11, Mideast Studies Program Funded by Saudis Implicated in Attacks," May 8, 2003; Alex Safian, "NPR's Special Bias," *Camera: Committee for Accuracy in Middle East Reporting in America,* Sept. 30, 2002, http://www.camera.org/indiex.asp?x_print=1&x_article=280&x_context=8, accessed 5/19/2005; John Laksin, "Arafat Supporter in American Academia," DiscoverTheNetwork.org, *FrontPage Magazine,* May 16, 2005, http://frontpagemagazine.com/Articles/ReadArticle.asp?ID=18074, accessed 5/16/2005.

3. Gayatri Chakravorty Spivak, "Can the Subaltern Speak?" in *Marxism and the Interpretation of Culture,* ed. Cary Nelson and Lawrence Grossberg (Urbana: University of Illinois Press, 1998), pp 271–313.

4. Donna Landry and Gerald Maclean, eds., *The Spivak Reader: Selected Works of Gayatri Chakravorty Spivak* (New York: Routledge, 1996). In this regard, Eric Adler raises an excellent point about postmodern academic writing styles. He notes that when Spivak wanted to defend her colleague, Professor Edward Said, who had been described as a "professor of terror" in the pages of *Commentary* magazine, she wrote very clearly; and when feminist academic Judith Butler, another postmodern (non-) writer, defended her own "disastrously cloudy style" in the pages of the *New York Times,* she did so with great clarity. Adler concludes: "It seems as though Spivak and Butler's bursts of limpidity are revealing in a way not intended by their authors. Sure, language might be an imperfect tool for discussing what surrounds us, but when words really matter, clarity is king. How simple." Eric Adler, "Clarity Is King—Eric Adler on Postmodernists' Limpid Bursts," *New Partisan,* May 7, 2004, http://www.newpartisan.com/display/ShowJournalEntry?moduledId=4763&entryId=40526&printer, accessed 5/4/2005. See also Terry Eagleton, "In the Gaudy Supermarket," *London Review of Books,* vol. 21, no. 10, May 13, 1999, and Butler, Judith, "Letters: Exacting Solidarities," *London Review of Books* 21 (13), July 1, 1999.

5. Suha Sabbagh, *Arab Women: Between Defiance and Restraint.* New York: Olive Branch Press, 1996.

6. Bouthaina Shaabain, *Both Right and Left Handed: Arab Women Talk About Their Lives* (Bloomington: Indiana University Press, 1991).

7. Elizabeth Fernea and Basima Qattan Bezirgan, eds., *Middle Eastern Women Speak* (Austin: University of Texas, 1977). Lois Beck and Nikki Keddie, eds., *Women In the Muslim World* (Cambridge, MA: Harvard University Press, 1978). Nikki Keddie and Beth Baron, eds. *Women in Middle Eastern History: Shifting Boundaries in Sex and Gender* (New Haven, CT: Yale University Press, 1991).

8. Margot Badran and Miriam Cooke, eds., *Opening the Gates: A Century of Arab Feminist Writing* (Bloomington: Indiana University press, 1990).

9. Phyllis Chesler, *Woman's Inhumanity to Woman* (New York: Thunder's Mouth/Nation Books, 2001; pbk. ed., New York: Plume Books, 2003).

10. Jane Alpert, *Growing Up Underground* (New York: William Morrow, 1981).

11. Amnesty International, "Israel and the Occupied Territories: Conflict, Occupation and Patriarchy: Women Carry the Burden," March 2005, AI Index: MDE 15/016/2005. Jerusalem Center for Public Affairs, "Amnesty International Exploits 'Women's Rights,'" *NGO Monitor,* distribution@www.ngo-monitor.org, Apr. 20, 2005.

On June 20, 2005, Wafa Samir Ibrahim Bas, a 21-year-old female resident of the Jabaliya refugee camp in Northern Gaza, attempted to detonate a suicide bomb in Soroka Medical Center in Beersheba, where she was scheduled to have an appointment that morning and where she had been treated for burns a few months earlier. According to the June 20, 2005 *Online Edition of the Jerusalem Post,* this is one of several recent illustrations of Palestinians taking advantage of the humanitarian efforts of Israeli hospitals to serve sick Palestinians. The would-be suicide bomber is at least the third Palestinian, since December 2004 to attempt to detonate a massive explosive, under the guise of health issues. Margot Dudkevitch, "Female Bomber: Attack Aimed at Youth," *Online Edition Jerusalem Post,* June 20, 2005.

12. Robin Morgan, *Saturday's Child* (New York: W. W. Norton, 2001).
13. Robin Morgan, *The Demon Lover: The Roots of Terrorism* (New York: Washington Square Press, 1989).
14. James Tisch, "UNRWA's Hamas Problem," *Jerusalem Post,* Dec. 18, 2004, http://www.jpost.com/servlet/Satellite?pagename=JPost/JPArticle/Printer&cid=1103356 913322& . . . , accessed 1/21/2005; David Bedein, "How the West Weakens Israel," *FrontPageMagazine.com,* Oct. 15, 2003, http://www.frontpagemag.com/Articles/Printable.asp?ID=10331, accessed 1/21/2005; Aluf Benn and Arnon Regular, "Israeli Pressure Unseats UNRWA's Controversial Chief," *Haaretz,* Jan. 21, 2005, http://www.haaretz.com/hasen/objects/pages/PrintArticleEn.jhtml?itemNo=530117, accessed 1/21/2005; Phyllis Chesler, "The Race Against Lies," *FrontPageMagazine.com,* Aug. 11, 2004, http://www.phyllis-chesler.com/articles/race-against-lies.htm, accessed 5/5/2005; Moshe Dann, "Jerusalem Summit Condemns UNRWA," *FrontPageMagazine.com,* Dec. 7, 2004, http:www.frontpagemag.com/Articles/Printable.asp?ID=16226, accessed 1/21/2005; Yaakov Lappin, "UNRWA's Shady Donors," *Jerusalem Post,* Nov. 23, 2004, http://www.jpost.com/servlet/Satellite?pagename=JPost/JPArticvle/Printer&cid=1101183314284& . . . , accessed 1/21/2005; Daniel Pipes, "[UNRWA]: The Refugee Curse," *New York Post,* Aug. 19, 2003, http://www.danielpipes.org/pf.php?id=1206, accessed 1/21/2005.

In Pierre Rehov's film *Hostages of Hatred,* there is a very good discussion of the incredibly corrupt and clever machinations of UNRWA.

15. Jan Goodwin, *Price of Honor: Muslim Women Lift the Veil of Silence on the Islamic World* (New York: Little, Brown, 1994). Updated and published by Plume Penguin in 2003. This is the edition I have read. Please allow me to disclose that Goodwin and I once briefly worked together on a feminist magazine. We never discussed any of this. Her view of Afghanistan was highly colored by the book she wrote about the mujihadeen, who later became the Taliban. I thought she overly romanticized them; she felt that what I had to say about Afghan misogyny put a damper on such romanticization. We never discussed this directly or fully nor did we ever discuss Israel and the Palestinians.

Goodwin's very well written work is nevertheless somewhat disingenuous. She gives no dates for her interview or travels and has no footnotes or bibliography. (The book does have an index). This allows the work to apparently remain up to date for a long time but the absence of sources and dates renders the work somewhat vague, even disorienting for scholars.

16. Please see my book, *The New Anti-Semitism, The Current Crisis and What We Must Do About It* and my subsequent 2003, 2004, 2005 columns posted on my website, and Alan Dershowitz's book *The Case for Israel* for another point of view and for another set of facts about almost everything Goodwin discusses: The history of Zionism; the 2000 Intifada; the cause and nature of Palestinian suffering and poverty; Israeli curfews, checkpoints, and use of torture; what happened to Rachel Corrie, etc. Goodwin also quotes women in this chapter who are telling blatant and unbalanced lies without noting this. For example, she quotes one woman who told her that Palestinian women "realize that UN Resolutions are only implemented against Arab and Muslim states." Goodwin gives Israeli government absolutely no credit for stopping Jewish terrorism against Arabs and she does not really fault the Palestinian Authority for failing to stop terrorism or for promoting terrorism.

17. Jean Sasson, *Princess: A True Story of Life Behind the Veil in Saudi Arabia* (USA: Sasson Corporation, 2001; New York: William Morrow, 1992).

18. Carmen Bin Laden, *Inside the Kingdom: My Life in Saudi Arabia* (New York: Warner Books, 2004).

19. Lila Abu-Lughod, ed., *Remaking Women: Feminism and Modernity in the Middle East* (Princeton, NJ: Princeton University Press, 1998). Lila Abu-Lughod, *Writing Women's Worlds: Bedouin Stories* (Berkeley: University of California Press, 1993). Lila Abu-Lughod, *Veiled Sentiments: Honor and Poetry in Bedouin Society* (Berkeley: University of California Press, 1986).

20. Deborah Scroggins, "The Dutch-Muslim Culture War: Ayaan Hirsi Ali has Enraged Muslims with her Attacks on their Sexual Mores," *The Nation* (June 27, 2005): 21–25.

21. For a more extensive history of listener-sponsored hate speech against Jews and against Israel, please see the following articles: "The Chesler Wars," *FrontPage Magazine,* June 18, 2004, discusses the Los Angeles-based KPFK's history in this area, "Listener Sponsored Hate," *FrontPage Magazine,* June 24, 2004, discusses New York City-based WBAI's history in this area.

In May 2005, I asked Tricia Roth for an update. This is what she told me:

The petition against us is still online, but there's been no new names added to it in probably at least 6 months. Very occasionally I'll see something posted to a chat room where Feminist Magazine is vilified, but there seems to be no repercussions from any of it. Every time one of us attends station meetings, we're greeted very well, and at least once our programs were singled out for praise. There does seem to be a sentiment at the station that more feminist programming is needed, so it would make sense, they want to keep us. There's been no activity against us, besides one of its members writing a history of Pacifica piece which talks about the Women's Coalition as part of those who are purposely trying to ruin Pacifica (but no *official* business mentioning us).

I'm still with the Women's Coalition, but only in an administrative capacity. I really don't like being at the station, and no longer agree with 99% of what their programming stands for. This whole experience, from the beginning of my sensing anti-Semitism there, to our program, to the present, has really opened my eyes about the use of propaganda and the manipulation of information. So for now, I'm with the Women's Coalition only generating the minutes and agendas for each of our meetings. I probably won't remain in that capacity for long, as I feel like a hypocrite contributing to Pacifica Radio at all.

Middle East in Focus (w/ Don Bustany) continues to follow our show. He promotes his show as a way for listeners to really know what's going on in the Middle East, yet neglects almost every Mideast issue except those where he can demonize Israel. I think he may have not even done any programming on what's going on in Lebanon these last couple of months. Initially, I tried listening for a couple of weeks, and was amazed that his programming even then was "still all Israel, all the time"—nothing about Lebanon! I have an Armenian girlfriend from Lebanon and it's so important to her what's going on there. Her family's business and home were taken over by Hezbollah and the Syrian armed forces, and her family had to flee the country to America. She's waiting to go back home—so it's unreal that Middle East in Focus not give blow-by-blow coverage to this significant turn of events. And of course, the status of women in that region never even merits a mention on his program.

I've really backed off the whole Middle-east, Antisemitism on the left thing for a while now. I' m still interested, but it's just such a hard battle to fight and I was feeling too consumed and drained by it.

Chapter Six

1. Amnesty International, "Women in Afghanistan: The Violations Continue," June 1997. The report attributes this account "to a filmmaker in Kapisa": "Although Human Rights Watch did not visit Parwan and Kapisa provinces, just north of Kabul, news reports indicated that local commanders are committing rapes in these areas as well." Institute for War and Peace Reporting, "Child Sex Abuse Alarm," Afghan Recovery Report, Feb. 24, 2003, http://www.iwpr.net/index.pl?archive/arr/arr_200302_49_1eng.t, accessed 5/14/2003.

Chapter Seven

1. Bat Ye' or, *Eurabia: Land of Dhimmitude, Land of Islam* (2004).
2. Ibid.
3. Robert Spencer, "Fox Kowtows to CAIR," FrontPageMagazine.com, Jan. 19, 2005; "Terror Suspect Gets Invitation to have dinner with President," http://www.wftv.com/irresistible/4457901/detail.html, May 6, 2005, accessed 5/10/2005; Hugh Fitzgerald, "Lisa Anderson: Apologist for Academic Radicalism," FrontPageMagazine.com, May 3, 2005; "Dhimmitude at Manchester Community College," April 16, 2005, http://www.jihadwatch.org/dhimmiwatch/archives/005778.php, accessed 5/10/2005; "UK: More University Dhimmitude: Students Want Bibles in Rooms Ban," from the BBC, April 19, 2005, http://www.jihadwatch.org/dhimmiwatch/archive/005807.php, accessed 5/10/2005; Maha Akeel, "New Twist in Nour Miyati Torture Case Baffle All," Arab News, May 8, 2005, www.arabnews.com/?page=1&section=0&article=63389&d=8&m=5&y=2005, accessed 5/10/2005.
4. George Melloan, "Making Muslims Part of the Solution," *Wall Street Journal,* March 29, 2005; Robin Shepard, "In Europe, Is It a Matter of Fact, or Loathing?" *Washington Post,* Jan. 25, 2004, http://www.washingtonpost.com/ac2/wp-dyn?pagename=article&contentId=A43493–2004Jan23&notfound=true, accessed 5/10/2005. Omar Taspinar, "Europe's Muslim Street," *Foreign Policy,* Mar. 2003, http://www.brookings.edu/views/oped/fellows/taspinar20030301.htm, accessed 4/4/2005.

    According to the Russell Sage Report published in 2002, 14 to 15 million Muslims live in Europe. Four to 5 million Muslims, mainly from North Africa, live in France; 3 million live in Germany; nearly 2 million live in England; more than 1 million live in Bulgaria; just under 1 million live in Italy. According to Bat Ye' or, given the pattern of clandestine immigration throughout Europe, the actual number is undoubtedly much higher. The 4 million other Muslims live in at least thirteen other European countries including Holland (695,600); Greece (370,000); Spain (300,000–400,000); Sweden (250,000–300,000); Switzerland (310,000). Frank J. Buijs and Jan Rath, "Muslims in Europe: The State of Research," essay prepared for the Russell Sage Foundation, New York City, USA, Oct. 2002.

    "According to the Central Bureau of Statistics, there are 1.7 million 'non-western' immigrants or their children among the 16.3 million people in Holland. Almost 1 million are Muslim. In 2003, people of non-western descent accounted for a third of the population in Amsterdam, Rotterdam, and the Hague." Christopher Caldwell, "Daughter of the Enlightenment," *New York Times Magazine,* April 3, 2005. Gareth Harding, "Europe's Muslim Victims," *Washington Times,* Dec. 4, 2004, http://washingtontimes.com/upi-breaking/20041203–105630–7837r.htm, accessed 4/4/2005.
5. Eric Waugh, "Concern over Absence of Shared Allegiance," *The Belfast Telegraph,* March 17, 2004, accessed 3/8/2005.

6. Mark Steyn, quoted by Robin Sheperd, "In Europe, Is It a Matter of Fear, or Loathing?," *Washington Post,* January 25, 2004.

7. *Washington Post,* ibid., "The Americanization of Pennsylvania Germans is Beyond Doubt," http://www.bridgewater.edu/~slongene/nolt.htm, accessed 5/10/2005; "Irish," http://64.233.161.104/search?q=cache:GsJSIYYoTrIJ:www.able.state.pa.us/able/lib/able/pr ofdev/GEDlesson13-Bratton.pdf+assimilated+Irish+minority&hl=en, accessed 5/10/2005; "Irish," www.nyu.edu/classes/blake.map2001/ireland.html, accessed 5/10/2005; "Japanese Fully Assimilated," http://www.aajalink.com/2001/news/aug3fri/03ethnic.shtml, accessed 5/10/2005; "Majority of Arabs in America Are Christian," http://www.aaiusa.org/defini- tion/htm., http://aaiusa.org/PDF/Grolier'sEncyc.pdf, http://www.aaiusa.org/images/reli- gion2.jpg, accessed 5/10/2005; "Majority of Muslim Americans are not Arabs; Majority of Arab Americans are Christians, and have assimilated," http://www.uu.edu/center/ christld/academicforum/faculty/article.cfm?ID=12, accessed 5/10/2005; D'Vera Cohn and Sarah Cohen, "Statistics Portray Settled, Affluent Mideast Community," *Washington Post,* http://www.allied-media.com/Arab-American/Arab%20in%20DC.htm, accessed 5/10/2005; "Greeks," http://people.westminstercollege.edu/faculty/dstanley /folklore/Edoted%20Foma;%20Draftfoi9anagnostou.htm, accessed 5/10/2005.

8. Alison Spencer. The article is based on a talk Spencer delivered in France in May 2002. "Women and Immigration in France." Reprinted from "Women and Revolution," *Spartacist,* English Edition, no. 57 (Winter 2002–03),
    http://www.icl-fr.org/SPARTACI/immig–57.htm, accessed 4/4/2005. The article fo- cuses on how the oppression of working-class immigrant Muslim women is "directly re- lated to the anti-working class, anti-immigrant policies of the French state, which for years has been run by a so-called 'left government.'" Spencer's article is a left-wing ideo- logical analysis.

9. Charles Bremner, "Stoned to Death. . . . Why Europe Is Losing its Faith in Islam," Timesonline.co.uk, Dec. 4, 2004, http://www.timesonline.co.uk/article/ 0,3–1387077,00.html, accessed 4/4/2005.

10. Walid Phares, "Terrorism in France," *Washington Times,* Jan 8, 2004, http://www.wash- ingtontimes.com/op-ed/20040107–084241–5047r.htm, accessed 4/4/2005.

11. Arjun Appadurai, "Disjuncture and Difference in the Global Cultural Economy," *Public Culture* 2, 2 (1990): 1–24. Rachel Bloul, "Engendering Muslim Identities: Deterritorial- ization and the Ethnicization Process in France," Feb. 1998, http: //www.wluml.org/eng- lish/pubsfulltxt.shtml?cmd%5B87%5D=i–87–2682#_ftn3, accessed 4/5/2005.

12. Stephen Stalinsky, "Arab TV Instructs on Wife-Beating," *New York Sun,* Oct. 20, 2004, http://dailynysun.com/Repository/getFiles.asp?Style=OliveXlib:ArticleToMail&Type=te xt/html_Path=NYS/2004/10/20&ID=Ar00901, accessed 4/4/2005; BBC News, "France Deports Controversial Imam," Oct. 5, 2004.

13. Stalinsky, Ibid.

14. Jamie Glazov, "Sexual Amputation and Silence," *FrontPage Magazine,* Dec. 2, 2004. Http://www.frontpagemag.com/Articles/authors.asp?ID=3, accessed 4/4/2005.

15. Alison Spencer, "Women and Immigration in France."

16. Glazov, "Sexual Amputation and Silence."

17. Val MacQueen, "Honor Thy Father—or Else," TechCentralStation.be, Feb. 2, 2005, http://www.techcentralstation.be/020205.html, accessed 4/4/2005.

18. Ibid.

19. Ibid.

20. Katherine S. Newell, Elin Ross, Carrie McVicker, and Jen Cromwell, *Discrimination Against the Child: Female Infanticide, Female Genital Cutting and Honor Killing,* Youth Ad- vocacy Program International, 2000, pp. 4–5, 32.

21. "Honor Killings in America and Abroad," http://www.soundvision.com/info/misc/honor.asp, accessed 4/4/2005.

22. Mark Rice-Oakley, "Britain Examines Honor Killings," *Christian Science Monitor,* July 7, 2004, http://www.kwahk.org/index.asp?id=53, accessed 4/4/2005.

23. Alison Spencer, "Women and Immigration."

24. In 1995, 1,740 Pakistani men used a wife's status to enter Britain; in 1999, approximately 3,510 Pakistani men did so—an increase of more than 100 percent. In 2000, the number of visas issued to a spouse rose an exponential 500 percent—from 255 in 1999 to 1,132—in 2000. "Huge Rise in Forced Marriages," *The Independent* Jan. 2000, http://wluml.org/english/pubsfulltxt.shtml?cmd[87]=i-87-2732, accessed 4/4/2005. And that was only for immigrants from Pakistan.

25. "School Guide to Forced Marriages," BBC, Jan. 26, 2005, http://news.bbc.co.uk/1/hi/uk/4205173.stm, accessed 4/4/2005. Sarah Womack, "Police Told to Treat Forced Marriages as Serious," *The Telegraph,* May 21, 2002, http://news.telegraph.co.uk/news/main.jhtml, accessed 4/4/2005.

    According to Home Secretary Charles Clarke, "Forced marriage is nothing less than an abuse of human rights. It can involve serious forms of duress, including physical assault." Clarke heads a six-member Forced Marriage Unit, with an annual budget of £300,000. British law allows prosecution with charges of kidnap, false imprisonment, or rape.

26. Rice-Oxley, "Britain Examines Honor Killings."

27. Ibid.

28. "The Case of the Reluctant Brides, *Guardian Unlimited,* Jan. 15, 1999, http://www.guardian.co.uk/weekend/story/0,3605,321664,00.html, accessed 4/4/2005.

29. Suzanne Goldenberg, "A Question of Honor," *The Guardian,* May 27,1999, http://www.guardian.co.uk/women/story/0,3604,296033,00.html, accessed 4/4/2005.

30. "Pakistan Attacks on Justice 2000," August 13, 2001, International Commission of Jurists. hhtp://www.icj.org/news.php3?id_article=2584&lang=en, accessed 5/22/2005.

31. Goldenberg, "A Question of Honor."

32. Isherwood, Julian, "Protests over Father's Execution of Daughter," *The Telegraph,* Jan. 28, 2002, http://telegraph.co.uk/news/main.jhtml;sessionid+OMJLSKWOEJ4NZQ-FIQMGCM54AVCBQUJVC?xml=/news/2002/01/28/whonor28.xml&secureRefrsh=true&_requestid=31588, accessed 4/4/2005.

33. Isherwood, Ibid. Shahrzad Mojah and Amir Hassanpour, "In Memory of Fadime Sahindal, Thoughts on the Struggle Against 'Honour Killing,'" *Kurdish Library,* http://www.kurdishlibrary.org/Kurdish_Library/Aktuel?Fadime_Sahindal/Article1_Hassanpour_Fa . . . , accessed 5/17/2005.

34. Tony Paterson, "How Many More Women Have to Die before This Society Wakes Up?" *The Telegraph,* Feb. 27, 2005, http://news.telegraph.co.uk/news/main.jhtml?xml=/news/2005/02/27/wturk27.xml, accessed 4/4/2005. Jody K. Biehl, "The Death of a Muslim Woman: 'The Whore Lived Like a German,'" *Der Spiegel,* Mar. 2, 2005, http://service.spiegel.de/cache/international/0,1518,344374,00.html, accessed 5/22/2005.

35. Sonis Phalnikar, "Berlin's Honor Killings," *Deutsche Welle,* Mar. 2, 2005, reprinted in http://www.frontpagemag.com/Articles/ReadArticle.Asp?ID=17201, accessed 4/4/2005.

36. Paterson, "How Many More Women Have to Die . . ." War Blog by *FrontPage Magazine,* "When Political Correctness Kills: Honor Killings Plague Berlin," Feb. 27, 2005, http://www.frontpagemag.com/Article/ReadArticle.asp?ID-17177, accessed 4/4/2005.

37. War Blog.

38. Yann Olivier, "Germany Shaken by Honor Killings in Its Turkish Community," *Agence France Press,* Mar. 4, 2005, http://www.metimes.com/articles/normal.php?StoryID=20050304-054539-2242r, accessed 4/4/2005.

39. Ibid.

40. Abigail R. Esman, "Hirsi Ali Leaves Hiding to Spotlight Honor Killings," *Women's ENEWS*, Jan. 23, 2005, http://www.womensenews.org/article.Cfm/dyn/aid/2157/context/archive, accessed 4/4/2005.

41. "Family Link Denied in Maja Murder," *Expatica*, Dec. 1, 2003, http://www.expatica.com/source/site_article.asp?channel_id=1&story_id=2749, accessed 4/4/2005.

42. "Third Maja Murder Suspect Jailed," April 27, 2005, http://www.expatica.com/source/site_article.asp?subchannel_id=19&story_id=19521&name=Dutch+news+in+brief%2C+27+April+2005=.

43. Nadia Hasmi, "Gender and Discrimination: Muslim Women Living in Europe," European Political-Economy Infrastructure Consortium, Ionian Conference 2000, http://www.epic.ac.uk/documents/ICHashmi.pdf, accessed 4/4/2005.

44. Glenn Bezalel, "Murder Shines Spotlight on ' Honor Killings,' " *CNN.com*, Oct. 2, 2003, http://www.cnn.com/2003/WORLD/europe/10/01/honor.killings, accessed 4/4/2005. See also MacQueen, "Honor Thy Father."

45. BBC News, "'Honour Killing' Father Begins Sentence," Sept. 30, 2003. http://news.bbc.co.uk/2/hi/uk_news/england/london/3149030.stm, accessed 5/22/2005.

46. MacQueen, "Honor Thy Father" and Rice-Oxley, "Britain Examines Honor Killings"; BBC News, "Bride's Snub Led to Murder," Oct. 15, 2003, http://news.bbc.co.uk/1/hi/england/west_midlands/3193918.stm, accessed 5/22/2005.

47. Charles Bremner, "Stoned to Death . . . Why Europe Is Starting to Lose Its Faith in Islam," *Times of London*, Dec. 4, 2004, http://www.timesonline.co.uk/article/0.3-1387077.00.html, accessed 4/4/2005. "Une jeune femme lapidée à Marseille," ("A Young Woman Is Stone in Marseille"), Jeuvers 18 de noviembre de 2004. En la misma sección Otros breves, http://www.mediterraneas.org/breve.php3?id_breve=3, accessed 5/22/2005.

48. Carin Pettersson, "Porn Star Receives Death Threats," netavisen, Aug. 20, 2004, http://pub.tv2.no/nettavisen/english/article267959.ece, accessed 4/4/2005.

49. Arthur Max, "In Europe, Muslim Women Speaking Out Against Extremism Risk Backlash," *North Country Times*, Nov. 30, 2004, http://www.nctimes.com/articles/2004/12/01/special_reports/religion/13_38_3111_30_04.txt, accessed 4/4/2005.

50. BLADI.NET, "Le Portail de la Diaspora Morocaine." http://www.bladi.net/modules/news/article-5767-bruxelles-1-auteur-des-menaces-contre-mimount-bousakla-devant-la-justice.html, accessed 5/22/2005.

51. Clare Chapman, "Voice for Muslim Women Terrorised by Their Families," *Scotland on Sunday*, Oct. 5, 2003, http://scotlandonsunday.scotsman.com/international.cfm?id=1102842003, accessed 4/4/2005.

52. Warren Hoge, "Deadly Affair: Pakistanis in England Who Wed for Love," *International Herald Tribune*, Hong Kong Edition, Oct. 20, 1997, pp. 1, 8, http://www.wluml.org/english/pubsfulltxt.shtml?cmd[87]=I-87-2682, accessed 4/4/2005; Geraldine Bedell, "Death before Dishonor," *The Observer*, Nov. 21, 2004, http://observer.guardian.co.uk./print/0,3848,5067876-110648,00.html, accessed 4/4/2005. "So Called Honour Crimes," March 7, 2003, http://assembly.coe.int/Documents/WorkingDocs/doc03/EDOC9720.htm, accessed 5/22/2005.

53. Zaffar Abbas and Jamie Wilson, "British Woman in Forced Marriage Freed," *The Guardian*, May 2003, http://www.guardian.co.uk/pakistan/Story/0,2763,951204,00.html, accessed 4/4/2005.

54. Richard Bernstein, "A Runaway Personifies Germany's ' Multi-Kulti' Debate," *New York Times*, Dec. 19, 2004, p. 16.

55. "Europe Grapples with Honor Killing," *Deutsche Welle,* June 23, 2004, http://www.dw-world.de/dw/article/0,1244406,00.html.accessed 4/4/2005.
56. Rice-Oxley, "Britain Examines Honor Killings."
57. Kathleen Moore, "Europe Grapples with Honor Killings of Women," Radio Free Europe, Mar. 8, 2005, http://www.rferl.org/features/features_article_old.aspx?id=0274f5ff-a54d–4e42–87b2–8ded26551db7&y=2005&m=03, accessed 4/4/2005.
58. Shahrzad Mojab, "Honor Killing: 'Culture, Politics and Theory,'" *MEWS Review,* Association for Middle East Women's Studies, 17, nos. 1–2 (Spring/Summer 2002), http://www.amews.org/review/reviewarticles/mojabfinal.htm, accessed 4/4/2005.
59. Rice-Oxley, "Britain Examines Honor Killings."
60. Paterson, "How Many More Women Have to Die . . ." War Blog by *FrontPage Magazine.*
61. Christopher Caldwell, "Daughter of the Enlightenment," *New York Times Magazine,* Apr. 3, 2005.
62. Ellen Francis Harris, *Guarding the Secrets: Palestinian Terrorism and a Father's Murder of His Too-American Daughter* (New York: Scribner, 1995).
63. Ellen Francis Harris, ibid.
64. Souad, *Burned Alive: A victim of the Law of Men.* (New York: Warner Books, 2003).

According to the Palestinian women's affairs ministry, quoted in the *London Guardian* in 2005, "20 girls and women were murdered in honor killings (on the West Bank and in Gaza in 2004) and 50 committed forced suicide. Another fifteen women survived attempts to kill them." (Chris McGreal, "Murdered In Name of Family Honour," *The Guardian,* June 23, 2005.)

In addition, the *London Guardian* reported a series of honor killings that had taken place on the West Bank in May 2005. One woman, 22-year-old Faten Habash, a *Christian* Arab who lived in Ramallah, wanted to marry a Muslim. Her father, Hassan Habash, tried to murder her but she escaped with only a broken pelvis. A Bedouin mediated the matter; Hassan wept and took a sacred vow that there would be no more beatings and that Faten could marry Hamis, the man she loved. Hassan lied. He bludgeoned poor Faten to death with an iron bar.

Two days later, in Jerusalem, Maher Shakirta, a bus driver in his thirties, held a family meeting with this three sisters, one of whom had been accused of adultery by her husband; he suspected that his two innocent sisters were protecting the allegedly guilty sister. Maher made all three sisters drink bleach and then he strangled both his sister Rudaina, who was eight months pregnant, and his sister Amani. His third sister, Leila, escaped but was "badly injured by the bleach." Maher went into hiding but his parents were arrested. Amin, the father of the two dead women, explained the murders this way: "They dishonored the family. A married woman who goes with another man is not good."

Women's rights groups do not blame patriarchal or Arab tribal customs for honor killing but, like Dr. Suha Sabbagh and journalist Jan Goodwin (whom I discussed in chapter five) they do blame the *increase* in such crimes on the Israeli occupation. Why? Because the women are employed and the men are not. This "loss of dignity" has led men to try and uphold the family honor by killing their sisters and daughters. Mrs. Abu Dayyeh Shamas also said "there is an incredible amount of incest."

However, this blame-the-occupation theory does not explain the role that women play in Palestinian honor killings. In one horrifying case, reported by *The Guardian,* a mother, Amira Abu Hanhan Qaoud, murdered her 22-year-old daughter, Rafayda, because she became pregnant after being raped by her two brothers. The mother placed a plastic bag over her daughter's head, sliced her wrists, and beat her with a stick. Mrs. Qaoud spent two years in jail; her two sons were sentenced to ten years for the rape. According to *Guardian* reporter, Chris McGreal, Mrs. Qaoud has "purged her home of all pictures of her older children, and declines to discuss the killing, saying all she wants to do is forget about it."

65. Karin Scholz, "'We Can't Separate Family,' Says Parents Who Want Proof Nephews Killed Their Daughter," *The Cleveland Plain Dealer,* May 17, 1999, p. 1A; Karin Scholz, "Prosecutor Argues 2 Men Killed Cousin for Shunning Culture," *The Cleveland Plain Dealer,* May 26, 1999, p. 1A; James Ewinger, "Honor-Slaying Trial Is Delayed, Statement to Police Backs Prosecution," *The Cleveland Plain Dealer,* Mar. 7, 2000 p.1B.; James Ewinger, "Victim's Cousin Cleared in Honor-Slaying Case, Prosecution's Case Too Weak, Judge Rules," *The Cleveland Plain Dealer,* May 6, 2000 p. 1A; Amanda Garrett, "Move to Force Testimony Merely Sets Witness Free," *The Cleveland Plain Dealer,* July 22, 2000, p. 2B; Amanda Garrett, "Cousin Acquitted in Killing," *The Cleveland Plain Dealer,* July 26, 2000, p.1A.

I have not reviewed the legal paperwork in this case and am forced to rely on multiple newspaper accounts. Apparently, two witnesses were intimidated and fled the jurisdiction. Methal's mother had been "visited" (or threatened) as well.

66. Alan Fernandes, "Doc Wanted for Four Murders Nabbed," *Rediff On the Net,* Sept. 14, 1999, www.rediff.com, accessed June 3, 2005; M. J. Shenoy, "Her Client Killed, Attorney Tries to Restore Kids to Grandmother," *Rediff on the Net,* Sept. 16, 1999, www.rediff.com, accessed June 3, 2005, http://www.prodeathpenalty.com/pending/04/nov04.htm, accessed on May 22, 2005; Victim: Lubaina Ahmed.

67. Bill Broadway, "Studies Offer Conflicting Estimates of U.S. Muslim Population," *Washington Post,* Nov. 21, 2001, http://www.detnews.com/2001/religion/0112/05/religion–351148.htm, accessed 4/4/2005; Barry Kosmin and Egon Mayer, "Profile of the American Muslim Population," American Religious Identification Survey, City University of New York Graduate Center, 2001, http://www.gc.cny.edu/studies/aris_part_two.Htm, accessed 4/4/2005; "Exploring Tensions within America's Muslim Community," PBS, http://www.pbs.org/wgbh/pages/frontline/shows/muslims/portraits/us.html, accessed 4/4/2005; Jane Smith, "Patterns of Muslim Immigration," U.S. State Department, http://usinfo.state.gov/products/pubs/muslimlife/immigrat.htm, accessed 4/4/2005; "Michigan Has Largest U.S. Muslim Population," *Psychiatric News,* Jan. 21, 2005, http://pn.psychiatryonline.org/cgi/content/full/40/2/13-b, accessed 4/4/2005.

68. AP report, "Census Report Details Lives of U.S. Arabs," *New York Times,* Mar. 9, 2005.

69. Daveed Gartenstein-Ross, "Insidious Inroads," *Commentary,* Feb. 2005, http://www.commentarymagazine.com/article.asp?aid=11902068_1HYPERLINK(http://www.commentarymagazine.com/article.asp?aid=11902068_1"/t(_blank(, accessed 4/4/2005.

70. Daniel Pipes, "Denying Terrorism," *New York Sun,* Feb. 8, 2005, http://www.danielpipes.org/article/2396, accessed 4/4/2005; Daniel Pipes, "More Incidents of ' Denying Terrorism,' " Feb. 8, 2005, http://www.danielpipes.org/blog/403, accessed 4/4/2005.

71. Daniel Pipes, "Which Privileges for Islam?," *New York Sun,* March 15, 2005.

72. Mel Gussow, "A New Play Encounters Muslims' Ire in Cincinnati," *New York Times,* Feb. 3, 2003, p. 1.

73. Tounushree Jaggi, "Apna Ghar: Domestic Violence and Reaching Out to Chicago's Faith Communities," The Pluralism Project, Harvard College, http://www.pluiralism.org/affiliates/student/jaggi/index/php, accessed 4/4/2005; "Muslim Wife Burned to Death in Chicago: Lessons for Muslims," Soundvision.com, undated, http://www.soundvision.com/Info/domesticviolence/shahpara1.asp, accessed 4/4/2005.

74. "Domestic Violence Blamed for Triple Murder," *wnbc.com,* July 30, 2002; Ralph R. Orega and Bill Hutchinson, "Mother, Aunt, Grandma Slain," *New York Daily News,* July 30, 2002, http://www.nydailynews.com/borough/story/7095p–6600c.htm, accessed

4/4/2005; Gloria Suhasini and Jyotirmoy Datta, "All 3 Women of Family Killed Over Religion," *News India-Times,* online edition, Aug. 9, 2002, http://www.newsindia-times.com/2002.08/09/dias-women.html, accessed 1/29/2005.

75. Robert Spencer, "New York: Man Killed Wife for 'Honor,' He Tells Cops," Jihadwatch.org, Apr. 25, 2004, http://www.jihadwatch.org/dhimmiwatch/archives/001706.php, accessed 4/4/2005.

76. "Muslim Population Statistics,"Muslim-Canada.org, http://muslim-canada.org/muslimstats.html, accessed April 4, 2005; Justin Hayward, "Religious Observance in Canada," CBC radio, transcripts, May 13, 2003, http://www.cjc.ca/ptemplate.php?Story=270&action=itn, accessed 4/4/2005; Abdul Malik Mujahid, "Profile of Muslims in Canada," *Soundvision.com,* ND http://soundvision.com/info/muslims/muslimsincanada.asp, accessed 4/4/2005.

77. Amrita Chaudhry, "Shame and Scandal in the Family," *The Indian Express,* Jan. 30, 2005, http://www.indianexpress.com/print.php?content_id63662, accessed 4/3/2005.

78. "Murder Convictions for Farah's Parents," *CBC News,* Apr. 22, 2004.

79. Margaret Wente, "Life under Sharia, in Canada," *Globe and Mail,* May 29, 2004, p. 21A, http://www.theglobeandmail.com/servlet/Page/document/v$/sub/MarketingPage?user_url=http:///www.theglobeandmail.com%2Fservlet%2FArticleNews%2FTPStory%2FLAC%20040529%2FCOWent29%2FTPColumnists%2F&ord=1108399525601&brand=theglobeandmail&force_login=true, accessed 4/4/2005.

80. Nosharia, http://www.nosharia.com, accessed 4/4/2005.

81. Sally Armstrong, "If there's a Place for Sharia, It's not Ontario," *International Herald Tribune,* Feb. 11, 2004, http://www.iht.com/articles/2005/02/10/opinion/edarmstrong.html, accessed 4/4/2005.

82. Gartenstein-Ross, "Insidious Inroads."

83. Robert Spencer, http://jihadwatch.org; Daniel Pipes, http://www.danielpipes.org; Maria Sliwa, http://www.freeworldnow.com.

Chapter Eight

1. Iraqi councilwoman Fatima Yaqoub is a devout Shiite Muslim. According to Farnaz Fassihi in the *Wall Street Journal,* Yaqoub "favors allowing Iraqi men to have as many as four wives" and has campaigned for the Iraqi adoption of Sharia law. A distraught young wife came to Ms. Yakoub for guidance. Her husband was about to marry a second wife. Ms. Yakoub told her that: "our country has had three wars and there are not enough men for every woman to marry. So she should not be so selfish, and [should] share her husband like a good Muslim wife."

According to another Iraqi woman, forty-six-year-old Salama al-Khafaji, a leading Islamist politician, "Forcing secularism on our society is also a form of dictatorship."

Of course, many Iraqi women are anti-Sharia and are both bitter and terrified that the American liberation of Iraq has not yet yielded—and may never yield—the kind of freedom they require.

Farnaz Fassihi, "Iraqi Shiite Women Push Islamic Law on Gender Roles," *Wall Street Journal,* Mar. 9, 2005, p. 1.

According to Liz Sly, in *The Chicago Tribune,* armed men in the streets are forcing Iraqi women to veil themselves, and there is pressure from husbands and fathers, as well. One hairdresser is quoted as saying: "If George Bush thinks this is liberation, then he should make his own wife and daughter wear hijab." Another hairdresser said: "He will have to issue visas for America with this new constitution, because we will all be leaving. Do they need hairdressers in America?"

Liz Sly, "Women Fear Losing Rights in New Iraq: Worry Islamic Law Will Be Instituted," *The Chicago Tribune,* Mar. 4, 2005, http://www.chicagotribune.com/news/nationworld/chi–0503040273mar04,1,2379934.story?ctrack=1&cset=true, accessed 4/7/2005.

Leila Al-Marayati and Semeen Issa, writing in the *Los Angeles Times,* take another view entirely. In their opinion, Muslim women are not victims but are "active, assertive and engaged in society." They say that traditional Muslim populations will be "more receptive to change that is based on Islamic principles of justice, as expressed in the Koran, than they will be to change that abandons religion altogether or confines it to private life."

Laila Al-Marayait and Semeen Issa, "An Identity Reduced to a Burka," *LA Times* Sunday Opinion, Jan. 20, 2002, reprinted in *Muslim Women's League Publications,* http://www.mwlusa.org/publications/opinion/veil.html, accessed 1/26/2005.

2. In December 2004, Amnesty International presented a briefing to the United Nation's Convention on the Elimination of all Forms of Discrimination Against Women (CEDAW) Committee regarding Algeria's failure to implement changes required under its status as a state party to the convention. The briefing focused on issues of legal discrimination, various kinds of violence against women, and the impact on women when men are kidnapped or "disappear."

In 1992, Algeria's first multiparty elections were abruptly cancelled in what amounted to a preemptive coup that displaced the Islamic Salvation Front, which most likely would have won. The country was launched into a downward spiral of violence and chaos, with civilians caught in the middle between warring factions.

Rape has been used as a political weapon against Muslim women by Muslim men in Algeria. In 1992, in "S.O.S. Algeria: Women's Human Rights Under Siege," Karima Bennoune described the "kidnapping and repeated raping of young girls as sex slaves for armed fundamentalists. The girls are also forced to cook and clean for God's warriors . . . one seventeen-year-old girl was repeatedly raped until pregnant. She was kidnapped off the street and held with other young girls, one of whom was shot in the head and killed when she tried to escape."

"Unveiled," educated, independent Algerian women have been seen as "military targets" and increasingly shot on sight. According to Bennoune, "the men of Algeria are arming, the women of Algeria are veiling themselves. As one woman said: 'Fear is stronger than our will to be free.'"

Bennoune says: "Terrorist attacks on women [in Algeria] have had the desired effect: widespread psychosis among the women; internal exile—living in hiding, both physically and psychologically, in their own country." In Bennoune's view, "the collective psychosis" is due to the "escalation of violence" by the "soldiers of Islamic state."

Should a rape case be actually brought to trial, numerous problems thwart prosecution. Algerian law does punish rape, but fails to define it. Conviction may hinge on medical evidence, but due to officials' lack of training such evidence often is improperly obtained or even lost. Even if a rape victim is examined by a doctor, there are few resources available to meet her physical, psychological, and other post-trauma needs.

People—mainly men—"disappear" off the streets in Algeria. They have either been arrested by the state or seized by paramilitary groups. The open-ended nature of "disappearances" takes a powerful toll on families. Under Algeria's Family Code, a father is his children's legal guardian until they reach the age of nineteen. Custody passes to the mother in the event of the father's death. Until she has been appointed their guardian, the mother has little ability to conduct her children's affairs. She can't enroll them in school, request a passport, or approve many other activities that require the father's signature. The law does allow for a person to be officially declared "missing," which provides some administrative reprieve for the wives of "disappeared" men in addressing their children's needs. However, because state agents are often implicated in men's disappearance, and because Algerian authorities are so unhelpful, families are usually reluctant to seek their help with guardianship issues.

Algerian divorce law, which blatantly discriminates against women, may contribute to violence. A husband may dissolve the union at will, but the wife must prove that one of seven legitimate causes has been met. Adultery is considered a crime for both men and women. However, *male* adulterers ignorant of the partner's marital status may be released; in such cases, *females* are still punished.

Prosecution of family violence is rare. Injuries must be fairly severe before the courts will sentence, and the injuries must be medically documented. Social stigma is also a powerful deterrent to reporting family violence. In 2001, the women's organization SOS Femmes en détresse (SOS Women is Distress) was prevented from running a public awareness TV spot that would have publicized its help lines. Nor has it received authorization for toll-free help lines. For all these reasons, violence in the family is rarely reported and even more rarely prosecuted.

3. Women and men in Saudi Arabia are separated both publicly and privately. Women are not allowed to drive nor are they allowed to go out without male "minders." Women must be veiled from head to toe or risk grave consequences. Until 2005, they had to submit to arranges marriages or risk death. Polygamy is legal; a man can divorce a wife instantly, assume immediate or eventual custody of the children, and must support his ex-wife for only three menstrual cycles. Domestic violence statistics are almost impossible to obtain. It is known, however, that husbands are allowed to discipline their wives for "disobedience."

Although Saudi women attend college in high numbers, their education is supposedly in preparation for the domestic duties of wife and mother. According to the US Department of State, even though 55 percent of Saudi university graduates were women by the mid-1990s, only 5.5 percent of the workforce was female. The segregation imposed on the workforce by the labor code, and the restrictions on women's movement help explain the disparity between graduation and employment. In September 2000, Amnesty released a report entitled "Gross Human Rights Abuses Against Women" in Saudi Arabia. The vast majority of domestic workers in Saudi Arabia are women, and almost all are foreign nationals. Therefore they are subject to some of the worst human rights abuses in the country.

Women tend to be charged with "crimes" of immoral conduct (which usually criminalize sexual activity) far more frequently than men. In these cases, domestic workers are particularly vulnerable to sexual abuse and torture during interrogation and imprisonment. Flogging is an acceptable and frequent penalty in Saudi Arabia for crimes of immorality. Amnesty International considers flogging inhumane and to constitute torture.

Since 1990, of the twenty-eight known executions of women in Saudi Arabia, seventeen have been foreigners—and foreigners comprise perhaps 25 percent of the population. The Saudi male and female abuse of female foreign domestic workers is particularly egregious. The Amnesty International interviews reported sleep deprivation, nonpayment of wages, refusal of holidays or time off, beatings, verbal abuse, rape, destruction of mail, and refusal of the police to intervene when such abuse was actually reported. Domestic workers frequently reported confiscation of their passports, which kept them from leaving the county. In many cases, these women essentially worked as slaves.

One Indonesian domestic worker came to Saudi Arabia at sixteen and was raped almost immediately following her arrival, an abuse that continued. "Apart from the repeated rape, which was about twice a week, and the unprovoked beatings, [the husband] would verbally abuse me all the time. He would call me a 'pig' and a 'dog,' she said. "I didn't think of going to the police. I wouldn't in any event have known where the police station was. I had not had a day off in seventeen months, had not been out, and had been locked up in the house."

According to Carmen Bin Laden, even royal women are subject to the most savage restrictions and punishments. Bin Laden recounts the well-known story of the tragic Princess Mish' al whose execution was the subject of a movie in the 1990s.

When Princess Mish'al dared refuse an arranged marriage to a much older man, dared to fall in love with someone, and tried to flee the country—she was apprehended and shot to death at the express order of her grandfather, Prince Mohamed, King Khaled's brother. (The king was willing to spare her, her own grandfather was not). Saudi princes, however, not only have four wives and many mistresses; they are rumored to fly in planeloads of Paris-based prostitutes for sex parties every week; both Jean Sasson and Carmen Bin Laden refer to this.

Jean Sasson recounts the chilling tale of one Sameera who had once wanted to be an engineer, who had studied abroad, and who had been planning to wed a non-Muslim American and never to return to Saudi Arabia. Her parents were exceptionally progressive. However, they died and her fiancée changed his mind. Sameera's male next-of-kin lured her back to Saudi Arabia, forced her into an abusive arranged marriage as a third wife. When that abusive husband returned the defiant and "dishonored" Sameera to the male head of her family—he had Sameera put in solitary confinement for the rest of her life. Sasson tells us that Sameera eventually went mad. Servants reported that she screamed for days, then babbled, spoke in gibberish, sobbed—but that she still kept eating.

4. For example, the mystical Egyptian novelist and short story writer, Alifa Rifaat, describes girls who fully (and normatively) expect their fathers "to slit their throats" if they do not accept a repugnant arranged marriage. Souad writes that as a child, she was "always sick with fear." Her father not only administered life-threatening beatings and imprisonment almost daily, he also forced her to watch him kill chickens, rabbit, sheep. She writes: "My sister and I were convinced that he could twist out necks just like the chickens, drain our blood, just like the sheep." Nevertheless, she also admits that she continued to obey her father in all things; as she puts it, she could not shed "the skin of [a] consenting slave."

How can society allow adults to abuse so many children so seriously? How can so many adults refuse to expose child-abuse practices but instead insist on silence? Usually adults who have been abused as children behave this way. They utterly fail to see themselves in their child victims and instead persecute those victims who, unlike themselves, dare to speak out.

Alifa Rifaat, *Distant View of a Minaret and Other Stories,* trans. Denys Johnson-Davies (London: Quartet Books, 1983).

5. Let us recall how three of Tina Isa's own sisters, envious of her freedom and fearful of its consequences for the family's reputation, demanded her death. The fact that their father was an Abu Nidal terrorist did not compromise their family reputation in the way that Tina's Americanization did. See Ellen Harris, *Guarding the Secrets: Palestinian Terrorism and a Father's Murder of His Too-American Daughter* (New York: Scribner, 1995).

Souad's mother, who was herself a beaten woman, did not allow her eldest daughter to stay for more than a few hours when she returned home, a savagely beaten bride. Remember how my former mother-in-law in Afghanistan treated her female servants: very badly indeed. Souad, *Burned Alive: A Victim of the Law of Men* (New York: Warner Books, 2003). Finally, Alifa Rifaat, in "The Flat in Nakshabandi Street," shows how the aging spinster Aziza treats her female servant, Waheeba. She criticizes Waheeba constantly, both to her face and behind her back, curses her, threatens to have her beaten, goes through her few private possessions when she is not at home, and, what's more, refuses to pay her any wages. "Every now and again Waheeba would lose her temper and rebel and demand her money so that she could take herself off to her village as she had done once many years ago. Aziza would agree and explain to her that Mahmoud would have to go to the post office and withdraw the money, and in the meantime she would remind her of how hard life was in the countryside and Waheeba would calm down and agree to stay."

Rifaat, *Distant View of a Minaret and Other Stories.*

6. According to the NCWDI report, "NGO Alternative/Shadow Report on Iran, submitted to: Conference of NGOs in Consultative Relationship with the United Nations," which Ramesh Sepehrrad and Soona Samsami shared with me, in 2002, 40,000 teachers participated in a January 12th demonstration outside the Iranian parliament, or Majlis, for increased human rights. As a result of that demonstration, many women were arrested and imprisoned. In August 2004, apparently alarmed that women had secured 63 percent of the nation's 195,000 university seats, Tabriz University shut down its female dormitories and told out-of-state female students to search for other universities. In October 2004, more than 650 women students demonstrated against the poor living conditions at Tehran's Allameh Tabatabai University. The government sent anti-riot police. The same month, Azad University in Meybod ordered its women students to wear the head-to-toe Islamic chador or face expulsion.

But if women's rights are curtailed in the most barbaric and brutal of ways, they are also curtailed in mundane matters. Bicycling for women was ruled unbecoming and unIslamic, and the sport was banned for women expect in indoor stadiums without men.

Whereas men achieve adulthood at age fifteen, girls become "women" at age nine. They lose their childhoods. Married women must have their husband's permission to apply for a passport. Iranian law denies marriage rites performed in other countries unless the rites are repeated in Iran. Consequently, divorces granted outside Iran are invalid in Iran. Divorces of Iranian couples must be repeated in the Islamic embassy or consulate, otherwise women returning to Iran could be tried for adultery, and stoned to death.

Given such oppression, an increasing number of Iranian women are suffering from clinical depression and are killing themselves.

Some Iranian clerics also sexually exploit the same female population which they themselves sexually repress. Widows from the Iran-Iraq war who asked for assistance became the victims of clerics' sexual exploitation. According to Professor Donna Hughes in "Defeating the Woman-haters," sex trafficking, slavery, and prostitution are increasing in Iran; government officials frequently run the sex slave rings. According to *Time* magazine in 2002, there were 84,000 prostitutes on the streets of Tehran and in 250 brothels, including some linked to high officials. Forty percent of all drug-addicted women in Iranian prisons had AIDS.

Iranian women are forced to endure lives under the strict control of fathers or husbands, but they are also often forced into "temporary marriages," which the religious authorities revived in 1998. These arrangements allow a man to marry a woman for as little as one hour, in exchange for money.

Reports from the notorious Evin prison in 1997 documented that the number of female prisoners had risen substantially in recent years. Women there endure the most barbaric of tortures. In March 2000, the Sunday *Times* of London described a horrific 50-minute film of a stoning smuggled out of Iran by the National Council of Resistance to Iran (NCRI). According to the *Times,* there had been 600 executions in the two years since "moderate" Mohammed Khatami came to power, 11 of them stonings. Stoning women in Iran is an all-too-common state phenomenon. Within a three-month period in 2001, at least four women were stoned to death. Women are also periodically and publicly hung from cranes in the city streets.

222 / THE DEATH OF FEMINISM

Iran has introduced Islamic human rights, which differ sharply from rights guaranteed under the 1948 United Nations international "Universal Declaration of Human Rights." According to UN watchdog, David Littman, Iran kept rewriting and essentially nullifying the human rights provisions contained in the UN document and in the International Covenant on Economic, Social and Cultural Rights, and the Covenant on Civil and Political Rights.

In 1999, after UN Special investigator on Iran, Maurice Danby Copithorne, filed a 26-page report charging that minority groups and women continued as targets of human rights violations, Iran's security of the Islamic Human Rights Committee said that "rapporteurs of the United Nations" should not "compare the Islamic values in our society with the values of western countries." They should recognize that "in a religious society, human rights are applied according to Islamic principles and not western values."

On June 8, 2005, in Washington D.C., a conference called The Plight of Iranian Women and Children under the Islamic rule was held by the Alliance of Iranian Women. It was sponsored by Senator Sam Brownback and co-sponsored by Senators Rick Santorum and Norm Coleman. Among the speakers were Senator Brownback; under secretary of State, Paula Dobrianski; Professor Donna Hughes; and Iranian dissident writer and human rights activist Banafsheh Zand-Bonazzi. According to Zand-Bonazzi's speech:

"One of the bones of contention for Iranian authorities is women's love for soccer! Iranian women are banned from attending soccer matches, yet thousands of women and teenage girls always turn up outside and around the stadium calling for an overthrow of the mullahs! In November 2001, Irish women were allowed to attend the Iran-Ireland playoff match for a berth in the 2002 World Cup. The Iranian Soccer Federation concluded that the Irish women will not understand the bad language that most Iranian men use during the matches.

"What women had to surrender in the process of the theocratic revolution was extremely critical and as such it has been none other than women themselves who have continued fighting to expose this blight year after year. They have vehemently [exposed] the absurdity of adhering to archaic social models of the Arabian peninsula of 1400 years ago . . . The theocrats have mocked women's claims and denied them as anti-religio[us]. Finally, after 26 years, their brutality is being more and more scrutinized by the world at large."

7. Condoleeza Rice, "Remarks at the American University in Cairo," speech: June 20, 2005, http://www.state.gov/secretary/rm/2005/48328.htm#democracy, accessed 6/23/2005.

The *Wall Street Journal* editorial, "Review and Outlook: Condi in Cairo," *Wall Street Journal,* June 22, 2005, A10. William F. Buckley, "Silence, Condi is Talking," *New York Sun,* June 22, 2005.

8. Condoleeza Rice, "Remarks at the American Israel Public Affairs Committee's Annual Policy Conference," speech: May 23, 2005.

References

Abu-Lughod, Lila, ed. *Remaking Women: Feminism and Modernity in the Middle East.* Princeton, NJ: Princeton University Press, 1998.

———. "Feminist Longings and Postcolonial Conditions" and "The Marriage of Feminism and Islamism in Egypt: Selective Repudiation as a Dynamic of Postcolonial Cultural Politics." In Abu-Lughod, Lila, ed.

———. *Writing Women's Worlds: Bedouin Stories.* Berkeley, CA: University of California Press: 1993.

———. *Veiled Sentiments: Honor and Poetry in a Bedouin Society.* Berkeley, CA: University of California Press, 1986.

Adler, Eric. "Clarity Is King—Eric Adler on Postmodernists' Limpid Bursts." *New Partisan* (May 7, 2004). http://www.newpartisan.com/display/ShowJournalEntry?moduledId=4763&entryId=40526&printer, accessed 5/4/2005.

Adler, Eric, and Jack Langer. "The Intifada Comes to Duke." *Commentary* (January 2005). http://www.commentarymagazine.com/Archive/digitalarchive.aspx, accessed 4/14/2005; print edition: 56–58.

Afkhami, Mahnaz, ed. *Faith & Freedom: Women's Human Rights in the Muslim World.* Syracuse, NY: Syracuse University Press, 1995.

———. *Women in Exile.* Charlottesville: University Press of Virginia, 1994.

Ahmad, Leila. "Western Ethnocentrism and Perceptions of the Harem." *Feminist Studies* 8:3 (Fall 1982).

———. *Women and Gender in Islam.* New Haven, CT: Yale University Press, 1992.

Al-Huweidar, Wajiha. "Arab Feminists on Women's Rights: Cats and Dogs in the Developed World Have More Rights than Women in the Arab and Muslim World," "Covert Animosity and Open Discrimination Against Women Prevail in Arab Countries," MEMRI, special dispatch, no. 890, April 12, 2005, http://www.memri.org/bin/opener_latest.cgi?ID=SD89005, accessed 4/13/2005.

Alireza, Marianne. *At the Drop of a Veil: The True Story of an American Woman's Years in a Saudi Arabian Harem.* Boston: Houghton Mifflin, 1991.

Al-Marayati, Laila, and Issa Semeen. "An Identity Reduced to a Burka." *Los Angeles Times Sunday Opinion*, January 20, 2002; reprinted in Muslim Women's League Publications, http://www.mwlusa.org/publications/opinion/veil.html, accessed 01/26/2005.

Alpert, Jane. "Mother Right: A New Feminist Theory." *Know, Inc.*, 1974; http://scriptorium.lib.duke.edu/wlm/mother, accessed 5/3/2005. This article or versions of it was reprinted in the feminist media, including *Ms. Magazine.*

Alpert, Jane. *Growing Up Underground.* New York: William Morrow, 1981.

Al-Sawaihi, Munjiyah. "I Look Beyond the Horizon and See Nothing but the Tightening of the Noose Around the (Arab) Woman," MEMRI, http://www.memri.org/bin/opener_latest.cgi?ID=SD89005, accessed 4/13/2005; http://frontpagemagazine.com/blog/printable.asp?ID=449, accessed 4/14/2005.

Amnesty International. "Israel and the Occupied Territories: Conflict, Occupation and Patriarchy: Women Carry the Burden," March 2005, AI Index: MDE 15/016/2005.

———. *Algeria Newsletter* (January/February 2005), http://www.amnesty-volunteer.org/uk/algeria/Current.php, accessed 4/8/2005. Amnesty International cites Decree no. 97–49 of February 12, 1997, published in *Journal Office* (Algerian official bulletin) and Decree n. 99–47 dated February 13, 1999, published February 17, 1999.

———. "Algeria: Briefing to the Committee on the Elimination of Discrimination Against Women." December 2004.

———. "Turkey: Women Confronting Family Violence." June 2004.

———. "Afghanistan: 'No one listens to us and no one treats us as human beings': Justice denied to women." October 2003.

———. "Pakistan: Insufficient Protection of Women." April 2002.

———. "Saudi Arabia: Gross Human Rights Abuses Against Women." September 2000.

———. "Women in Afghanistan: Pawns in men's power struggles." November 1999.

———. "Women in Afghanistan: The Violations continue." June 1997.

Andreatta, David. "Columbia Jews Want Outside Probe." *New York Post,* April 1, 2005.

Angier, Natalie. "Spiking the Punch: In Defense of Female Aggression." In *Woman: An Intimate Geography.* Boston: Houghton Mifflin, 1999.

Anna Akhmatova. http://www.uvm.edu/!sgutman/Akhmatova.htm; http://www.odessit.com/namegal/english/ahmatova.htm. Accessed 4/18/2005.

Ansary, Tamim. *West of Kabul, East of New York: An Afghan American Story.* New York: Picador, 2002.

Arab News (Saudi Arabia), Human Rights Watch, Amnesty International, 2002. "Schoolgirls Die Because Their Heads Were Not Covered." http://www.sossexisme.org/english/schoolgirls.htm, accessed 4/7/2005.

Arenas, Reinaldo. "Bio." http://www.cubaheritage.com/subs.aps?sID=135&cID=3, accessed 4/18/2005.

Armstrong, Sally. *Veiled Threat: The Hidden Power of the Women of Afghanistan.* New York: Four Walls Eight Windows, 2002.

Asad, Talal, ed. *Anthropology and the Colonial Encounter.* New York, Humanity Books: 1973.

Associated Press. "A Matter of Honour: Egyptian Style"; 'Dishonored' Father Beheads Bride who Eloped." *Indian Express Newspapers* (Bombay), © 1997. http://www.financialexpress.com/ie/daily/19970821/23350273.html, accessed 4/14/2005.

Badran, Margot, and Miriam Cooke, eds. *Opening the Gates: A Century of Arab Feminist Writing.* Bloomington: Indiana University Press, 1990.

Baraheni, Reza. *The Crowned Cannibals: Writings on Repression in Iran.* New York: Vintage, 1977.

Bartlett, Bruce. "Wanted: Intellectual Diversity." *New York Sun,* December 8, 2004.

Bauerlein, Mark. "Liberal Groupthink Is Anti-Intellectual." *Chronicle of Higher Education,* November 12, 2004.

BBC. "Vladimir Bukovsky." http://bbcbias.org/html/body_background.html, accessed 4/19/2005.

BBC News. "Harry Public Apology 'Not Needed,'" January 14, 2005. http://news.bbc.co.uk/1/hi/uk/4170623.stm, accessed 4/15/2005.

———. "Harry Says Sorry for Nazi Costume," January 13, 2005. http://news.bbc.co.uk/go/pr/fr/-/2/hi/uk_news/4170083.stm, accessed 4/15/2005.

———. "Saudi police 'stopped' fire rescue," March 15, 2002. http://news.bbc.co.uk/1/hi/world/middle_east/1874471.stm, accessed 4/7/2005.

Beck, Lois, and Nikki Keddie, eds. *Women in the Muslim World.* Cambridge, MA: Harvard University Press, 1978.

Beckwith, Leila. "Marketplace of Ideas Has Gone Sour at UCSC." *Santa Cruz Sentinel,* March 7, 2004.

Bell, Diane, and Renate Klein, eds. *Radically Speaking: Feminism Reclaimed.* North Melbourne, Australia: Spinifex Press, 1996.

Benda, Julien. *The Treason of the Intellectuals.* Tr. Richard Aldington. New York: William Morrow, 1928.

Benjamin, Ilan, and Tammi Rossman-Benjamin. "Moderate Islam Should Not Be Ignored." *Santa Cruz Sentinel,* May 23, 2004.

Bennoune, Karima. "S.O.S. Algeria: Women's Human Rights Under Siege." In *Faith and Freedom: Women's Human Rights in the Muslim World.* Syracuse, NY: Syracuse University Press, 1995.

Berman, Paul. *Terror and Liberalism.* New York: W. W. Norton, 2003.

Bin Laden, Carmen. *Inside the Kingdom: My Life in Saudi Arabia.* New York: Warner Books, 2004.

Bjorkquist, Kaj, and Pirkko Niemela, eds. *Of Mice and Women: Aspects of Female Aggression.* San Diego: Academic Press, Harcourt Brace Jovanovich, 1992.

Blanch, Lesley. *The Wilder Shores of Love: The Story of Four Remarkable Women Who Fled the Conventional Life of 19th-Century Europe for the Romance and Passion of the East.* New York: Simon & Schuster, 1954.

Bodansky, Yossef. *Islamic Anti-Semitism as a Political Instrument.* Houston, TX: The Freeman Center for Strategic Studies, 1999.

Bostom, Andrew G., ed. *The Legacy of Jihad—Islamic Holy War and the Fate of Non-Muslims.* Amherst, NY: Prometheus Books, 2005.

Brooks, David. "The Art of Intelligence," *New York Times,* April 2, 2005, p. A15.

Brooks, Geraldine. *Nine Parts of Desire: The Hidden World of Islamic Women.* New York: Anchor Books, 1995.

Brown, Lyn Mikel, and Carol Gilligan. *Meeting at the Crossroads: Women's Psychology and Girl's Development.* Cambridge, MA: Harvard University Press, 1992.

Brownmiller, Susan. *In Our Time: Memoir of a Revolution.* New York: The Dial Press, 1999.

Bruce, Tammy. *The New Thought Police: Inside the Left's Assault on Free Speech and Free Minds.* California: Prima Publishing, 2001.

Campbell, Anne. *Men, Women, and Aggression.* New York: Basic Books, 1993.

Caplan, Paula J. "Try Diagnosing Men's Mind Games Instead of Pathologizing Women." *On the Issues,* Winter 1997.

———. *They Say You're Crazy: How the World's Most Powerful Psychiatrists Decide Who Is Normal.* Reading, MA: Addison-Wesley, 1995.

———. *Lifting a Ton of Feathers: A Woman's Guide to Surviving in the Academic World.* Toronto: University of Toronto Press, 1992.

———. *The Myth of Women's Masochism.* New York: E. P. Dutton, 1985.

CBC Archives. "Marc Lepine, Mass Murderer," December 7, 1989, http://archives.cbc.ca/400i.asp?IDCat=70&IDDos=398&IDCLi=2237&IDLan=1&NOCli=3&type=clip, accessed 4/8/2005.

CBSNEWS.COM. "Charles to Harry: Visit Auschwitz," January 14, 2005. http://www.cbsnews.com/stories/2005/01/12/earlyshow/printable666570.shtml, accessed 4/15/2005.

Chesler, Phyllis. *The New Anti-Semitism: The Current Crisis and What We Must Do About It.* San Francisco: Jossey-Bass, 2003.

———. *Woman's Inhumanity to Woman.* New York: Thunder's Mouth/Nation Books, 2001; pbk ed. New York: Plume Books, 2003.

———. *Women and Madness.* Doubleday, 1972.

———. *Mothers on Trial: The Battle for Children and Custody.* New York: McGraw-Hill, 1986.

———. *About Men.* New York: Simon & Schuster, 1978.

———. "Duke's Terror Conference: A Postmortem." *FrontPageMagazine,* October 22, 2004.

———. "A Survivor of Palestinian Tyranny: The Global Cultural Wars Continue." *FrontPageMagazine,* October 13, 2004.

———. "The Truth Is No Longer 'Politically Correct' at Duke: Round II." *FrontPage Magazine,* October 5, 2004.

———. "Free Speech and Hate Speech at Duke, Round I." *FrontPageMagazine,* September 28, 2004.

———. "'Gender Cleansing' in the Sudan." *FrontPageMagazine.com,* July 26, 2004.

———. "Listener-Sponsored Hate." *FrontPageMagazine.com,* June 24, 2004; *www.phyllis-chesler.com.*

———. "The Chesler Wars." *FrontPageMagazine.com,* June 18, 2004; *www.phyllis-chesler.com.*

———. "The Psychoanalytic Roots of Islamic Terrorism." *FrontPageMagazine.com,* May 3, 2004; *www.phyllis-chesler.com.*

———. "The Anti-Semitic Intelligentsia." *FrontPageMagazine.com,* August 21, 2003.

Chesler, Phyllis, and Donna M. Hughes. "Feminism in the 21st Century." *The Washington Post,* February 22, 2004, p. B07.

Chesler, Phyllis, and Nancy H. Kobrin. "Osama, Bush and a Little Girl." *FrontPageMagazine.com,* November 1, 2004; *www.phyllis-chesler.com.*

Chowdry, Geeta, and Sheila Nair. *Power, Postcolonialism, and International Relations: Reading Race, Gender and Class.* New York: Routledge, 2004.

Cockburn, Alexander. "A Whiner Called David Horowitz." *CounterPunch,* May 31, 2003. http://www.counterpunch.org/cockburn05312003.html, accessed 4/14/2005.

Cohen, Marcia. *The Sisterhood: The True Story of the Women Who Change the World.* New York: Simon & Schuster, 1988.

Collectif 95 Maghreb Egalite: Les Maghrebines entre violences symboliques et violences physiques: Algerie, Maroc, Tunisie. Rapport annuel: 1998–1999.

Constable, Pamela. "In Pakistan, Women Pay the Price of Honor." *Washington Post,* May 8, 2000; http://www.washingtonpost.com/ac2/wp-dyn/A23279–2000May7?language=printer, accessed 2/21/2005.

Cowan, Gloria. "Women's Hostility toward Women and Rape and Sexual Harassment Myths," *Violence against Women,* 6(3) (2000): 238–246.

Cowan, Gloria, C., J. DeLaMoreaux, Neighbors, and C. Behnke. "Women's Hostility toward Women." *Psychology of Women Quarterly* 22 (1998): 267–284.

Darwish, Nonie. "Escaping Submission." http://www.noniedarwish.com/pages/745443/page745443.html?refresh=1110343832775, accessed 5/3/05.

———. "Impossible Family Dynamics of Islam." *FrontPageMagazine.com,* January 29, 2003.

———. "The Veil: A Form of Female Jihad." *WorldNetDaily.com,* 2002; also posted http://www.noniedarwish.com/pages/745437/index.htm, accessed 4/7/2005.

Davis, Caroline. "Clarence House Must Tackle the Wayward Prince," January 15, 2005, http:www.telegraph.co.uk/core/Content/displayPrintable.jhtml;sessionid=GDQL4MST-NDTy1Q, accessed 4/15/2005.

De Rooij, Paul. "David Horowitz's Corrosive Projects." *CounterPunch,* April 11, 2005. http://www.counterpunch.org/rooij04112005.html, accessed 4/14/2005.

Dunsheath, Joyce, and Eleanor Baillie. *Afghan Quest: The Story of The Abinger Afghanistan Expedition 1960.* London: George G. Harrap & Co., 1961.

DuPlessis, Rachel Blau, and Ann Snitow. *The Feminist Memoir Project: Voices from Women's Liberation.* New York: Three Rivers Press, 1998.

Dworkin, Andrea. *Scapegoat: The Jews, Israel and Women's Liberation.* New York: Simon & Schuster, 2000.

———. *Mercy.* New York: Avalon, 1992.

———. *Woman Hating.* New York: E. P. Dutton, 1974.

Eder, Donna, and David A. Kinney. "The Effect of Middle School Extracurricular Activities on Adolescents' Popularity and Peer Status." *Youth and Society* 26:3 (1995): 298–324.

Edmunds, Marlene. "Rotterdam Drops van Gogh Movie." *Variety.com,* January 27, 2005. http://www.variety.com/story.asp?I=story&a!=story&a=VR1117917006&c=1444, accessed 4/14/2005.

Elliot, Jason. *An Unexpected Light: Travels in Afghanistan.* New York: Picador, 2001.

El-Saadawi, Nawal. *Woman at Point Zero.* London: Zed Books, 1983.

———. *Hidden Face of Eve: Women in the Arab World.* London: Zed Books, 1980.

Esman, Abigail R. "Hirsi Ali Leaves Hiding to Spotlight Honor Killings." *Women's Enews,* January 23, 2005. http://www.womensenews.org/article.cfm/dyn/aid/2157/context/archive, accessed 4/14/2005.

Fallaci, Oriana. *The Rage and the Pride.* New York: Rizzoli International, 2002.

Farah, Joseph. *Taking America Back: A Radical Plan to Revive Freedom, Morality, and Justice.* Nashville, TN: Thomas Nelson, 2003.

Farah, Joseph. WorldNetDaily.com. Founder, editor, CEO.

Fassihi, Farnaz. "Iraqi Shiite Women Push Islamic Law on Gender Roles." *Wall Street Journal,* March 9, 2005, p. 1.

Feldman, H. "Children of the Desert: Notes on Arab National Character." *Psychoanalytical Review* 45 (1958): 41–50.

Fernea, Elizabeth Warnock. *In Search of Islamic Feminism: One Woman's Global Journey.* New York: Anchor Books, 1998.

Fernea, Elizabeth W., and Basima Qattan Bezirgan, eds. *Middle Eastern Muslim Women Speak.* Austin, TX: University of Texas Press, 1977.

Firestone, Shulamith. *The Dialectic of Sex.* New York: William Morrow, 1970.

Flattum, Jerry. "Honor Killing Demands Global Response." *The Minnesota Daily,* Editorials/Opinions, January 29, 1999. http://www.mndaily.com/daily/1999/01/29/editorial_opinions/oo0129/, accessed 4/13/2005.

Fordham, Signithia. *Blacked Out: Dilemmas of Race, Identity, and Success at Capital High.* Chicago: University of Chicago Press, 1996.

Fortunecity.com. "Marc Lepine." http://www.fortunecity.com/roswell/hammer/73/lepine.html, accessed 4/8/2005.

Galileo Galilei. *Stanford Encyclopedia of Philosophy.* http://plato.stanford.edu/entries/galileo, accessed 4/10/2005.

Gershman, Jacob. "Faculty Denounce 'Right-Wing Attack.'" *New York Sun,* April 5, 2005.

———. "Bollinger Criticized for Embracing Report Clearing Faculty." *New York Sun,* April 1, 2005.

Gilligan, Carol. *In a Different Voice: Psychological Theory and Women's Development.* Cambridge, MA: Harvard University Press, 1982.

Ginat, J. *Blood Disputes among Bedouin and Rural Arabs in Israel.* Pittsburgh: University of Pittsburgh Press, 1987.

Glazer, Ilsa M., and Wahiba Abu Ras. "On Aggression, Human Rights, and Hegemonic Discourse: The Case of a Murder for Family Honor in Israel." *Sex Roles* 30:3/4 (1994): 269–289.

Glazov, Jamie. "The People v. Harvard Law." *FrontPageMagazine.com,* April 21, 2005. http://www.frontpagemag.com/Articles/Printable.asp?ID=17801, accessed 4/21/05. I am pleased to note that my friend Alan Dershowitz has behaved in very principled ways as these matters arose at Harvard Law.

———. "Symposium: Why the Mullahs Murdered Atefeh Rajabi." *FrontPageMagazine,* September 17, 2004. http://www.frontpagemag.com/Articles/Printable.asp?ID=15129, accessed 4/14/2005.

———. "Frontpage Interview: Christopher Hitchens." *FrontPageMag.com,* December 10, 2003.

Glick, Peter, and Susan T. Fiske. "Hostile and Benevolent Sexism: Measuring Ambivalent Sexist Attitudes toward Women." *Psychology of Women Quarterly* 21 (1997): 119–135.

Goodwin, Jan. *Price of Honor: Muslim Women Lift the Veil of Silence on the Islamic World.* New York: Little Brown, 1994.

Goodwin, Jan. *Caught in the Crossfire: The True Story of an American Woman's Secret and Perilous Journey with the Freedom Fighters through War-torn Afghanistan.* New York: E. P. Dutton, 1987.

Gould, Carol. "An American Scapegoat in London." *The Guardian,* October 16, 2004.

Gray, Seymour. *Beyond the Veil: The Adventures of an American Doctor in Saudi Arabia.* New York: Harper & Row, 1983.

Guha, Ranajit, and Gayatri Chakravorty Spivak. *Selected Subaltern Studies.* New York/Oxford: Oxford University Press: 1988.

Haddad, Yvonne Yazbeck, and Jane I. Smith. "Women in Islam: 'The Mother of All Battles.'" In Sabbagh, ed., *Arab Women.*

Hakakian, Roya. *Journey from the Land of No: A Girlhood Caught in Revolutionary Iran.* New York: Crown Publishers, 2004.

Halkin, Hillel. "Nationalism's Undeserved Reputation." *New York Sun,* December 28, 2004.

Harris, Ellen Francis. *Guarding the Secrets: Palestinian Terrorism and a Father's Murder of His Too-American Daughter.* New York: Scribner, 1995.

Harrison, Paul. "A History of Pantheism: Giordano Bruno—Pantheist Martyr." http://members.aol.com/pantheism0/brunlife.htm, accessed on 4/19/2005.

Hatem, Mervat F. *The Demise of Egyptian State Feminism and the Politics of Transition, 1980–1991.* Los Angeles: G.E. von Grunebaum Center for Near Eastern Studies, UCLA, 1991.

Herman, Judith. *Trauma and Recovery: The Aftermath of Violence—from Domestic Abuse to Political Terror.* New York: Basic Books, 1992.

Hirshmann, Lisa. "Students Respond to Ad Hoc Report." *Columbia Spectator,* April 1, 2005.

Horowitz, David. *Unholy Alliance: Radical Islam and the American Left.* Washington, D.C.: Regnery Publishing, 2004.

———. *Left Illusions: An Intellectual Odyssey.* Dallas: Spence Publishing, 2003.

———. *The Politics of Bad Faith: The Radical Assault on America's Future.* New York: Simon & Schuster, 1998.

———. "From the Desk of David Horowitz." E-mail, April 14, 2005.

———. "David's Blog." *FrontPageMagazine,* April 7, 2005. http://frontpagemagazine.com/blog/printable.asp?ID=451, accessed 4/14/2005.

———. "Why an Academic Bill of Rights Is Necessary." *FrontPageMagazine,* March 15, 2005. http://www.frontpagemag.com/Articles/ReadArticle.asp?ID=17369, accessed 4/14/2005.

———. "Correction: Some of Our Facts Were Wrong; Our Point Was Right." *FrontPageMagazine,* March 15, 2005. http://www.frontpagemag.com/Articles/Printable.asp?ID=17370, accessed 4/14/2005.

———. "In Defense of Intellectual Diversity." *Chronicle of Higher Education,* February 10, 2004; reprinted in *FrontPageMagazine,* http://www.frontpagemag.com/articles/Printable.asp?ID-12116, accessed 4/14/2005.

Hoskin, Fran. *The Hoskin Report, 1978.* Editor, Women's International Network.

Hosseini, Khaled. *The Kite Runner.* New York: Riverhead Books, 2003.

Hughes, Donna. "Defeating the Woman-haters." *FrontPageMagazine,* January 17, 2005. http://www.frontpagemag.com/Articles/ReadArticle.asp?ID=16640, accessed 4/14/2005.

———. "The Mullah's Killing Fields." *FrontPageMagzine.com,* December 14, 2004.

———. "Iran's Sex Slaves." *FrontPageMagzine.com,* June 11, 2004.

———. "Not Unfamiliar: Images of Sexual Abuse and Humiliation in Abu Ghraib." *National Review Online,* May 6, 2004.

———. "Nyet to Trafficking." *National Review Online,* June 18, 2003.

Hughes, Donna E., Nancy Kobrin, and Banafsheh Zand-Bonazzi. "Symposium: Why the Mullahs Murdered Atefeh Rajabi." *FrontPageMagzine.com,* September 17, 2004.

Human Rights Watch. "Honoring the Killers: Justice Denied for 'Honor' Crimes in Jordan." Vol. 16:1(E), April 2004.

Human Rights Watch. "Killing you is a very easy thing for us": Human Rights Abuses in Southeastern Afghanistan. Vol. 15:5(C), July 2003.

Hunter, Edward. *The Past Present: A Year in Afghanistan.* London: Hodder and Stoughton, 1959.

Hymowitz, Kay S. "Why Feminism Is AWOL on Islam." *City Journal,* Winter 2003, accessed 8/14/2005.

Ignatieff, Michael. *The Lesser Evil: Political Ethics in an Age of Terror.* Princeton, NJ: Princeton University Press, 2004.

Institute for the Secularisation of Islamic Society. "An Interview with ISIS: Taslima Nasrin and the Struggle Against Religious Fundamentalism." http://www.secularislam.org/skeptics/taslima.htm, accessed 2/17/2005.

Isis International. "Schoolgirls Die in Burning Building for Lack of Headscarves." No. 4 (March 2002). http://www.isiswomen.org/pub/we/archive/msg00069.html, accessed 4/7/2005.

Jacobs, Charles. "Becoming Columbia." *The Columbia Spectator,* April 11, 2005. http://www.columbiaspectator.com/vnews/display.v?TARGET=printable&article_id=4259dce9c9, accessed 4/14/2005.

Jacobsen, Jennifer. "Columbia U. Report Criticizes Professor's Classroom Conduct but Finds No Pattern of Anti-Semitism." *Chronicle of Higher Education,* April 1, 2005.

Jenkins, Robin. *Dust on the Paw.* New York: G. P. Putnam's Sons, 1961.

Jerusalem Center for Public Affairs. "Amnesty International Exploits 'Women's Rights.'" *NGO Monitor:* distribution@www.ngo-monitor.org, April 20, 2005.

Jilani, Hina. "Women Killed in the Name of Honour." *Amnesty International,* AI Index: ASA 33/20/99, September 21, 1999.

Katz, Naomi, and Nancy Milton, eds. *Fragment from A Lost Diary and Other Stories: Women of Asia, Africa and Latin America.* New York: Pantheon Books, 1973.

Keddie, Nikki R., and Beth Baron, eds. *Women in Middle Eastern History: Shifting Boundaries in Sex and Gender.* New Haven, CT: Yale University Press, 1991.

Kessler, John J. "Giordano Bruno: The Forgotten Philosopher." http://www.infidels.org/library/historical/john_kessler/giordano_bruno.html, accessed 4/19/2005.

Klein, Daniel B., and Andrew Western. "How Many Democrats per Republican at UC-Berkeley and Stanford? Voter Registration Data Across 23 Academic Departments." *Ratio Working Papers* no. 54 (November 18, 2004).

Klein, Daniel B., and Charlotta Stern. "How Politically Diverse Are the Social Sciences and Humanities? Survey Evidence from Six Fields." *Academic Questions.* Forthcoming.

Klug, Brian. "The Myth of the New Anti-Semitism." *The Nation,* February 2, 2004.

Kobrin, Nancy. "Political Domestic Violence in Ibrahim's Family: A Psychoanalytic Perspective." In J. Piven, C. Boyd, and H. Lawton, eds., *Eroticisms: Love, Sex, and Perversion: Psychological Undercurrents of History,* vol. 5. New York: iUniverse Inc., 2003.

———. "The Death Pilots of September 11th, 2001: The Ultimate Schizoid Dilemma." In J. Piven, Boyd, C., and H. Lawton, eds., *Jihad and Sacred Vengeance: Psychological Undercurrents of History,* vol. 3. New York: Writers Club Press, 2002.

———. "A Psychoanalytic Approach to bin Laden, Political Violence and Islamic Suicidal Terrorism." *MAMFT News: The Newsletter of the Minnesota Association for Marriage and Family Therapy* 20:3 (September 2002): 7–10.

———. "Psychoanalytic Notes on Osama bin Laden and His Jihad against the Jews and the Crusaders." *Annual of Psychoanalysis* 23 (2002): 211–220.

Kobrin, Nancy H., and Yoram Schweitzer. "The Sheikh's New Clothes: Islamic Suicide Terrorism and What It's Really All About." Introduction by Phyllis Chesler. Unpublished manuscript.

Kristof, Nicholas D. "A Free Woman." *The New York Times,* June 19, 2005.

———. "Raped, Kidnapped and Silenced." *The New York Times,* June 14, 2005.

Kurtz, Howard. "College Faculties a Most Liberal Lot, Study Finds." *Washington Post,* March 29, 2005, p. C01.

Lamb, Sharon. *The Secret Lives of Girls: What Good Girls Really Do—Sex Play, Aggression, and their Guilt.* New York: Free Press, 2001.

Landry, Donna, and Gerald Maclean, eds. *The Spivak Reader: Selected Works of Gayatri Chakravorty Spivak.* New York: Routledge, 1996.

Legh-Jones, Alison. *English Woman Arab Man.* London: Paul Elek, 1975.

Leonowens, Anna H. *Siamese Harem Life.* New York: E. P. Dutton & Company, 1873.

Leuchtag, Erika. *Erika and the King.* New York: Coward-McCann, 1958.

Lewis, Bernard. *The Crisis of Islam: Holy War and Unholy Terror.* New York: Modern Library, 2003.

———. *The Middle East: a Brief History of the Last 2,000 Years.* New York: Touchstone, 1995.

———. *The Jews of Islam.* Princeton, NJ: Princeton University Press, 1984.

Liben, Noah. "Anti-Semitism and Discrimination: Case Analyses." Jerusalem Center for Public Affairs, no. 1, April 13, 2005, http://www.jcpa.org/phas/phas-liben-05.htm, accessed 4/13/2005.

Lindholm, Jennifer, Alexander Astin, Linda Sax, and William Korn. "The American College Teacher: National Norms for the 2001–2002 HERI Faculty Survey." Higher Education Research Institute, UCLA Graduate School of Education and Information Studies.

Littlegreenfootballs.com. "Honor Killing in Iran, Tehran." Reuters, September 2, 2002. http://www.littlegreenfootballs.com/weblog/?entry=4046, accessed 4/14/2005.

Macintyre, Ben. *The Man Who Would Be King: The First American in Afghanistan.* New York: Farrar, Straus, Giroux, 2004.

Macintyre, Donald. "Hamas Admits Its Gunmen Shot Betrothed Women in 'Honour Killing.'" *The Independent,* April 13, 2005. http://news.independent.co.uk/world/middle_east/story.jsp?story=628859, accessed 4/15/2005.

Mackinnon, Catherine A. *Towards a Feminist Theory of the State.* Cambridge, MA: Harvard University Press, 1989.

———. *Feminism Unmodified: Discourses on Life and Law.* Cambridge, MA: Harvard University Press, 1987.

Mackworth, Cecily. *The Destiny of Isabelle Eberhardt.* New York: Ecco Press, 1975.

Madre. 2004, http://www.madre.org, accessed 4/17/2005.

Mahl, from *Women in Black,* "Ordinary Fascism, Fundamentalism and Femicide." ND, http://geocities.com/inizjamed/algeria_femicide.htm, accessed 4/8/2005.

Mahoney, Daniel J. "Traducing Solzhenitsyn." *First Things* 145 (August/September 2004): 14–17. http://www.firstthings.com/ftissues/ft0408/opinion/mahoney.htm, accessed 4/19/2005.

Malkin, Michele. "Minority Conservatives and the Sellout Smear." Michelle Malkin.com, January 12, 2005. http://michellemalkin.com/archives/001212.htm, accessed 4/6/2005.

Manji, Irshad. *The Trouble with Islam: A Muslim's Call for Reform in her Faith.* New York: St. Martin's Press, 2003.

Mernissi, Fatima. *The Veil and the Male Elite: A Feminist Interpretation of Women's Rights in Islam.* Reading, MA: Addison-Wesley, 1987.

———. *Beyond the Veil: Male-Female Dynamics in a Modern Muslim Society.* New York: John Wiley & Sons, 1975.

Middle East Newsline. "Saudis Question Value of Religious Police." March 20, 2002. http://www.menewsline.com/stories/2002/march/03_20_1.html, accessed 4/8/2005.

Miller, Miranda. *A Thousand and One Coffee Mornings: Scenes from Saudi Arabia.* London: Peter Owen, 1989.

Millett, Kate. *Going to Iran.* New York: Coward McCann, 1982.

———. *Sexual Politics.* New York: Doubleday, 1970.

———. *The Basement.* New York: Simon and Schuster, 1979.

Morgan, Robin. *Saturday's Child.* New York: W. W. Norton, 2001.

———. *The Demon Lover: The Roots of Terrorism.* New York: Washington Square Press, 1989.

———. *Sisterhood Is Global: The International Women's Movement.* New York: Anchor Press/Doubleday, 1984.

Morrow, Lance. *Evil: An Investigation.* New York: Basic Books, 2003.

Ms. Magazine. "V-Day 2001: To End Violence Against Women." March 30, 2001. http://www.msmagazine.com/news/printnews.asp?id=5954, accessed 4/14/2005.

Nafisi, Azar. *Reading Lolita in Tehran: A Memoir in Books.* New York: Random House, 2003.

Narasimhan, Sakuntala. *Sati: Widow Burning in India.* New York: Penguin Books, 1990.

National Committee of Women for a Democratic Iran (NCWDI), exiled NGO. "NGO Alternative/Shadow Report on Iran, Submitted to: Conference of NGOs in Consultative Relationship with the United Nations," February 27, 2005.

Newby, Eric. *A Short Walk in the Hindu Kush.* Middlesex, England: Penguin Books, 1958.

Nimmo, Kurt. "The Delusions of David Horowitz." *CounterPunch,* October 31, 2002. http://www.counterpunch.org/nimmo1031.html, accessed 4/14/2005.

O'Connor, J. J., and E. F. Robertson. "Galileo Galilei." http://www-groups.dcs.st-and.ac.uk/~history/Printonly/Galileo.html, accessed 4/19/2005.

Okin, Susan Moller. *Is Multiculturalism Bad for Women?* Princeton, NJ: Princeton University Press, 1999.

Orwell, George. *1984.* New York: Harcourt Brace and Company, 1949.

Ostroff, Ken. "Sincerely Yours, LibLove." *The Jewish Press,* June 3, 2005, p. 7.

PeaceWomen, Women's International League for Peace and Freedom. "Schoolgirls Die Because Their Heads Were Not Covered," March 17, 2002. http://www.peacewomen.org/news/news%20, archive/2002/schoolgirls.html, accessed 4/7/2005.

Pew Research Center. "Foreign Policy Attitudes Now Driven by 9/11 and Iraq: Eroding Respect for America Seen as Major Problem," released August 18, 2004. http://people-press.org/reports/display.php3?PageID-862, accessed 2/4/2005.

———. "Americans Favor Force in Iraq, Somalia, Sudan and . . . ," released January 22, 2002. http://people-press.org/reprots/display.php3?ReportID=148, accessed 2/4/2005.

Piven, J., C. Boyd, and H. Lawton, eds. *Terrorism, Jihad, and Sacred Vengeance.* Giesson: Psychosocial-Verlag, 2004.

Pipes, Daniel. "Good News Could End in Mideast." *New York Sun,* March 8, 2005.

———. *Miniatures: Views of Islamic and Middle Eastern Politics.* Piscataway, NJ: Transaction, 2003.

Plato. *Euthyphro, Apology, Crito, Phaedo, Phaedrus.* Cambridge, MA: Harvard University Press, 1999.

Pogrebin, Letty Cottin. *Deborah, Golda, and Me.* New York: Crown, 1991.

Pollitt, Katha. "Andrea Dworkin, 1946–2005." *The Nation,* May 2, 2005. http://www.thenation.com/doc.mhtml?i=20050502&s=pollitt, accessed 4/16/2005.

Poullada, Leon. *Reform and Rebellion in Afghanistan, 1919–1929: King Amanullah's Failure to Modernize a Tribal Society.* Ithaca, NY: Cornell University Press, 1973.

Power, Samantha. *A Problem from Hell: America and the Age of Genocide.* New York: Perennial, 2002.

Rabin, Claire Low, ed. *Understanding Gender and Culture in the Helping Process: Practitioners' Narratives from Global Perspectives.* Introduction by Phyllis Chesler. Belmont, CA: Thomson, Wadsworth, 2005.

Rajan, Rajeswari Sunder. *Real and Imagined Women.* London/New York: Routledge, 1993.

Ramsland, Katherine. "Gendercide: The Montreal Massacre The Target," Court TV's Crime Library, http://www.crimelibrary.com/notorious_murders/mass/marc_lepine/index.html, accessed 4/8/2005.

Rashid, Ahmed. *Taliban: Militant Islam, Oil & Fundamentalism in Central Asia.* New Haven, CT: Yale Nota Bene, Yale University Press, 2000.

Raspail, Jean. *The Camp of the Saints.* Paris: Editions Robert Laffont-Fixot, 1973.

Raven, Arlene. *Crossing Over: Feminism and Art of Social Concerns.* Ann Arbor, MI: UMI Research Press, 1988.

Rebzani, Mohamed. "Incidence de l'activite professionnelle sur le role famililale." *Les Cahiers de l'Orient* 47 (1997): 96.

Reseau, Wassila. *Livre Blanc: Violences Contra Les Femmes et Les Infants* (*The White Book: Violence Against Women and Children*). Algiers, 2002.

Reuters. "Pakistani Woman Recalls Jury-Ordered Rape." *New York Times,* July 6, 2002. http://query.nytimes.com/gst/abstract.html?res=F60712FA3A550C758CDDAE0894DA404 482&incamp=archive:search, accessed 4/14/2005.

Rifaat, Alifa. *Distant View of a Minaret and Other Stories.* Tr. Denys Johnson-Davies. London: Quartet Books, 1983.

Rizvi, Muddassir. "'Honor Killing' Rises in Pakistan Despite State and Religious Opposition." JINN, November 28, 2000. http://www.pacificnews.org/jinn/stories/6.24/001128-honor.html, accessed 4/14/2005.

Rothman, Stanley, Robert S. Lichter, and Neil Nevitte. "Politics and Professional Advancement Among College Faculty." *The Forum* 3:1. http://www.bepress.com/forum/vol3/iss1/art2, accessed 4/15/2005.

Rotten.com. "Marc Lepine." http://rotten.com/library/bio/crime/spree-killers/marc-lepine/, accessed 4/8/2005.

Rubin, Barry, and Judy Colp Rubin. *Hating America: A History.* New York: Oxford University Press, 2004.

———. *Yasir Arafat: A Political Biography.* New York: Oxford University Press, 2003.

Sabbagh, Suha, ed. *Arab Women: Between Defiance and Restraint.* New York: Olive Branch Press, 1996.

Sahebjam, Freidoune. *The Stoning of Soraya M.* New York: Arcade Publishing, 1994.

Said, Edward W. *Orientalism.* New York: Random House, 1978.

Sakharov, Andrei. "The Time 100," by Fang Lizhi. http://time.com/time/time100/heroes/profile/sakharov02/html, accessed 4/19/2005.

Santiago, Fabiola. "Cuban Poet Heberto Padilla Dies." *Miami Herald,* September 26, 2000. http://www.latinamericanstudies.org/cuba/padilla-obituary.htm, accessed 4/18/2005.

Sasson, Jean. *Princess: A True Story of Life behind the Veil in Saudi Arabia.* USA: Sasson Corporation, 2001; New York: William Morrow, 1992.

Schmitt, Arno, and Jehoeda Sofer, eds. *Sexuality and Eroticism among Males in Moslem Societies.* New York: Harrington Park Press, 1992.

Schuster, I., and M. Glazer. "The Power of the Weak: Arab Women in Israel." *Reviews in Current Anthropology* 10 (1984): 37–43.

Sciolino, Elaine. *Persian Mirrors: the Elusive Face of Iran.* New York: Touchstone Books, 2000.

Scroggins, Deborah. "The Dutch-Muslim Culture War." *The Nation,* June 27, 2005, pp. 21–25.

Seaman, Barbara. *The Greatest Experiment Ever Performed on Women: Exploding the Estrogen Myth.* New York: Hyperion Books, 2003.

Seierstad, Asne. *The Bookseller of Kabul.* Boston: Little, Brown, 2002.

Shaabain, Bouthaina. *Both Right and Left Handed: Arab Women Talk about Their Lives.* Bloomington: Indiana University Press, 1991.

Shah, Saira. *The Storyteller's Daughter.* New York: Knopf, 2003.

Shalhoub-Kevorkian, Nadera. "Redefining and Confronting 'Honor Killings' as Femicide." In Cynthia Meillon with Charlotte Bunch, eds., *Holding on to the Promise: Women's Human Rights and the Beijing +5 Review.* New Brunswick, NJ: Rutgers Center for Women's Global Leadership, 2001.

Sharansky, Natan. "The View from the Gulag: An Interview with Natan Sharansky." *Weekly Standard* 9:39 (June 21, 2004).

Sharansky, Natan with Ron Dermer. *The Case for Democracy: The Power of Freedom to Overcome Tyranny and Terror.* New York: Perseus Books Group, 2004.

Simmons, Rachel. *Odd Girl Out: The Hidden Culture of Aggression in Girls.* Orlando, FL: Harcourt, 2002.

Simms, Norman. "Apologies and Reconciliation: A Report from Hamilton." *Chadashot* (December 2002): 14–15.

Simms, Norman. "Holocaust Denial in New Zealand Universities." *Clio's Psyche* 6:4 (2000): 173–174.

Simms, Norman. "Submission to Mr. Bill Renwick, the Kupka Inquiry at Waikato University." February 7, 2001.

Sly, Liz. "Women Fear Losing Rights in New Iraq: Worry Islamic Law Will Be Instituted." *Chicago Tribune,* March 4, 2005. http://www.chicagotribune.com/news/nationworld/chi–0503040273mar04,1,2379934.story?ctrack=1&cset=true, accessed 4/7/2005.

Souad. *Burned Alive: A Victim of the Law of Men.* New York: Warner Books, 2003.

Speed, Richard B. "Hating America: A History." *FrontPageMagazine,* January 21, 2005. http://frontpagemag.com/articles/Printable.asp?ID=16678, accessed 4/14/2005.

Spencer, Robert. *The Myth of Islamic Tolerance: How Islamic Law Treats Non-Muslims.* Amherst, NY: Prometheus Books, 2005.

———. *The Politically Incorrect Guide (and the Crusades).* Washington D.C.: Regnery Publishing, 2005.

———. *Onward Muslim Soldiers: How Jihad Still Threatens America and the West.* Washington, D.C.: Regnery Publishing, 2003.

———. *Islam Unveiled: Disturbing Questions About the World's Fastest-Growing Faith.* San Francisco: Encounter Books, 2002.

Spender, Dale. *For the Record.* London: The Women's Press Limited, 1985.

———. *Women of Ideas and What Men Have Done to Them from Aphra Behn to Adrienne Rich.* London: Routledge, Kegan and Paul, 1982.

Spivak, Gayatri Chakravorty. *Outside in the Teaching Machine.* New York: Routledge, 1993.

———. *In Other Worlds: Essays in Cultural Politics.* New York: Routledge, 1988.

Staff Editorial. "Intimidation at Columbia." *New York Times,* April 7, 2005.

Stark, Freya. *The Southern Gates of Arabia: A Journey in the Hadhramaut.* New York: Modern Library, 2001.

———. *East Is West.* London: John Murray, 1945.

Students for Academic Freedom. "The Academic Bill of Rights." http://www. Studentsforacademicfreedom.org, accessed 4/14/2005.

Taheri, Amir. "The London and Paris 'Street' Is Still Roiling." *Jerusalem Post,* March 9, 2005.

Tanenbaum, Leora. *Catfight: Women and Competition.* New York: Seven Stories Press, 2002.

———. *Slut! Growing Up Female with a Bad Reputation.* New York: Seven Stories Press, 1999.

Tannen, Deborah. "Dangerous Women: The Hard, Mean World of Post-Feminist Competition." *Washington Post,* March 10, 2002, p. 1.

Think Quest. "The World Hunger Problem: Fact, Figures and Statistics." http://library.thinkquest.org/C002291/high/present/stats.htm, accessed 2/16/2005.

Thomas, Andrew Peyton. *The People v. Harvard Law: How America's Oldest Law School Turned Its Back on Free Speech.* New York: Encounter Books, 2005.

Timmerman, Kenneth R. *Preachers of Hate.* New York: Crown Forum, 2003.

Tracy, Laura. *The Secret Between Us: Competition Among Women.* Boston: Little, Brown, 1991.

U.S. Department of State: Saudi Arabia country report on human rights practices for 1998. Published February 26, 1999.

Valladares, Armando. "Bio." The Valladares Foundation. http://www.valladaresfoundation.org/site/content.php?content.7, accessed 4/19/2005.

Vickers, Melana Zyla. "An Empty Room of One's Own: A Critical Look at the Women's Studies Programs of North Carolina's Publicly Funded Universities." *Inquiry* no. 22 (March 30, 2005).

Victor, Barbara. *Army of Roses: Inside the World of Palestinian Women Suicide Bombers.* New York: Rodale, 2003.

Wakili, Shekaiba, and Sultana, Wakili. "Out of Kabul." In Warren Lehrer and Judith Sloan, eds., *Crossing the Boulevard*. New York: W.W. Norton, 2003.

Walker, Lenore, E. *Terrifying Love: Why Battered Women Kill and How Society Responds*. New York: Harper & Row, 1989.

————. *Battered Women*. New York: Harper & Row, 1979.

Wallach, Janet. *Desert Queen: The Extraordinary Life of Gertrude Bell: Adventurer, Adviser to Kings, Ally of Lawrence of Arabia*. New York: Anchor Books, 1996.

Warraq, Ibn, ed. *Leaving Islam: Apostates Speak Out*. New York: Prometheus Books, 2003.

White, Emily. *Fast Girls: Teenage Tribes and the Myth of the Slut*. New York: Scribner, 2002.

Williams, Walter E. "Higher Education in Decline." *The New York Sun*, December 8, 2004, p. 11.

Winfrey, Oprah. "About Oprah." January 9, 2001. http://www.oprah.com/about/press/about_press_vday.jhtml, accessed 4/14/2005.

Women Living Under Muslim Law Organization. "Algeria: Justice for Women in Hassi Messaoud." December 12, 2004. http://www.wluml.org/english/actionsfulltxt.shtml?cmd[156]=i–156–90813, accessed 4/8/2005.

————. "Algeria: Attacks on Women in Hassi Messaoud." August 8, 2001. http://www.wluml.org/english/newsfulltxt.shtml?cmd[157]=x–157–3429,accessed 4/7/2005.

Worker-Communist Party of Iran. Briefing No. 158. "On Atefeh Rjabi's Execution in Iran: Interview with Maryam Kousha." September 29, 2004. http://www.wpibriefing.com.

Ye'or, Bat. *Eurabia: The Euro-Arab Axis*. Cranbury, NJ: Fairleigh Dickinson University Press/Associated University Presses, 2005.

————. *Islam and Dhimmitude: Where Civilizations Collide*. Cranbury, NJ: Fairleigh Dickinson University Press/Associated University Presses, 2002.

————. *The Decline of Eastern Christianity Under Islam: From Jihad to Dhimmitude*. Cranbury, NJ: Fairleigh Dickinson University Press/Associated University Presses, 1996.

————. *The Dhimmi: Jews and Christians Under Islam*. Cranbury, NJ: Fairleigh Dickinson University Press/Associated University Presses, 1985.

Zand-Bonazzi, Banafsheh. "Tehran's Killing Fields," *FrontPageMagazine.com*, January 27, 2005.

————. "Iranian Citizens Trash *Fahrenheit 9/11*." *FrontPageMagazine.com*, September 29, 2004.

Zinsmeister, Karl. "Diversity on Campus? There Is None." *American Enterprise Institute*, December 13, 2004.

Zogby International. "Today's College Students and Yesteryear's High School Grads: A Comparison of General Cultural Knowledge." *National Association of Scholars* (Winter 2002–2003). http://www.nas.org/reports/senior_poll/senior_poll_report.pdf, accessed 4/14/2005.

Index